Nepal's Peace Process

This volume provides a holistic overview of the long peace process in Nepal following the signing of the Comprehensive Peace Agreement (CPA) in 2006.

The date of 21 November 2021 marked the 15th anniversary of the CPA which concluded the decade-long civil war that had ravaged Nepal. Despite avoiding a resurgence of statewide conflict, Nepal's post-conflict era has been far from perfect. This era has witnessed ethnic violence, rampant corruption, the politicisation of key public institutions, and a failure to fully implement the provisions of the CPA. The resulting lack of socio-economic progress has led to large-scale dissatisfaction within the country and even given rise to elements within Nepal who reject the framework of the CPA and the 2015 constitution.

With a focus on the years following the 2015 constitution, this book offers an analysis of post-conflict Nepal and explores issues relating to ex-combatants, transitional justice, women, socio-economic affairs, and federal governance. The contributors are all scholar-practitioners, some of whom had direct involvement in the peace process and are therefore able to offer unique insights into the processes and challenges of Nepal's long journey to addressing past grievances and promoting future peace in the country.

This book will be of interest to students of peace studies, Asian politics, security studies, and International Relations.

Raunak Mainali is a Research Fellow at the Centre for Social Change, Nepal.

Prakash Bhattarai is Executive Director at the Centre for Social Change, Nepal.

Routledge Studies in Conflict, Security and Development

Designed to meet the needs of researchers, teachers and policy makers in this area, this series publishes books of new, innovative research in to the connections between conflict, security and development processes. The series encourages a multidisciplinary approach to the links between these thematic issues, including the nature of conflict itself and the underlying conflict drivers, the underlying characteristics and drivers of insecurity, and the effects and use of development strategies in post-conflict environments and how that relates to broader peacebuilding strategies.

Series Editors: Paul Jackson, *University of Birmingham*, and Mark Sedra, *University of Waterloo*

The Politics of Peacebuilding
Emerging Actors and Security Sector Reform in Conflict-affected States
Safal Ghimire

Military Interventions in Civil Wars
The Role of Foreign Direct Investments and the Arms Trade
Kamil C. Klosek

Civil Resistance and Democracy Promotion
A Comparative Study Analysis
Michael Schulz

Nepal's Peace Process
Issues and Challenges
Edited by Raunak Mainali and Prakash Bhattarai

For more information about this series, please visit: www.routledge.com/Routledge-Studies-in-Conflict-Security-and-Development/book-series/CSD

Nepal's Peace Process
Issues and Challenges

**Edited by Raunak Mainali and
Prakash Bhattarai**

LONDON AND NEW YORK

First published 2024
by Routledge
4 Park Square, Milton Park, Abingdon, Oxon OX14 4RN

and by Routledge
605 Third Avenue, New York, NY 10158

Routledge is an imprint of the Taylor & Francis Group, an informa business

© 2024 selection and editorial matter, Raunak Mainali and Prakash Bhattarai; individual chapters, the contributors

The right of Raunak Mainali and Prakash Bhattarai to be identified as the authors of the editorial material, and of the authors for their individual chapters, has been asserted in accordance with sections 77 and 78 of the Copyright, Designs and Patents Act 1988.

All rights reserved. No part of this book may be reprinted or reproduced or utilised in any form or by any electronic, mechanical, or other means, now known or hereafter invented, including photocopying and recording, or in any information storage or retrieval system, without permission in writing from the publishers.

Trademark notice: Product or corporate names may be trademarks or registered trademarks, and are used only for identification and explanation without intent to infringe.

British Library Cataloguing-in-Publication Data
A catalogue record for this book is available from the British Library

ISBN: 978-1-032-26199-7 (hbk)
ISBN: 978-1-032-26776-0 (pbk)
ISBN: 978-1-003-28987-6 (ebk)

DOI: 10.4324/9781003289876

Typeset in Times New Roman
by Newgen Publishing UK

Contents

List of Contributors	*vii*
Introduction RAUNAK MAINALI	1
1 The Road to the Comprehensive Peace Agreement PRAKASH BHATTARAI	9
2 Evaluating the Comprehensive Peace Agreement RAUNAK MAINALI	28
3 Rural Attitudes Towards the Peace Process in Nepal: Voice of the Villages RAUNAK MAINALI	43
4 Transitional Justice in Nepal: An Insider's Perspective MANCHALA JHA	58
5 Governing Conflict Victims in Nepal RAM KUMAR BHANDARI	72
6 Reflection on Past Assumptions Vs Present Realities of Social Reintegration in Nepal CHIRANJIBI BHANDARI	85
7 The Post-Conflict Context of Marginalised Groups in Nepal: Unmet Expectations RAM PRASAD MAINALI	100

vi   *Contents*

8 Analysing the Peace Process of Nepal through a Gender Lens   115
SUSAN RISAL

9 Governance Challenges and Opportunities in Young
Federal Nepal: Growing Pains   137
SHUVAM RIZAL

   Conclusion   154
   RAUNAK MAINALI

   Index   *163*

Contributors

Chiranjibi Bhandari is an Assistant Professor at the Department of Conflict, Peace and Development Studies, Tribhuwan University. He previously served at the Secretariat of the Special Committee for Supervision, Integration and Rehabilitation of Maoist Army Combatants.

Ram Kumar Bhandari is the Co-founder and President of the International Network of Victims and Survivors of Serious Human Rights Abuses (INOVAS).

Prakash Bhattarai is the Executive Director of the Centre for Social Change, Nepal.

Manchala Jha is a former Commissioner at the Truth and Reconciliation Commission, Nepal.

Raunak Mainali is a Research Fellow at the Centre for Social Change, Nepal.

Ram Prasad Mainali is an Under-Secretary at the Ministry of Finance, Nepal.

Susan Risal is the Chief Executive Officer at Nagarik Awaz (Citizens' Voice).

Shuvam Rizal is the Research Lead for the Governance Monitoring Centre, Nepal.

Introduction

Raunak Mainali

The following words penned by Chandra Gurung encapsulate the gradual dampening of revolutionary fervour in Nepali society within the last few years:

> The nation's joy has frayed
> Like roads and railings
> Gutted together with tires
> By people unfurling flags of their own interests
> Singing the songs of their own concerns
>
> Chandra Gurung (2020)

For the nation, 2006 was a turning point. The second *Jana Andolan* (People's Movement) much like its predecessor in 1990 saw countrywide support for democratic reforms and once again forced the monarchy to concede to its citizens. The 1990 *Jana Andolan* established a constitutional monarchy which was quickly embroiled in an armed struggle that arose out of various factors, of which the failure of the government to address economic and social marginalisation was a major component. However, 2006 and the successive years provided various reasons to be optimistic. The beginning of the peace process, marked with the signing of the Comprehensive Peace Agreement (CPA), promised revolutionary changes to the country that went further than the democratisation efforts of 1990. After all, the Maoists, who now intended to join mainstream politics, had waged a decade-long armed struggle on the basis of improving the lives of ordinary Nepalese and especially those who had faced century-long discrimination based on caste, region, gender, and ethnicity. Enthusiasm was further encouraged when on 28 May 2008, the newly elected Constituent Assembly voted to abolish the 240-year-old Shah dynasty of Nepal transforming the nation into a federal democratic republic. On 20 September 2015, the Constitution of Nepal was promulgated ushering in the framework of federalism in which three tiers of government were introduced: local, provincial, and federal. This was also perceived to be a progressive development as the historical concentration of power in Kathmandu had left rural areas vastly underdeveloped. Nevertheless, concerns were brewing within the

DOI: 10.4324/9781003289876-1

populace despite the introduction of progressive policies and optimism slowly turned into caution and disappointment. The Madesh region witnessed three different movements from the years 2006 to 2015 which revolved around federalism and the socio-political and cultural rights of ethnic Madhesis. These protests were often met with violence and more than 50 combined deaths were reported across the movements. Further disillusionment occurred as the peace process itself ran into roadblocks, particularly concerning transitional justice. Victims' groups emerged to challenge the nature of impunity that surrounded the transitional justice mechanisms. Ex-child soldiers relayed their grievances concerning the lack of state support they received with the conclusion of the war. Women were vocal about the persisting gender inequalities within the state which was even reflected in the lopsided citizenship laws embedded within the constitution. The problems that affected pre-conflict Nepal continued to plague the new Nepal as corruption, instability, and poor governance persisted even with a new governance framework. The 2017 general election was a proverbial last straw for Nepali citizens as a coalition party comprising the Unified Marxist-Leninists and Maoists won with a decisive majority. However, the period since then has been markedly similar. Instability caused by political wrangling has become the norm as opposed to the exception as parties vie for power to pursue their own self-interest at the detriment of the country as reflected in the poem of Gurung.

The Nepali civil war that was fought from 1996 to 2006 led to an estimated death toll of around 15,000 and disappearances of around 1,300 individuals. The economy was also devastated through the loss of tourism, corporate investment, labour disruptions, and high defence spending which pushed the already economically challenged country further into precarity (Pradhan, 2009; Upadhayaya & Sharma, 2010). Economic hardship was also significant at the individual level, especially around conflict areas, as agricultural lands went uncultivated, local businesses were destroyed, and households lost breadwinners. Additionally, the conflict hosted severe human rights violations resulting in unmeasurable physical and psychological harm to the civilian population leading to long-term consequences. The fighting was conducted mostly in rural western Nepal as the lack of state presence made it easier to conduct an armed conflict and the disenfranchised citizenry were easier to recruit due to the lack of state support they received. The ensuing peace process, which was set in motion with the signing of the CPA in 2006, provided an impetus to address the difficulties that arose as a consequence of the civil war. In line with peace treaties signed previously and around that time, the CPA embedded clauses relating to ceasefire, security sector reform (SSR), truth and reconciliation (TRC), as well as disarmament, demobilisation, and reintegration (DDR). Moreover, Nepali society was rife with inequalities relating to gender, caste, ethnicity, and region. Upper-caste men from Kathmandu Valley dominated the social, political, and economic landscape of the country resulting in the marginalisation of others which intensified depending on the intersections an individual occupied. It was within this context that the Maoists conducted their armed conflict as they were able to appeal to those who held grievances against a state that had largely marginalised them such as indigenous groups, Madhesis, Dalits, and women (Lawoti, 2010).[1] To ensure long-lasting peace, issues of marginalisation and poverty also had to be addressed. To redress the systematic failures of the past, the CPA envisioned a program of state restructuring that would be more inclusive and progressive in the administration of the state. This was reflected in the interim constitution of 2007 as well as the 2015 constitution which formalised Nepal's transformation into a secular and federal democracy.

Current Discourse Surrounding the Armed Conflict and Peace Process in Nepal

More than 15 years after the official end of the conflict and seven years after the promulgation of the 2015 constitution, the armed conflict and the peace process still finds a place in Nepali political discourse, albeit in a limited manner. For some, the peace process has been a source of national pride due to the limited involvement of international bodies. India played a significant role in initiating the peace talks between the parties and the role of the United Nations Mission in Nepal (UNMIN) was restricted mainly to the DDR process. Whilst conducting interviews for this volume, it was noticed that this sense of pride was mostly observed amongst those involved in state mechanisms such as civil servants and politicians. In a recent article concerning 15 years of the CPA, Pushpa Kamal Dahal, alias Prachanda, celebrated the achievements of the peace process such as democratic reforms and inclusive policies and highlighted the fact that the process itself was nationally led (Dahal, 2021).[2] As the chapter on transitional justice highlights later, the national ownership of the peace process was positively viewed by some within rural Nepal as they had often felt like they were used by international development actors who they engaged with. To them, it showed a nationally led peace process displayed the commitment of political actors to the people of Nepal, a far cry from the exclusion they had faced in the hands of the state in previous administrations. However, this honeymoon period would soon end as the transitional justice process was delayed as a result of various factors.

There is a general sense that the peace process ended with the promulgation of the constitution in 2015 and this is viewed differently amongst the population. Those with a favourable view, particularly elites, refer to the establishment of democracy, the transformation of the Maoists from a rebel group to a political party, the increase in the political representation of marginalised groups, and the fact that Nepal has not reverted to a large-scale political violence as successes. The DDR process, particularly the disarmament, demobilisation, and army reintegration aspects are regarded to be relatively successful when compared to other international case studies (Ansorg & Strasheim, 2019; Bhandari, 2015). Numbers are used to reinforce the success of these aspects such as the number of rebels demobilised, rebels that were integrated

4 *Raunak Mainali*

into the National Army, or the increase of marginalised groups within parliament. As will be discussed later, these numbers provide an incomplete picture of these so-called successes. Political reform is perceived to be mostly positive. Even those who are dissatisfied with the current government due to lack of economic development or rampant corruption mainly regard this as an issue of political will and a perversion of constitutional norms as opposed to fundamental flaws within the constitution and the laws. However, criticisms of the constitution have come from progressive and conservative elements within Nepal. The constitution and its corresponding laws have been criticised by civil society, particularly women's groups, for their unequal citizenship rights provisions. Conservatives within the country have been vocal against post-conflict reforms such as federalism, secularism, and even democracy and opting for a return of Nepal to a constitutional Hindu monarchy. Their ideas are gaining credence due to the dissatisfaction of the general populace with the current mainstream parties which are synonymous with kleptocracy and instability (Poudel, 2021). Opposition to undo the achievements of the peace process are gaining popularity even before a full electoral cycle under the framework for the 2015 constitution. Whilst discourse surrounding development in Nepal is ubiquitous, it is often not linked to the civil war or the peace process itself. For example, many civil servants that were interviewed were not worried about a reversion to a civil conflict despite agreeing that development has not been equitably distributed and that the root causes of the war persisted.

An aspect of the peace process that does find a place in current Nepali political discourse is transitional justice as there is a collective acceptance that the process is incomplete. Even Prachanda has accepted transitional justice has not been completed and that it can be regarded as a failure of the peace process (Dahal, 2021). K.P. Oli, former Prime Minister of Nepal, has regularly brought up the issue of transitional justice but his motives for doing so have been questioned. Oli and Prachanda's relationship are best described as tumultuous as the two were formal rivals who unified their respective political parties in order to contest the 2017 elections. After a resounding victory in the 2017 elections, the party eventually dissolved in March 2021 due to internal disputes leading to a renewal of the Oli-Prachanda rivalry. Oli has been accused by civil society of weaponising transitional justice to exert pressure on Prachanda's faction (Ghimire, 2020). Civil society has also been integral to the advocation of transitional justice within Nepal. Human rights activists, victim's groups, journalists, and NGOs have been essential in keeping transitional justice advocacy alive. The lack of progress regarding transitional justice has also led to the vilification of political leaders, particularly Prachanda and Nepali Congress leader Sher Bahadur Deuba. Both Deuba and Prachanda were in leadership positions during the war and have been accused of watering down the process of transitional justice in order to protect themselves and their party members from persecution (Dixit, 2022; Giri, 2022).

Objectives and Structure of the Volume

Since 2006, there have been several volumes, countless academic articles, and policy papers concerning the armed conflict and the subsequent peace process. Lawoti and Pahari's edited volume titled *The Maoist Insurgency in Nepal: Revolution in the Twenty-first Century* primarily explored the armed conflict as the peace process was relatively new at the time of publication (Lawoti & Pahari, 2010). Aditya Adhikari's *The Bullet and the Ballot Box: The Story of Nepal's Maoist Revolution* is a largely narrative account of the civil war and the second Jana Andolan that preceded the CPA and the peace process (Adhikari, 2014). Volumes focusing on specific aspects of the peace process have also been released in recent years such as gender (Kolås, 2017), transitional justice (Selim, 2018), and DDR (Subedi, 2018). Furthermore, there have also been edited volumes produced by Nepali NGOs in conjunction with donor organisations. The first of these, *The Remake of a State: Post-conflict Challenges and State Building in Nepal*, was edited by Nepalis and published by the Swiss National Centre of Competence in Research in conjunction with Kathmandu University (Upreti et al., 2010). The other is a volume by Nepal Transition to Peace Institute (NTTP-I) which aimed to offer a comprehensive analysis of the peace process after a decade and was published with the help of USAID.

This volume intends to add to the existing literature on the Nepali peace process with analysis relating to marginalised groups, gender, transitional justice, and DDR. There already exists an abundance of academic work related to these issues and Nepal; however, this volume has a unique approach concerning analysis. The majority of the contributors to this volume were involved within the peace process or post-conflict governance in some capacity. For instance, Manchala Jha served within the Truth and Reconciliation Commission of Nepal between the years 2014 to 2018. Ram Kumar Bhandari has worked as a victim's group advocate for all of the post-conflict era and is a leading figure aiming to create a united victim's front. Susan Risal has been an active member of civil society and leads a peacebuilding organisation that works with conflict-affected youth and women. Ram Prasad Mainali is an under-secretary at the Ministry of Finance who has worked for the Government of Nepal for more than two decades. He also has an academic background in developmental economics concerning marginalised castes in Nepal. Chiranjibi Bhandari is a former member of the Special Committee for Supervision, Integration and Rehabilitation of Maoist Army Combatants and was directly involved in the DDR process. Finally, Shuvam Rizal has led projects concerning the efficacy of health, education, and migration policy at different federal levels. Although not all of their chapters are strictly auto-ethnographic, their experience within their respective fields provides valuable insights. The fact that this is an edited volume also means that methodologies differ by chapters. For instance, Jha's chapter draws insights from experience in the field offering a unique perspective on the transitional justice process in the country. On the other hand, the

6 Raunak Mainali

chapter on the DDR process and local voices were mainly formulated through primary sources.

The volume is structured as follows. The first chapter gives a brief overview of the causes of the war and analyses the events and agreements that ultimately led to the signing of the CPA in 2006. The second chapter analyses the agreement itself in order to evaluate whether it provided a strong framework to establish peace in Nepal. The chapter also provides the rationale for the inclusion of the constitution and post-conflict governance in the analysis of the peace process. Following this, the next chapter explores the current attitudes towards the peace process and governance in rural Nepal. This is an important contribution as Nepal's discourse is often hijacked by elites within Kathmandu and the Maoists themselves were trying to address this urban/rural divide. The fourth chapter is based on the experiences of an ex-TRC commission member and the challenges they faced in delivering transitional justice. The following chapter explores the difficulties encountered by victims and argues that victims have appeared as a new marginalised group in Nepal with their identity being separate from traditional identities in Nepal. The next chapter explores the contemporary situation of ex-combatants with a particular focus on social integration which was a shortcoming of a relatively successful DDR program. The chapter following analyses the progress and shortcomings regarding marginalised groups and their development. It aims primarily to answer the question: Why has there been limited progress concerning marginalised groups despite constitutionally embedded provisions relating to their empowerment? The experiences of women within conflict and post-conflict Nepal are unique and challenges facing their progress is analysed in the ensuing chapter. The final chapter before the conclusion concerns itself with post-constitution governance in Nepal and the challenges that are currently hindering more efficient governance.

Several issues arose during the research phase of this book. The first of these was the Covid-19 pandemic. The pandemic meant that the population census of Nepal which was meant to be conducted in mid 2021 was not completed until later that year. Additionally, the National Living Standard Survey (NLSS) had not been conducted in Nepal since 2010/11 and the pandemic led to further unfavourable conditions to do so. The NLSS survey and census would have provided data relating to household income, years of schooling, health status, and more. Quantitative data could then be compared across the years to assess the effectiveness of governance in post-war Nepal and the large-scale nature of this data means it could be generalised. This would be particularly beneficial for the final three chapters of the volume as one could assess the quantitative progress regarding inequalities between groups across different cleavages. This was the original intention for the chapter regarding marginalised groups, but a lack of data meant that the chapter had to be slightly reconstituted. Instead of national-level data, NGO reports had to be consulted which do not possess the same level of generalisability as those of national datasets such as the NLSS and census. The pandemic also made it difficult to conduct in-person interviews and therefore most of these were primary data collected from before

Introduction 7

the pandemic. There were still in-person interviews conducted when lockdown rules that were put in place in Nepal were not breached.

Originally, this volume also intended to include a chapter based on the experiences of politicians who were directly involved in the peace process. We intended to ask them about concessions they may have made, the logic behind the provisions they included, the problems they encountered during peace negotiations, and other questions relating to their experiences. However, arranging interviews with senior politicians proved to be a frustrating and ultimately fruitless task. Despite being relatively well connected, we were only able to speak to assistants or relatives of politicians and the furthest we got was a quick introduction before we were told to arrange another time for a more in-depth talk. Needless to say, this interview never materialised, and the chapter was eventually omitted. The logic behind including this anecdote is to highlight the inaccessibility of the political class in Nepal and the culture of sycophancy that exists. As several respondents stated during our interviews, it is really hard to do anything in Nepal without strong political connections.

Notes

1 It is important to clarify that the Maoists did not enjoy unanimous support from these groups. Madhesis in the Terai region had their own movement independent of the Maoists and even came into conflict with the ruling Maoist party in post-conflict Nepal (Kantha, 2010). Similarly other marginalised groups also did not identify themselves with the Maoist cause and chose to oppose their status quo independently (Boquérat, 2006). Not everyone who joined the Maoists was ideologically aligned with them as many joined due to coercion or security reasons. This will be explored in a later chapter.
2 Within the article Prachanda also cited transitional justice and a lack of economic development as the shortfalls of the peace process.

References

Adhikari, A. (2014). *The Bullet and the Ballot Box: The Story of Nepal's Maoist Revolution.* Verso.

Ansorg, N., & Strasheim, J. (2019). Veto Players in Post-Conflict DDR Programs: Evidence From Nepal and the DRC. *Journal of Intervention and Statebuilding, 13*(1), 112–130. https://doi.org/10.1080/17502977.2018.1501981

Bhandari, C. (2015). The Reintegration of Maoist Ex-Combatants in Nepal. *Economic and Political Weekly, 50*(9), 63–68.

Boquérat, G. (2006). Ethnicity and Maoism in Nepal. *Strategic Studies,* 26(1), 79–99.

Dahal, P. (2021, November). *Nepal Peace Process as a Global Model. The Kathmandu Post.* Retrieved May 29, 2022, from https://kathmandupost.com/columns/2021/11/20/the-nepali-peace-process-as-a-global-model

Dixit, K. (2022). *How Nepal's Transitional Justice Process, the Only of Its Kind in South Asia, is being Undermined. Scroll.In.* Retrieved August 28, 2022, from https://scroll.in/article/1030020/how-nepals-transitional-justice-bill-the-only-one-of-its-kind-in-south-asia-is-being-undermined

8 Raunak Mainali

Ghimire, B. (2020). *Transitional Justice is Once again Being used as a Tool for Political One-upmanship, Conflict Victims say*. *The Kathmandu Post*. Retrieved August 15, 2022, from https://kathmandupost.com/national/2020/12/03/transitional-justice-is-once-again-being-used-as-a-tool-for-political-one-upmanship-conflict-victims-say

Giri, A. (2022). International Community Expresses Concern over Transitional Justice Process. *The Kathmandu Post*. Retrieved August 28, 2022, from https://kathmandup ost.com/politics/2022/08/21/international-community-expresses-concern-over-trans itional-justice-process

Gurung, C. (2020). *My Father's Face*. Rubric Publishing.

Kantha, P. (2010). Maoist–Madhesi dynamics and Nepal's peace process. In M. Lawoti & A. Pahari (Eds.), *The Maoist Insurgency in Nepal: Revolution in the Twenty-first Century*. Routledge.

Kolås, Å. (2017). *Women, Peace and Security in Nepal: From Civil War to Post-Conflict Reconstruction* (1st ed.). Routledge.

Lawoti, M. (2010). Ethnic dimensions of the Maoist insurgencies: Indigenous groups' participation and insurgency trajectories in Nepal, Peru, and India. In M. Lawoti & A. Pahari (Eds.), *The Maoist Insurgency in Nepal: Revolution in the Twenty-first Century*. Routledge.

Lawoti, M., & Pahari, A. (2010). *The Maoist Insurgency in Nepal: Revolution in the Twenty-First Century*. Routledge.

Poudel, S. S. (2021). In Nepal, Calls Grow for the Restoration of a Hindu State. *The Diplomat*. Retrieved May 18, 2022, from https://thediplomat.com/2021/12/growing-calls-for-restoring-hindu-state-in-nepal/

Pradhan, G. (2009). Nepal's Civil War and Its Economic Costs. *Journal of International and Global Studies*, *1*(1), 114+.

Selim, Y. (2018). *Transitional Justice in Nepal* (Y. Selim, Ed.). Routledge.

Subedi, D. (2018). *Combatants to Civilians: Rehabilitation and Reintegration of Maoist Fighters in Nepal's Peace Process*. Palgrave Macmillan.

Upadhayaya, P., & Sharma, S. (2010). Sustainable tourism and post-conflict state building. In B. Uprety, S. Sharma, K. Pyakuryal, & S. Ghimire (Eds.), *The Remake of a State: Post-conflict Challenges and State Building in Nepal* (pp. 87–110). Swiss National Centre of Competence in Research (NCCR North-South) and Human and Natural Resources Studies Centre (HNRSC) of Kathmandu University.

Upreti, B. R., Sharma, S. R., Pyakuryal, K. N., & Ghimire, S. (Eds.). (2010). *The Remake of a State: Post-conflict Challenges and State Building in Nepal*. South Asia Regional Coordination Office of the Swiss National Centre of Competence in Research (NCCR North-South) and Human and Natural Resources Studies Centre (HNRSC), Kathmandu University.

1 The Road to the Comprehensive Peace Agreement

Prakash Bhattarai

Introduction

This chapter mainly provides an overview of Nepal's journey from a situation of intensified armed violence to the signing of the Comprehensive Peace Agreement (CPA). International experiences demonstrate that several contextual factors contribute to the signing of a peace agreement between state and non-state parties or rebel groups. In some cases, conflicting parties have signed an agreement when both parties reach the stage of Mutually Hurting Stalemate (MHS) and realised that they cannot continue fighting as the cost is too high. In other cases, conflicting parties have considered the signing of a peace agreement as a face-saving strategy to enter an orthodox political environment by securing their democratic spaces. Often politically motivated groups take this approach. Some rebel groups have signed peace agreements as a strategic move to regain power or reduce additional damages on their side if the conflict were to continue.

The reasons for signing a peace agreement may vary from one place to another. One common phenomenon that can be observed in most cases relates to the status of power and position of conflicting parties. Peace agreement signing is not an overnight process where conflicting parties engaged in an aggressive armed struggle make decisions to sign an agreement immediately; rather it has to go through a tumultuous dialogue and negotiation process. More importantly, each conflict-affected country has their own journey of peace agreement signing process. Nepal also has its unique journey to the 2006 CPA signing process between the Maoist rebels and the Government of Nepal (GoN).

Three major contextual factors are particularly important to consider for better understanding of Nepal's journey to the 2006 CPA signing process. First, it is imperative to understand the trajectory of peace negotiation processes and the CPA signing ground prepared by these events. This section mainly explains the major peace negotiation events that took place between the Maoists and the government in different phases of armed conflict and the impact of those negotiations for preparing a ground for the signing of the CPA.

DOI: 10.4324/9781003289876-2

10   *Prakash Bhattarai*

Second, it is also important to bring some key events into the context that prepared an enabling environment for the CPA. This section explains five major events, namely: (a) Maoist's own strategic shift; (b) the unpopularity of King Gyanendra and his desire to rule the country in an autocratic manner; (c) the 12-point agreement signed between the Seven Party Alliance (SPA) and Maoists in October 2005; (d) the 2006 April Uprising; and (e) the role of international community and local civil society actors and the impacts of each of these events on the CPA signing process.

Finally, the chapter provides an overview of the processes and dynamics of renegotiating the agreements signed between the Maoists and the Seven Party Alliance[1] in the past. This section highlights how the former agreements such as the 12-point agreement were renegotiated between conflicting parties before the actual signing of the CPA in November 2006.

This chapter begins by presenting a brief historical context of the armed conflict and its causes and consequences. The chapter also undertakes the challenge of analysing the events that led to the manifestation of the CPA. In doing so, it first provides an overview of peace attempts that took place during the decade-long armed conflict. Following this, the chapter explains the exclusive as well as shared contribution of various political events that prepared a ground for the CPA. Finally, this chapter provides an account of the negotiation efforts that took place between the conflicting parties within the period of April–November 2006.

Armed Conflict in Nepal: Evolution, Causes, and Consequences

An armed conflict began in Nepal on 13 February 1996. The Communist Party of Nepal-Maoist (CPN-Maoist)[2] prompted an armed struggle against the state by undertaking several violent attacks on police posts and government offices in the hilly districts of Mid Western Nepal. The Maoists articulated three broad objectives of their armed struggle: to wipe out the 'capitalist class and the state system' that had traditionally existed; to abolish the Monarchy[3] that protected and promoted feudalism; and to establish a democratic republic ruled by the people (Mahat, 2005). Based on these three objectives, the Maoists were driven to radically transform Nepalese society economically, socially, and politically. They therefore named their struggle a 'People's War', through which they sought to establish a communist government. The Maoists articulated the key objective of the armed struggle as "to capture political power for the people" (UCPN-Maoist, 1995). They sought to control state power by "completing the new democratic revolution after the destruction of feudalism and imperialism, then immediately moving towards socialism and, by way of cultural revolutions based on the theory of continuous revolution under the dictatorship of the proletariat, marching to communism" (UCPN-Maoist, 1995). This armed conflict has also been recognised as "a competition for control over the state", with the simultaneous use of violence and non-violent political means (Kievelitz & Polzer, 2002).

The Rise of the Maoists

Before the upsurge of armed conflict, the Maoists were a small and a less influential political party in the Nepalese political landscape. Yet, it was somewhat influential in its base areas, the hilly districts of Mid Western Nepal. Before the eruption of armed revolt, the Maoist's 'genealogy' can be divided into various parts. One of its wings, the United People's Front (UPF), had participated in the general election of 1991 and won nine seats in the parliament out of 205 (Chalmers, 2007). The UPF, after a few years of experience within the multiparty democratic system, realised that their desired change could not be obtained under the existing political and social system, which they had named as semi-feudal, semi-colonial, and fascist. The UPF subsequently boycotted the second general election in 1995, claiming that the existing political system did not work in favor of the people. This conclusion was most likely drawn because of their intense groundwork for beginning an armed movement. Dr Baburam Bhattarai, then Chairman of the UPF, submitted a 40-point list of demands to the government, expressing an intense dissatisfaction over the existing socio-economic and political practices adopted by the mainstream political parties (ICC, 2005). The UPF wanted immediate action to be taken to address their concerns relating to socio-political change, nationality, and foreign policy, which were specified in their 40-point memorandum submitted to the government (Suhrke, 2009).

It was unlikely that the government would address all of their demands within a short time-span, especially given the unstable political environment of that time. The UPF did not expect their demands to be addressed immediately; rather, it appeared to be a strategy by the Maoists to legitimise their armed struggle as a pro-people political struggle. At the same time, the government undervalued the UPF's demands, anticipating that nothing serious was going to happen. Even if the government had taken initiatives to pay attention to their demands, the Maoists would not have stopped their armed movement because the demands were put forward as a warning to the government on the eve of the formal beginning of the armed struggle.

The Maoist armed conflict eventuated and expanded nationwide due to the perceived failure of multiparty democracy from 1990 to 1995, built on the expectations of people who were historically poor, discriminated against, and marginalised. There had initially been hope amongst these groups of people that their lives would significantly improve after the restoration of multiparty democracy in 1990. However, multiparty democracy up until this time had failed to fulfil the expectations of the Nepalese people due to the lack of people-centric economic and development policies, a high level of political corruption, the unheard voices of people from disenfranchised groups, and exclusion and discrimination based on caste, gender, ethnicity, and place of residence (Crossette, 2005; Kievelitz & Polzer, 2002; Sharma, 2009). The Maoists took advantage of the chaotic political atmosphere of the country, drew attention to the unheard groups, and convinced marginalised people to

12 *Prakash Bhattarai*

wage war against the state authorities with an ultimate aim of emancipating the people from the existing exploitative practices of Nepalese society.

The lack of a cordial and interdependent relationship between the state and society is another reason behind the eruption of the armed conflict, where marginalised groups had always been exploited for the benefit of state authority (Riaz & Basu, 2007). The failure of the democratic government and political parties to fulfil the expectations of the people contributed to a sharp increase in public anger and frustration towards the government. Instead of working together to fulfil the demands of various groups, the government and the mainstream political parties were involved in corruption, inter- and intra-party rifts related to grabbing political power, and neglect of the people's aspirations (R. Bhattarai, 2005; Kievelitz & Polzer, 2002; Suhrke, 2009; Thapa & Sijapati, 2004). The enjoyment of existing resources by only a small number of citizens resulted in the side-lining of historically marginalised groups[4] in Nepalese society. In this light, the armed struggle was due in large part to the accumulated grievances felt by underprivileged people against the Nepalese government (Dahal, 2004; Gobyn, 2009; Mahat, 2005; Thapa & Sijapati, 2004).

Three Phases of Armed Conflict

The 10-year period of armed conflict can be divided into three phases. The chapter considers 1996–mid 2001 as the beginning phase; late 2001 until October 2005 as the middle phase; and November 2005 until April 2006 as the final phase of the armed conflict.

In the beginning phase of armed conflict, the Maoists' strategy was to strengthen their local political influence with direct military action against political party structures and local government institutions, while in the national political domain they were attacking the Monarchy politically. The Maoists were very successful in accomplishing their mission. Initially, they were involved in the struggle with limited military capability and very limited support from the public. For this reason, the armed struggle was not perceived as a serious matter in its initial stage. The government wanted to treat the armed movement as a problem of 'law and order'. However, the armed struggle grew like wildfire and became a nationwide movement. By that time government security forces, particularly the police force, had already lost their capacity to quell the rebel group through military means (Whitfield, 2008).

It was only around 2000–2001 that the armed police force, and later on the Royal Nepal Army (RNA), was mobilised against the Maoists. By the time the government paid serious attention to this problem, the Maoists had already developed a strong military capacity, with more than 15,000 combatants and a force capable of challenging the state's security forces. As a result, within five years of the armed struggle the Maoists were able to expand into an armed movement with a nationwide scope, strong military and political strength, and a strong support base among the historically marginalised groups of Nepalese society. The decade-long armed struggle of Nepal can be considered as one of the most strategically sound and successful (both militarily and politically) communist armed revolts of the twenty-first century. Its success can be measured by its rapid expansion from a few hilly districts to the entirety of Nepal, and its positive as well as negative contribution to shaping the socio-political and economic dynamics of the country (Mishra, 2004). A favourable political climate, social upheavals, topographic advantages, and strategically sound political and military actions are some of the broader factors that determined the dynamics and direction of the Maoist armed struggle.

The second phase of the Maoist armed struggle began after the rise of King Gyanendra following the royal massacre[5] in mid 2001 and the King's widely criticised undemocratic move in 2002 to dissolve the democratically elected government. In this phase the political conflict was triangular in nature, with the Maoists, the King, and the mainstream political parties in conflict with each other. None of these forces were powerful enough to rule over the other (Dahal, 2004). The triangular nature of conflict remained until the King's absolute takeover of power in February 2005.

The third phase of the conflict began in early 2005 and lasted until April 2006. Now there were only two parties involved in the conflict: the Maoists and the mainstream political parties were on one side, and the King was on the other side. The formal peace process began in November 2006 after the government and the Maoists signed a peace agreement.

Peace Attempts

Peace talks were crucial political events that influenced the dynamics and direction of Nepal's decade-long armed conflict. Peace talks at one point brought hope that the conflict was going to be resolved peacefully, with limited social, human, and economic costs. The failure of these peace talks brought devastating results, with a massive escalation of violence from both conflicting parties.

Before the 2006 April Uprising, only two rounds of formal talks were undertaken between the government and the Maoists. The first round of peace talks was in 2001 and they were held in a series of three meetings, on 30 August, 13 September, and 13 November. This round of peace talks began after a large-scale Maoist attack on government offices and security barracks in Dunai, in the Dolpa district of Midwestern Nepal (Sharma, 2009). Although both parties had agreed to attend the peace talks, they were not moving smoothly, mainly due to the huge differences in ideologies which obstructed a negotiated solution. Both parties were also using the ceasefire period as an opportunity to re-strengthen and re-organise their military capacities and assess each other's weaknesses. At the same time, they used this time for improving their public image, particularly the Maoists, by conveying a message that they wanted to find solutions to the conflict through peaceful means. No such policy decisions were made from the Maoist side regarding their approach to the struggle. The first round of peace talks broke down in late November 2001 after a massive

14 *Prakash Bhattarai*

attack from the Maoists on a military barrack in Dang district of Mid Western Nepal. This event forced the government to declare a state of emergency and return to war with the mobilisation of the RNA for the first time. Human rights violations greatly increased after late November 2001 due to the larger scale of insurgency and counter-insurgency actions.

The second round of peace talks began in April 2003. Once again, three series of peace talks were convened, on 27 April, 9 May, and 17 August. This round of talks was considered more serious than the first round for two main reasons. First, the Maoists had sent Dr Baburam Bhattarai, one of their top ranked leaders, as their chief negotiator, along with three other high-profile leaders. One of them, Krishna Bahadur Mahara, had already become a chief negotiator in 2001, and another, Ram Bahadur Thapa (Badal), was the military strategist for the Maoists. In other words, negotiators from the Maoists' side were comprised of high-profile leaders.

In addition, during the second round of peace talks, the newly crowned King Gyanendra was already active in the day-to-day state affairs of the country and had even nominated the Prime Minister of his choice. It was believed that this round of peace talks would take the country in a peaceful direction. However, the peace talks broke down again on 27 August 2003. The Doramba massacre, where government security forces killed 17 unarmed Maoists and two civilians, is considered as the key reason for the breakdown of the talks. Other reasons included growing mistrust between the two sides, the absence of ceasefire-monitoring mechanisms, the absence of confidence-building measures, single-track negotiation, a focus on differences rather than on commonalities, inflexibility in the adjustment of goals, the lack of defined roles for facilitators, and a lack of support from the mainstream political parties for the negotiations (Dahal, 2004; Sharma, 2009).

Both of these rounds of talks were facilitated by local individuals without the use of formal international third-party involvement (Sharma, 2009). Until 2004, external third-party interventions consisted of development aid, humanitarian assistance, military assistance to the RNA, and providing some good offices and back-channel support. Informal active third-party interventions in all domains had begun only after the King's takeover in February 2005.

Key Events that Prepared a Ground for the CPA

Nepal's peace process had moved ahead not just because of the successful negotiations between the conflicting parties. Other supplementary intervention efforts which accompanied the negotiations have also determined the trajectory of the peace process. For example, the Maoists' own strategic shift to choose from a violent struggle to more democratic space remained crucial. The unpopularity of King Gyanendra and his desire to rule the country in an autocratic way also prepared a ground for the CPA. Likewise, India played a vital role in devising the 12-point agreement between the SPA and the Maoists in October 2005. The 2006 April Uprising was another vital political event, which not only forced the King to step down from central political power, but also created a conducive environment for the signing of a peace pact between the government and the Maoist rebels. The role of informal mediators was crucial in convening secret talks and back channels between the Maoists, the palace, and the mainstream political parties. Moreover, the role of the UN during the period of conflict, particularly after the signing of the CPA, also remained crucial for monitoring the Constituent Assembly (CA) election and the management of arms and armies (Mehta et al., 2010). This section further elaborates on these points.

Maoists' Own Strategic Shift

The Maoists' strategic shift from a violent struggle to a nonviolent struggle, along with the mainstream parties' decision to include the Maoist rebels in their struggle against the King, was an important political event heralding the beginning of a more hopeful peace process. Considering the complex political environment of Nepal in 2002 and afterwards, the Maoists found those complexities unfavourable for accomplishing their ultimate goal of establishing a communist government. A significant number of Maoist leaders lobbied within their party for a peaceful solution in order to institutionalise their agenda for change with an alternative approach, rather than the violent approach. As a result, the Maoist plenum meeting in 2005, popularly known as the Chunwang plenum meeting, decided "to forge an alliance with the parliamentary political parties against the monarchy and push for the formation of the federal democratic republic" (Basnet, 2011). This decision was a paradigm shift in the Maoists' policy, redefining the course of their struggle. Gobyn has pointed out the key factors that compelled the Maoists to move towards finding a peaceful solution to the conflict:

> From 2002 onward, they [Maoists] started to realise that there was no direct military solution of the conflict, that they lacked the internal support from the urban middle class, and that the international community was not going to accept an armed communist takeover in Nepal. To overcome these obstacles, the Maoist leadership started to develop a more pragmatic and pluralistic approach and engaged with domestic and international forces. The 2003 peace talks with the government, the cease-fire at the end of 2005, and the agreement with the mainstream political parties were all concrete steps on that path.
>
> (Gobyn, 2009, p. 434)

There are additional explanations as to why the Maoists chose to compromise after 10 years of armed conflict. It is generally believed that the Maoists saw that the conflict had reached a stalemate that was not beneficial to them. It is also claimed that there was grassroots pressure from Nepali citizens to end violence and reinstate democracy. Maoists' strategic decision to look for a

16   *Prakash Bhattarai*

nonviolent as well as negotiated solution to their armed struggle motivated them to sign a 12-point agreement with the SPA, which eventually remained a turning point in the struggle against the Monarchy and led to the signing of the CPA for a sustainable solution to the armed conflict.

Unpopularity of King Gyanendra and His Autocratic Desires

The Maoists' and SPA's decision to collectively struggle against King Gyanendra was greatly supported due to the unpopularity of the King and his desire to rule the country in an autocratic way. King Gyanendra, shortly after coming to the throne in 2001, attempted to curtail democratic freedom of the people, stating that armed conflict was the product of the failure of democracy. However, his hidden motive behind such a statement was to enjoy the absolute power of the country with the help of his loyalists, particularly with the support of military force of the country (K. Bhattarai, 2006). This led King Gyanendra to dissolve the elected government and take control over the central power. He assumed that these actions would be popular as the citizens had lost faith in the mainstream political parties and suffered heavily from the armed conflict. Thus, he reinforced the wrongdoings of political parties and the heightening of the insurgency to legitimise his 2005 takeover (Dixit, 2006b).

When the king came to power, his actions were repeatedly unconstitutional, such as the arbitrary appointment of Prime Ministers and ministers, dissolving the democratically elected parliament and the government, gradual destruction of democratic institutions, government machineries and their "royalisation", militarisation of the country, and not paying much attention to development activities (Dixit, 2006a). In addition, attacking media, banning mass campaigns of political parties, and putting leaders under house arrest had also continued after his takeover. The King had also hoped to receive support from the international community, mainly from India and China. Outside of regional neighbours, the King also hoped to get support from the USA as he believed taking a stronger stance against the insurgency would please the USA due to their war on terror strategy.

However, all ill intentions of King Gyanendra backfired. His plans and prediction to grab absolute power did not work out. When the April Uprising was drawing the attention of people from all segments of Nepalese society, he could not think that the political movement would soon manifest into a wider people's movement. He incorrectly assumed that people supported him rather than the political parties and the Maoists. When the King observed the protesters from his helicopter on 21 April 2006, he got nervous seeing hundreds of thousands protestors everywhere around Kathmandu valley rallying against him. He did not fathom that such a great opposition of people would come to the streets to protest against him. Rather it created an enabling environment for the Maoist rebels and political parties to form an alliance and prepare a solid ground for the uprising of April 2006 (K. Bhattarai, 2006). The alliance formed between the Maoists and the SPA also garnered popular support to

The Road to the Comprehensive Peace Agreement   17

remove the King from power through a nonviolent revolution and eventually paved the way for conflicting parties to look for a negotiated solution to the conflict (Bhatt, 2006).

The 12-point Agreement

As pointed out in literature, it was India who took a lead role in having a 12-point agreement in place between the SPA and the Maoists in October 2005. India provided a venue and other logistical support to facilitate dialogue between the SPA leaders and the Maoists. The 12-point agreement paved the way for the 2006 April Uprising against the King, and ultimately the signing of the peace agreement between the Government and the Maoist rebels in November 2006.

The basic spirit of the 12-point agreement was that the Maoist and the SPA agreed to form an alliance for removal of the King from power, restoring democracy in the country, ending a decade-long armed conflict for building peace, and promoting political coexistence among the political parties and the Maoists (Dixit, 2006b). This historic agreement created a solid foundation for launching a nonviolent people's movement in the country. Likewise, more than a decade of long messy politics existed in the country and the power of nonviolent movement for broader political change, which was learned from the success of the 1990s mass movement of Nepal, were some other key factors behind preparing a favourable environment for the 2006 April Uprising. However, it took almost five months for a real people's movement to take place. Several months of political homework, strategy development, and a gradual motivation of people to join the movement, finally prepared an environment for an uprising. From the very first week of April 2006, people throughout the country started to get involved in the nonviolent struggle. Participation of the mass populace kept on increasing daily and ultimately compelled the King to accede. Bottom-up pressure from people to open the blocked path to democracy and peace had effectively forced the political parties and the Maoists to continue their agitation until the main goal of the movement would be fulfilled (Dixit, 2006b).

2006 April Uprising

The 2006 April Uprising (popularly known as People's Movement II or Jana Andolan II) can be considered as one of the key gateways that encouraged the GoN and the Maoist rebels to sign the CPA. The 12-point agreement signed between the SPA and the Maoists remained a catalyst for ushering the nonviolent movement (Pyakurel, 2008). The 2006 April Uprising took place with an immediate goal of restoring democracy in Nepal with the removal of King Gyanendra from central political power, whereas its ultimate goal was focused on the successful resolution of decade-long armed conflict by transforming the Maoists from a rebel group to a democratic political force (AHRC, 2006;

18   *Prakash Bhattarai*

Hachhethu & Gellner, 2010). This nationwide nonviolent movement was also considered as a means to construct the future political roadmap to Nepal based on the principle of democracy and peace. As a result, a significant portion of people supported the idea of the SPA and the Maoists jointly launching a nonviolent movement.

Maoist rebels were waging a war since 1996 and its intensity became very high since 2001 when they started attacking the military barracks and when government also adopted aggressive counter-insurgency measures against the rebels. Armed conflict remained devastating to any sense of normalcy due to its severe effect on the economy, politics, and societal affairs of the country. People desired the ceasing of this armed conflict, however speaking against the Maoists and convincing them from the people's level to stop their violent struggle was worthless unless they themselves were ready to transform their strategies for gaining power.

Maoist armed conflict was not the only factor behind the people's suffering; rather levels of suffering had heightened when King Gyanendra came into power since 2001 after a royal massacre. King Gyanendra, within less than a year after his arrival as a new king in the country, attempted to limit the executive role of democratically elected governments by blaming them as incapable in ruling the country, particularly in solving the armed insurgency. Thus, he gradually took control over the executive power of the country and eventually formed a puppet government of his favour. Such a side-lining approach of King Gyanendra contributed to increased tension between the King and the mainstream political parties. From February 2005, King Gyanendra totally ignored the political parties, took control over the executive power of the state, and formed a government under his direct authority (Pyakurel, 2008). This action further contributed to heightening the political crisis in the country. This political development brought the mainstream political parties into aggressive street agitation against the king; however political party led street protests could not get momentum until October 2005, as people did not trust the parties for a long time due to their failures to meet the expectations of people and their engagement in corruption and other malpractices during active multiparty democracy period from 1991 to 2002.

The 2006 April Uprising was started on the basis of five different propositions. First, the April Uprising was the climax of the success of a 12-point agreement between the Maoists and the SPA in October 2005, which was mainly a memorandum of understanding to take collective action against the authoritarian regime of the King. According to Peter Tobin:

> The Maoists kept to the agreement with the Seven Party Alliance (SPA), led by Nepali Congress (NP) and the CPN (UML) declaring a ceasefire in the Kathmandu Valley allowing the SPA a free hand to challenge the Royalist autocracy with their form of well-practiced mass mobilisation.
>
> (Tobin, 2006)

Second, the unpopularity of King Gyanendra created a favourable environment for nonviolent political movement, as that was the only way to fight against the King. Third, the Maoists in their central committee meeting in early 2005 took a historic decision to move from violent to nonviolent action for restoring democracy and enter into multiparty politics. Fourth, the extreme suffering of a decade-long armed conflict and three years of the oppressive King's regime also motivated people to be part of the people's movement. Fifth, there was popular support among the people to be part of a nonviolent action rather than a violent struggle that was already observed as being counterproductive for the nation.

The Role of the International Community and Local Civil Society Actors

Nepal's peace process is regarded as largely a homegrown process where the procedures and timings of peace talks were decided by the conflicting parties without formal involvement of external third parties (Suhrke, 2009). However, a number of local, regional, and external third parties had showed interest in de-escalating the armed conflict through military as well as peaceful approaches (Warisha & Hayner, 2009). The interventions have mostly been informal but often very influential, either changing the dynamics and direction of the armed conflict or supporting the peace process. For instance, military assistance to the RNA was provided by India, the USA, and the UK until early 2005, in support of suppressing the armed conflict. International donors, particularly from Europe, India, and the USA, provided support during the conflict, as well as post-agreement humanitarian and conflict management support. Deep interest shown by the international community on issues around security sector reform, human rights, transitional justice, and federalism are some of the visible examples of active third-party engagements in Nepal's peace process.

It was estimated that more than 600 NGOs in Nepal were directly engaged in the conflict management and peace intervention process between the period of 2001–2006. Nearly 50 bilateral and multilateral donor agencies and more than 100 INGOs are active in Nepal and many of these have focused on supporting the peace process (IA, 2006). The UN and its specialised agencies working in Nepal have made peace-making a core program. The UN also provided good offices during and after the conflict for the negotiation process (Dahal, 2005). Additionally, both official and unofficial external third parties, such as non-governmental peacemakers, the UN, India, China, the USA, the EU, and other Western donors have been involved in the intervention process since 2000, encouraging dialogue between the conflicting parties, sharing experiences from other conflict settings, and giving support to the negotiation process (Whitfield, 2010). The multiplicity of third parties indicates their deep institutional interests in conflict resolution and peacebuilding efforts in Nepal, which greatly pushed the conflicting parties to look for a negotiated solution to the conflict.

20 *Prakash Bhattarai*

It is obvious that international actors enter into a conflict system with various motives. The initial motivation of internal and external actors to get involved in conflict resolution efforts in Nepal was humanitarian, due to the increased number of conflict-related killings from one year to the next. Economic, social, and psychological costs were also increasing with each passing year. But humanitarian tragedy was not the only motivation for third-party assistance. Strategic and policy interests of both internal and external actors were equally as important (Whitfield, 2008). Nepal's geopolitical context, foreign aid dependency, and internal political dimensions are three broader reasons for the active third-party intervention in its conflict. Other factors such as the global war on terrorism, geo-strategic contests, and security considerations are major factors that have motivated third parties to get involved in Nepal's peace process through military cooperation, creative diplomacy, and humanitarian support to limit the harmful actions of the actors in conflict (Dahal, 2005). Neighbouring countries, particularly India and China, feared the spillover effect of Nepal's armed conflict. They were also concerned about preventing an active role for other external actors in the region. Other countries, particularly Western nations as global advocates of human rights, were deeply concerned about the deteriorating human rights situation and the deepening political crisis due to a dramatic increase in violent activities. The USA was further interested in Nepal because it wanted to restrain communist influences and expand its anti-terrorist global alliance (R. Bhattarai, 2005).

Third-party involvement was mostly prominent in the latter phase of the conflict when it was nearing the state of MHS. In the beginning phase (i.e. before 2001), there was no significant involvement from external third parties. In this phase, the international community did not deem it necessary to step in because the conflict was not serious enough in terms of human casualties and property damage. They also miscalculated the trend of expansion of the armed struggle. Moreover, third parties relied on the then government to find an adequate solution to the conflict. Similarly, local third parties' efforts in the beginning phase were limited to the role of messenger between the conflicting parties. Local third-party intervention in armed conflict began in 1998, just two years after the initiation of the Maoist armed conflict. Senior leaders from the Nepalese human rights community, who had close contact with the leaders from both conflicting parties, attempted to bring the parties together. However, dialogue did not properly materialise due to the lack of sincerity from both parties. Thus, the first phase of third-party involvement was less active and did not produce any substantial outcomes.

Active forms of third-party intervention began after November 2001 when the violence escalated, following the failure of the first round of peace talks between the Maoists and the government. As a response to the Maoists' attacks on military barracks and government offices in the Dang district of Mid Western Nepal, the government imposed a state of emergency that enabled it to mobilise the RNA against the Maoists. The post-November 2001 scenario

The Road to the Comprehensive Peace Agreement   21

attracted a number of external third parties to Nepal who were divided in their support of a military versus a non-military solution to the conflict. For example, India, the USA, and the UK were in favour of a military solution, which meant that they heavily supplied both lethal and non-lethal weapons to the RNA until the King's takeover of power in February 2005. In contrast, the European nations, Nordic countries, the UN, and local and international NGOs were in favour of a negotiated solution to the conflict. The scenario changed after February 2005 with the King's action against democracy. By then, almost all third parties more or less agreed that the correct response to the conflict was to help the parties to find a negotiated solution rather than prolonging the conflict.

The UN focused on Nepal's conflict starting in September 2002 after Secretary-General Kofi Annan offered to use his good offices for the peaceful solution of the conflict. Tamart Samual, an official from the UN Department of Political Affairs (DPA), made his first visit to Nepal in mid 2003, during which he "developed good relations with a wide variety of political actors in Nepal, consulted regularly with Indian officials (in recognition of the enduring importance of India's influence within Nepal) and other representatives of the diplomatic community" (Whitfield, 2010, p. 6). Officially, the UN was involved in Nepal's conflict from May 2005 through the establishment of the UN Office of the High Commissioner for Human Rights (OHCHR) to monitor the human rights situation and advise the government on the promotion and protection of human rights. After the signing of a peace agreement in November 2006, the United Nations Political Mission in Nepal (UNMIN) was established in 2007 for the management of arms and armies and the monitoring of the CA election (Warisha & Hayner, 2009).

In addition to the UN, both local and external third parties were involved in various conflict intervention initiatives at the local and national levels. Local third parties, particularly Civil Society Organisations (CSOs), human rights groups, and other professional groups were involved in conflict monitoring and peace advocacy work. At the same time, a block of external actors, particularly the Europeans, were putting diplomatic pressure on the government to find a negotiated solution to the conflict. They also condemned human rights violations committed by government security forces and Maoist combatants. A 12-point agreement was signed between the SPA and the Maoists in November 2005 under the indirect facilitation of India.

Renegotiating the Former Agreements

Over 50 agreements, understandings, and other documents related to the peace process have been signed by different parties between the period of November 2005 and the signing of the CPA in November 2006. Additionally, conflicting parties have proactively negotiated on a number of issues mentioned in the CPA before they were actually incorporated in the formal documents when they signed the CPA. This section provides an overview of negotiated events

22   *Prakash Bhattarai*

that took place between April to November 2006 to prepare a ground for signing the CPA and key documents signed between different stakeholders.

Several talks and agreements preceded the CPA that were instrumental in its formation. These fostered and consolidated trust between the rival groups through consistent negotiation and the commitment to independent monitoring bodies: both national and international. Additionally, they also laid the framework for provisions that would eventually be co-opted by the CPA in order to conduct post-conflict reconstruction. These documents, displayed chronologically, are:

- The Proclamation of the House of Representatives (18 May 2006);
- The Code of Conduct on Ceasefire Agreed between the Government of Nepal and the CPN-M (26 May 2006);
- Agreement Reached Between the GoN and the CPN-M at Kupondole (15 June 2006);
- 8-Point Agreement between the Leaders of Seven Political Parties and the CPN-M (16 June 2006);
- Terms of Reference and Mandate of the National Monitoring Committee on Code of Conduct on Ceasefire (26 June 2006);
- Letters to the United Nations Secretary General (9 August 2006);
- Decisions of the Meeting of the High-Level Leaders of the Seven Political Parties and the CPN-M, and Dissenting Opinion of the CPN-UML (8 November 2006).

These events warrant an exploration for various reasons. Firstly, provisions that would be adopted later by the CPA were negotiated and included within these agreements and therefore there is a direct relationship with the peace effort and agreement. Secondly, these events allude to the compromises made by the warring parties which eventually enabled the manifestation of a peace document that was accepted by both factions. Therefore, a chronological analysis of these documents must be conducted.

The first document, the Proclamation of the House of Representatives, outlines the actions to be taken concerning the legislature, executive, army, Royal Council, Royal Palace, and other miscellaneous agendas (Wakugawa et al., 2011). The document can be seen as a compromise by the government on several fronts. Firstly, the proclamation clearly displays the willingness of the parties to carry out extensive state restructuring through a new constitution. This can be perceived to be a compromise as a majority of the parties who made up the government were involved in the creation of the 1990 constitution. The start of the armed conflict in 1996 meant that the government could only effectively administer under the 1990 constitution for six years. Creating a new constitution despite limited use of the 1990 constitution they fought for can certainly be deemed as a compromise. However, a new constitution may also have been in the interest of the parties as co-opting the anti-monarchy sentiment within the population would allow them to severely undermine the powers of the royal palace or even remove the monarchy. This proclamation adopts this anti-monarchy sentiment as it places the control of the army, royal council, and royal assets in the hands of the government. Further compromises with the Maoists are also abundant within the proclamation. The proclamation states that those who are not members of the House of Representatives will also be permitted to be nominated into the Council of Ministers (CoM). This would allow Maoist leaders to be nominated to the CoM as they were not members of the House of Representatives. This is important as the CoM were the main actors in carrying out the post-conflict agenda. Other Maoist influences within the document are the declaration of Nepal as a secular state as well as the restructuring of the army to be more representative of Nepal.

The second document, Code of Conduct on Ceasefire, outlined how the nature of ceasefire would be conducted (ibid., pp. 13–16). The importance of this document should not be understated as large components would later be adopted by the CPA. The document called for both parties to cease all violent conduct, not provoke each other or obstruct public works, and more. Not only did this build and consolidate trust between the warring parties but it also facilitated negotiations as leaders could travel without obstruction and did not have to shoulder the burden of war. The document also introduced international bodies for the purpose of monitoring, something that would be consistent in the following documents and the CPA.

The Agreement between the GoN and CPN-M on 15 June 2006 reinforced the monitoring clauses that were introduced in the preceding document (ibid., pp. 17–18). The agreement introduced a 30-member National Monitoring Commission with the explicit goal of ensuring the Code of Conduct on Ceasefire. Whilst the previous document limited the role of international bodies to the ceasefire, this agreement sought to expand their mandate to monitor human rights issues in the country. This agreement further reinforced the trust between the parties as they were willing to be under the scrutiny of independent bodies, both national and international. However, the Code of Conduct on Ceasefire and this agreement both fail to include any binding mechanisms to coerce parties into submission.

The following day, on 16 June 2006, the parties signed the 8-point agreement. This agreement would reaffirm the points from earlier documents as well as introduce several that would be included in the CPA (ibid., pp. 19–21). Firstly, the agreement increases the role of international bodies by requesting assistance from the UN for the management of armies. This also alludes to a Disarmament, Demobilisation and Reintegration (DDR) process that would be expanded in future agreements. The 8-point agreement also introduces the creation of an interim constitution that would espouse the democratic values and dissolve the House of Representatives and the alternative People's Governments created by the Maoists in their respective districts. The influence of the Maoists is visible through the point calling for the restructuring of the state to address the needs of marginalised groups in the country, something that is consistent with their 40-point demand.

24 *Prakash Bhattarai*

On 26 June 2006, the parties agreed upon the Terms of Reference and Mandate of the National Monitoring Committee on Code of Conduct on Ceasefire. This provided a framework to conduct ceasefire monitoring activities for the National Monitoring Committee (ibid., pp. 22–4). These included investigation of ceasefire violations, conflict negotiation, assistance from UNCHR on human rights issues.

The final document of interest and the document preceding the CPA was the Decisions of the Meeting of the High-Level Leaders of the Seven Political Parties and the CPN-M, and Dissenting Opinion of the CPN-UML. This meeting was conducted just 13 days prior to the CPA and the content is focused on the interim constitution, the monarchy, interim legislature parliament, judiciary, and others (ibid., pp. 41–50). The document contains a rough framework guiding the DDR process which would later be included in the CPA. It designates cantonment sites for the Maoist army as well as the role of the UN and the Nepal Army during the process. It also inspires the creation of a Truth and Reconciliation Commission to "conduct investigations into those who have committed grave violations of human rights and those who were involved in crimes against humanity" (ibid., p. 49). Also included in the document, and which would later be addressed in the CPA and the 2015 constitution, was the socio-economic transformation of Nepal into a more egalitarian Nepal devoid of any social or economic marginalisation. This was to be achieved through the ending of the feudal system, promotion of Nepali industry, ensuring workers' rights, and more. Finally, unlike the preceding documents and the CPA, this agreement included an implementation timetable. However, it does not go far enough to create binding mechanisms to ensure implementation.

Analysis and Conclusions

The analysis suggests that conflicting parties in Nepal reached the point of signing the CPA not because of the success of peace negotiation attempts they made during the time of armed conflict; rather formal peace negotiation attempts took place in 2001 and 2003 produced some counterproductive results to the successful resolution of the conflict. Interestingly, other several factors as described above contributed to prepare a solid ground to the signing of the CPA. Yet, it is hard to claim a particular factor that contributed the most. It can be argued that the 12-point agreement signed between the SPA and the Maoist rebels prepared a foundation for bringing the two major political forces together to pave way towards restoring democracy and find a negotiated solution to the conflict. Willingness of the Maoist rebels to give up their armed movement and extending hands for cooperation with the SPA, who were also in a nonviolent struggle against the autocratic regime of King Gyanendra, remained another strong move that eventually contributed to sign the CPA. The success of the 2006 April Uprising remained at the crux in providing an enabling environment to remove the autocratic regime and further work on creating a solid roadmap for signing the CPA. The role of local and external third parties remained

The Road to the Comprehensive Peace Agreement   25

complementary to push for the conflicting parties to look for a negotiated solution. The post April Uprising phase where conflicting parties developed some tacit and documented understandings, such as a provision for ceasefire, inviting the UN to support the DDR process, as well as flexibility around the forthcoming governing structure of the state and the process of achieving that, remained crucial to sign the CPA. Although our analysis does not explicitly mention it, the role of political leadership from both sides and their commitment to peace and inclusive democracy remained extremely valuable to sign the CPA.

Ending a decade-long armed conflict which had already taken a nationwide shape was not an easy process. This process was further complicated due to an undemocratic move taken by the King to jeopardise the process with a motivation of a military solution to the conflict and compromising democracy. However, due to the series of formal and informal understanding developed by the key political leaders from the SPA and the Maoist rebels' side, the conflict has been safely landed through the signing of the CPA. In the next chapter, we discuss more on signatories' perspectives regarding the factors involved in reaching the CPA and their own analysis of the post-CPA process in achieving durable peace in Nepal.

Notes

1 The SPA were an alliance made up of the parties being represented in the GoN during the signing of the peace agreement.
2 Although this is the full name of the party that started the civil war, the volume will refer to them as Maoists.
3 There was an active Monarchy in Nepal until the 1990s. After the success of the People's Movement in 1990, the then King was ready to share power with parliamentary political parties and remain as a constitutional Monarch. However, the King still held some powers, such as Chief of Command of the then Royal Nepal Army.
4 This group includes Dalits (the so-called lower-caste group), Janjati (an ethnic group), Aadivasi (an endogenous group), and the people from remote geographical locations, particularly from the hilly and mountainous regions of the country.
5 In the Royal massacre, 17 royal family members were killed in the palace, including King Birendra, his wife and son, daughter, and other close relatives. As Birendra's family had all been killed, his brother Gyanendra took over as the monarch.

References

AHRC. (2006). *Nepal: The Human Rights Situation in 2006*. Asian Human Rights Commission.
Basnet, P. B. (2011). Plenum Fiasco. Himal South Asian. Retrieved February 7, 2021, from www.himalmag.com/plenum-fiasco/
Bhatt, S. (2006). Nepal: A people's Movement Grows with Fury. *Rediff News*. Retrieved February 7, 2021, from www.rediff.com/news/2006/apr/24nepal.html
Bhattarai, K. (2006). Consequences of April 2006 Revolutionary Changes in Nepal: Continuation of Nepalese Dilemma. *Indian Journal of Economics and Business*, 5(2).

26 Prakash Bhattarai

Bhattarai, R. (2005). *Geopolitics of Nepal and International Responses to Conflict Transformation*. Friends for Peace.

Chalmers, R. (2007). Toward a New Nepal? *Current History, 106*(699), 161–167. https://doi.org/10.1525/curh.2007.106.699.161

Crossette, B. (2005). Nepal: The Politics of Failure. *World Policy Journal, 22*(4), 69–76.

Dahal, D. R. (2004). *Nepal: Conflict Dynamics and Choices for Peace*. FES.

Dahal, D. R. (2005). *Nepal: Supporting Peace Processes Through a Systemic Approach*. Berghof Foundation for Peace Support.

Dixit, K. M. (2006a). Nepal: The Rising. *Open Democracy*. Retrieved February 24, 2021, from www.opendemocracy.net/en/nepal_rising_3471jsp/

Dixit, K. M. (2006b). People Power in Nepal. *The Nation*. Retrieved February 24, 2021, from www.thenation.com/article/archive/people-power-nepal/

Gobyn, W. (2009). From War to Peace: The Nepalese Maoists's Strategic and Ideological Thinking. *Studies in Conflict & Terrorism, 32*(5), 420–438. https://doi.org/10.1080/10576100902831578

Hachhethu, K., & Gellner, D. (2010). *Nepal: Trajectories of Democracy and Challenges of Restructuring the State*. (P. R. Brass, Ed.; 1st ed.). Routledge.

IA. (2006). *Donor Aid Strategies in Post-Peace Settlement Environments: International Lessons and Recommendations for Donors in Nepal's Transition Period*. International Alert.

ICC. (2005). *Nepal's Maoists: Their Aims, Structure and Strategy*. International Crisis Group.

Kievelitz, U., & Polzer, T. (2002). *Nepal Country Study on Conflict Transformation and Peace Building*. Deutsche Gesellschaft für Technische Zusammenarbeit (GTZ).

Mahat, R. S. (2005). *In Defence of Democracy: Dynamics and Fault Lines of Nepal*. Adroit Publishers.

Mehta, A. K., Pandey, N. N., & Rajan, K. V. (2010). Political Developments and Evolving Security Scenarios in Nepal. *Indian Foreign Affairs Journal, 5*(4), 395–425.

Mishra, R. (2004). India's Role in Nepal's Maoist Insurgency. *Asian Survey, 44*(5), 627–646. https://doi.org/10.1525/as.2004.44.5.627

Pyakurel, U. P. (2008). The Vision of The Jana Andolan II for a Future of Nepal. *Coalition for Environment and Development: Sustainable Cultures-Cultures of Sustainability, Background Paper 23*. Coalition for Environment and Development.

Riaz, A., & Basu, S. (2007). *Paradise Lost: State Failure in Nepal*. Lexington Books.

Sharma, R. K. (2009). *Changing Realities and Challenges for the Peace Process of Nepal*.

Suhrke, A. (2009). *UN Support for Peace Building: Nepal as the Exceptional Case*. Chr. Michelsen Institute.

Thapa, D., & Sijapati, B. (2004). *A Kingdom under Siege: Nepal's Maoist Insurgency, 1996 to 2004*. Zed Books.

Tobin, P. (2006). The People's Movement: Twenty Days That Changed Nepalese History. *Inside the Nepalese Revolution*. Athol Books.

UCPN-Maoist. (1995). Plan for the Historic Initiation of the People's War: Adopted by the Central Committee of the Party in September 1995. Retrieved February 9, 2021, from https://nepalconflictreport.ohchr.org/html/documents/1995-09-00_document_cpn-m_eng.html

UNMIN. (2009). *Press Statement on Registration and Verification of Maoist Army Personnel*. United Nations Mission in Nepal.

Wakugawa, I., Gautam, P., Shrestha, A., & Asian Study Center for Peace and Conflict Transformation. (2011). *From Conflict to Peace in Nepal: Peace Agreements 2005-10.* Asian Study Center for Peace & Conflict Transformation.

Warisha, F., & Hayner, P. (2009). *Negotiating Peace in Nepal: Implications for Justice.* International Center for Transitional Justice.

Whitfield, T. (2008). *Masala Peacemaking: Nepal's Peace Process and the Contribution of Outsiders.* Conflict Prevention and Peace Forum.

Whitfield, T. (2010). *Focused Mission, Not So Limited Duration: Identifying Lessons from the United Nations Mission in Nepal (UNMIN).* New York University.

2 Evaluating the Comprehensive Peace Agreement

Raunak Mainali

Introduction

There is no universally accepted framework to structure a peace agreement. They often follow a pragmatic framework in an attempt to address the needs of the conflict and these vary between documents. Christine Bell suggests that whilst there are difficulties with the legal classification of peace agreements, there is a common trend amongst these accords (Bell, 2008). Bell claims that a peace agreement "links ceasefires to agreed new political and legal arrangements for the holding and exercising of power" as well as using "third parties to develop, enforce and implement the agreement" (ibid., p. 106). In this respect, the main rationale of peace agreements is to consolidate the types of peace as conceptualised by Johan Galtung (1969). Whilst ceasefire clauses enforce the negative peace with an end to hostilities, the transformation of existing social, economic, and political structures aims to actualise positive peace. Seen through this lens, the Comprehensive Peace Agreement (CPA) signed in Nepal in 2006 aimed to accomplish both the positive and negative by creating a suitable framework for post-conflict peacebuilding.

The aim of this chapter is manifold. Initially, the chapter seeks to explain what the CPA is as well as a brief outline of the provisions. Following this, the chapter will explore the theoretical rationale for the inclusion of the provisions and assess if there is an adequate framework for these processes within the CPA. In order to do this, the chapter will categorise the key provisions as a means to address either the root causes or by-products of the conflict. An important contribution of this section, and indeed the volume, is the analysis of the 2015 constitution of Nepal as an extension of the CPA. To this end, the chapter will explore how the provisions within the accords were influential in the promulgation of the 2015 constitution. The importance of this should not be understated as the creation of a new democratic constitution was an explicit goal of the Maoists and serves as a means to treat the social, political, and economic grievances that plagued Nepal. Despite the importance of the constitution in delivering "positive peace" and its obvious links with the CPA, there remains a lacuna as it has not been analysed in regard to the peace process in Nepal. Finally, as a conclusion, the chapter will discuss whether the CPA can

DOI: 10.4324/9781003289876-3

Evaluating the Comprehensive Peace Agreement 29

be regarded as a "good" or "bad" peace agreement on the basis of it delivering a suitable framework for post-conflict reconstruction. This chapter will explore the CPA within the context of Nepal and limits cross references with those agreements outside the nation as this will be addressed in a later chapter.

Conceptualising the CPA

The CPA, signed on 21 November 2006, is a negotiated peace agreement between the Maoists and the Seven-Party Alliance that formed the Government of Nepal. It aimed to cease the hostilities between the belligerents whilst simultaneously outlining a framework for post-conflict peacebuilding. Explicitly stated in the preamble of the document, the CPA itself was heavily shaped by previous agreements and understandings negotiated between the parties (CPA, 2006). These include the 12-point understanding, 25-point Code of Conduct, 8-point agreement, and the 5-point letter to the United Nations which were all finalised in the several months preceding the CPA. As a result, these documents will be analysed in conjunction with the CPA.

Peace agreements, at the very least, are expected to create a ceasefire and end the hostilities between warring parties. The parties in Nepal had already agreed to an informal truce prior to signing any official documents. The Maoists and the Seven Party Alliance had agreed to a truce in order to lead agitations against the monarch, King Gyanendra, who had extended his reach beyond his constitutional role and imposed draconian measures on the nation (BBC, 2006; Adhikari, 2014). This ceasefire was then made official and extended by 25-point Code of Conduct (2006), which provided a guideline on how to conduct peaceful affairs, as well as the 8-point agreement (2006) before finally being cemented within the CPA (2006). Additionally, the 5-point letter to the United Nations also displays the commitments towards ceasefire as both parties request assistance in monitoring the Code of Conduct (Prachanda and Koirala, 2006). The fifth clause of the CPA is devoted entirely to the ceasefire efforts and details, amongst other things, the activities that correspond to violence which must be ceased (CPA, 2006). In essence, the CPA was an extension of commitment towards ceasefire that existed prior to the document as a result of the usurpation of power by King Gyanendra.

Staying within the realm of the monarchy, the CPA and the documents that preceded it favoured a republican model of governance as opposed to monarchic. The desire for democratic changes predated the conflict in Nepal and was even prime motivator for enabling it. The *Jana Andolan* (People's Movement) that took place in 1990 reigned in the powers of the king and devolved much of the executive power to the elected representatives (Dixit, 2006). The Maoists were even more staunch in their opposition to the monarchy and demanded its abolition in their 40-point demand prior to conducting their protracted conflict (ICC, 2005). The democratic aspirations of both the Maoists and the Government of Nepal are well reflected in the CPA and other documents. The election of a constituent assembly is highlighted in all the documents previously mentioned and clause 3.3 of the CPA explicitly stated that the status of the monarchy would be decided by the assembly (CPA, 2006). The democratisation of post-war Nepal is also reinforced throughout the CPA in other provisions by calls for free and fair multiparty elections. The democratic framework championed by the CPA is said to follow the patterns of other peace accords that call for a redefinition of the state, disaggregation of power, and dislocation of power (Bell, 2008).

Complementary to the political reform, as explored above, are the social and economic transformations also guaranteed by the CPA. The Maoists were successful in co-opting the marginalised groups of Nepal such as Dalits, Janajatis, Madhesis, Tharus, and women into their rank and file. This success can be partly credited to the perception of the Maoists as an anti-feudal force who represented the concerns of disadvantaged groups in Nepal (Lawoti, 2012; Kantha 2012; Sthapit and Doneys, 2017). This is represented in the third clause which calls for a political, social, and economic transformation of the country that is devoid from discriminatory practices against marginalised groups (CPA, 2006). Additionally, the commitment to the protection and elevation of marginalised groups is also highlighted in clause seven which guarantees universal human rights. As with the ceasefire, both parties also requested the continuation of human rights monitoring by the Office of the High Commissioner for Human Rights (OHCHR) (Prachanda and Koirala, 2006). This need to address the requirements of marginalised groups was also present in other documents signed by the parties.

Clause four of the CPA is devoted to outlining the management of the army, both Maoists and National, and armaments. This clause acts as a general guide to the Disarmament, Demobilisation and Reintegration (DDR) process that would be conducted later. The clause identifies the cantonment sites for disarmed Maoist combatants and the plans for democratisation process of the Nepal Army, who were previously the Royal Nepal Army and therefore were under the direct command of the king (CPA, 2006). Prior to the CPA, the 8-point agreement and the 5-point letter to the UN both hinted at a possible future role of the UN in the DDR process. The CPA expands on this by clearly outlining the role of the UN within the process. This is unlike other provisions where the request for international help has been along the ambiguous role of monitoring. As will be explored later, this was a contributing factor towards the comparative success of the DDR process.

Clause eight, although brief, includes provisions for the creation of transitional justice mechanisms. The National Peace and Rehabilitation Commission (NPRC) and the Truth and Reconciliation Commission (TRC) were created in order to properly address the human rights abuses that occurred during the conflict. The CPA designates the formation of terms of reference and working procedures of these commissions to the interim Council of Ministers (CPA, 2006). Unlike clause four, which highlights the role of the actors in the DDR process, clause eight does not dive into the intricacies of the transitional justice process. The roles of the NPRC and TRC are not specified which ultimately

Evaluating the Comprehensive Peace Agreement 31

would cause problems in the future and retard the process of transitional justice. Whilst assistance had been requested from international bodies for monitoring human rights, this clause does not provide a role for international actors in the transitional justice process.

The ninth clause aims to create accountability for the implementation of the accords by introducing certain measures. Here the role of the OHCHR and the UN in monitoring human rights and the DDR process is reinforced. Additionally, the UN is also given the responsibility of supervising the constituent assembly elections. The National Human Rights Commission (NHRC) is also mandated through this clause to carry out a monitoring role of Human Rights in a similar capacity to the OHCHR. This conflicting mandate is also of importance due to its negative impact on the peace process.

Key Provisions of the CPA

Despite the complexities of conflict, arising from its multifaceted motivators, there have been attempts at categorising wars based on their characteristics (Zartman, 1998; Kaldor, 2012). Similarly, there have been attempts to catalogue the different types of peace agreements that can be dated to the Romans who had agreements based on asymmetry of power, balance of power, and a treaty of alliance to consolidate future peace (Rich and Shipley, 1993; Baldus, 2004). More recently, Christine Bell has classified peace agreements according to when and how agreements are produced (Bell, 2008). However, there is limited literature on how to classify the provisions within the peace agreement itself which this volume hopes to address. This chapter proposes that the provisions within a peace agreement can be sorted into two distinct categories: those provisions that are produced to address the root causes of conflict and those that address the by-products of the conflict. However, this method of categorising provisions should not undermine peacebuilding which should be conducted in a comprehensive manner. Rather, this method of categorisation is conceptualised in order to understand the role of provisions in post-conflict processes. This will be expanded upon in this section by analysing the key provisions within the CPA.

By-products of the Conflict

Disarmament, Demobilisation and Reintegration (DDR)

The process of DDR usually finds itself a part of the larger Security Sector Reform (SSR) that occurs in post-conflict nations. According to the United Nations Secretary General (UNSG, 2008) the importance of SSR stems from its potential to consolidate peace and security, prevent countries from relapsing into conflict and in laying the foundations for sustainable peace. DDR itself is a process that can take many forms. As Özerdem (2013) claims, DDR processes vary according to eligibility criteria; actors involved such as armed forces or paramilitary groups; or even through timing as DDR can take place before or after the cessation of hostilities. The disarmament aspect of DDR aims to pacify the fighting forces by the collection of information and arms, stockpile management, and the destruction of weapons (DPKO, 2010). Demobilisation process refers to the registering, monitoring, and discharging of combatants. As in the case of Nepal, the demobilisation process may be lengthy and require the combatants to be contained within designated cantonment sites. The final phase of the process, reintegration, occurs when combatants are released into the civilian sphere. The aim of the final process is to ensure that ex-combatants can be successfully integrated socially, financially, and politically and reduce their likeliness of returning to a life of violence. Whilst the more comprehensive SSR process addresses both root causes of conflict and the by-products, DDR can be deemed to tackle the latter due to its focus on the combatants of the conflict.

As with every other aspect of peacebuilding, DDR is plagued with a multitude of deficiencies as reflected upon by Özerdem (2013). A strict definition of a combatant may exclude children and women. Feminist scholarship has emphasised that women are often excluded from the DDR process despite being actively involved in the conflict as a combatant (Henshaw, 2019; Shekhawat & Pathak, 2015). Additionally, in a vulnerable post-conflict climate, combatants may not be willing to disarm themselves due to worries of revenge killings. A poorly devised DDR framework may also not equip combatants with the necessary expertise to gain employment and therefore would increase the likelihood of them resorting to violence and banditry due to familiarity and financial pressures. DDR as a process should be clearly defined and work in conjunction with other post-conflict processes to ensure fruitful results.

A latter chapter will discuss the triumphs and failures of the DDR process in Nepal, but this section will analyse if the DDR provisions within the CPA itself was sufficient as a framework for the process. Although rare in practice, theory states that a DDR program should be negotiated and included in a peace treaty (Swarbrick, 2007). In this respect, Nepal is an anomaly as clause four of the CPA is entirely dedicated to a DDR program. The clause is detailed in outlining the cantonment sites as well as the storage of weapons and roles of the involved actors. However, this detail is not consistent within the framework as some aspects are ambiguous in nature. For example, whilst the CPA is very detailed about the types of violence that constitute a breakdown of the ceasefire, it is does not apply the same detail to define who a combatant is. This is problematic in the context of the Nepali civil war as large numbers of children and women fought for the rebel army which would legitimate the label of combatant. In hindsight, it is clear that this was a major reason why women and children combatants were excluded from the process.

Additionally, the reintegration aspect of DDR is largely underdeveloped within the CPA. Kingma (2004) classifies reintegration into political, economic, and social where each must be considered before reintegrating combatants. Özerdem (2013) stresses that the social reintegration requirements

Evaluating the Comprehensive Peace Agreement 33

are often overlooked in a DDR process and Nepal as a case study strengthens this claim. The caste and ethnic differences between the combatants are not even recognised within the clause, showing a lack of commitment to the social reintegration aspect. Moreover, the clause fails to detail other important aspects of the reintegration process such as a financial package, workshops to teach employable skills and more. Whilst this DDR framework is initially promising, there are several aspects which would ultimately go on to undermine the process.

In a stalemate conflict situation, where no party is the clear victor, Swarbrick (2007) emphasises the need for an impartial third party to mediate the DDR process. In such a situation, the central government does not have a monopoly on violence and therefore lacks the legitimacy that is needed to conduct the DDR. A security dilemma may also manifest as a consequence of mutual suspicion and hostility and combatants would be less willing to depart from their weapons for safety reasons. Additionally, a conflict would have depleted the financial capabilities of the state and intervention by third party becomes integral to the success of DDR.

The CPA acknowledged these constraints and added an impartial third party, the UN, to oversee the process of DDR. The UN's role, as mandated by the CPA, required them to monitor the cantonment sites, secure the key for the weapons cache and prepare technical detail. This can be considered to be a success as the presence of the UN would have alleviated suspicions and the rebels would be more willing to disarm themselves under the security and assurance of the impartial third party. The role of the UN was also beneficial to the Nepal DDR process in a unique way. Nepal is a top contributor of troops to the UN and has conducted DDR processes in other countries which made them accountable and motivated to conduct the process meticulously within their own home nation (Ansorg and Strasheim, 2018).

Transitional Justice

The extensive work on transitional justice by scholars and practitioners attests to its significance in a post-conflict environment. There are debates on how transitional justice should be conducted as some advocate for the truth telling commissions resulting in forgiveness whilst others emphasise the need for criminal justice with perpetrators receiving their fair dues (Hutchinson and Bleiker, 2013). However, transitional justice should be viewed as a more holistic process which is pragmatic in considering the context in which it is applied. The UN Secretary General's Report (2004) stresses that transitional justice should include mechanisms for criminal justice, truth-telling, reparations, and vetting. Reinforcing this, De Greiff (2012) also highlights the necessity of a comprehensive process as omitting certain aspects leads to paucity. Providing reparation schemes for victims whilst not addressing their abuses through a truth tribunal or criminal court gives the impression of "buying them out". Conversely, if a perpetrator is tried and found guilty, but the victim isn't compensated adequately, the impact of the trial loses personal significance as the victim isn't supported. Additionally, the process must also include reform and vetting of institutions as their role in enabling past abuses has led to a loss of trust and legitimacy amongst civilians. Ultimately, the role of transitional justice is to rectify past human rights abuses through the mechanisms stated previously with the goals of providing recognition to victims, fostering civil trust, contributing to reconciliation and democratisation (De Greiff, 2012). This role means that transitional justice, similar to DDR, can also be classified as a provision addressing the by-products of conflict.

Transitional justice, similar to DDR, can also be fraught with difficulties. Along with the problems of a non-holistic approach as aforementioned, the individual mechanisms also run into roadblocks derailing the process. Reparations, whilst providing victims with financial support, also raises some questions as how much compensation would be appropriate. Financial support is never adequate in post-conflict nations due to the reduced capacity of the state.

Acquiring testimonies and dispensing justice can be problematic due to the individuals that have the potential to be implicated. For example, high-ranking government and military officials may be accused and connected to human rights violations that took place during the conflict period. Additionally, in a stalemate conflict where there is no clear victor, the non-government belligerent groups may be co-opted within the political institutions despite being linked to human rights abuses. As these groups are pivotal in setting the post-conflict agenda, they may not see it in their best interests to involve themselves in the justice process which could lead to them being found guilty. This often leads to a situation where the rank and file of a force are subjected to trial whilst those giving the orders avoid justice mechanisms. Additionally, transitional justice can also be weaponised in a post-conflict situation as it may be deployed disproportionately by rival political factions in order to weaken one another. These undermine the overall goals of transitional justice as stated by De Greiff.

Clause 8.4 of the CPA mentions, albeit in a limited capacity, the creation of transitional justice mechanisms (CPA, 2006). It expresses the commitment of the parties in the creation of a National Peace and Rehabilitation Commission, a Truth and Reconciliation Commission, a High-Level State Restructuring Recommendation Commission, and other mechanisms. In clause 9, the document agrees to the continuation of human rights monitoring by the OHCHR as well as the NHRC which would facilitate the process of transitional justice. The CPA can be credited with the commitment of creating mechanisms for a holistic transitional justice process, the importance of which is outlined by scholars and academics alike. Additionally, the mandating of human rights monitoring for independent bodies such as the OHCHR is also a positive as they are able to mitigate the politicisation that usually plagues transitional justice processes in post-conflict nations. However, the omission of a detailed framework for transitional justice within the CPA far outweighs the minor positives from these inclusions.

Clause 8.2 of the CPA states that the formation and terms of reference of the National Peace and Rehabilitation Commission is to be determined by the interim Council of Ministers (CPA, 2006). Firstly, this delays the process of transitional justice as the workings of the institutions have not been included. The CPA omits details such as the actions that constitute human rights abuses, the compensation a victim is entitled to, what kind of high-level state-restructuring will take place and more. The inability of the CPA to distinguish these vital aspects undermines the effectiveness of the transitional justice process.

Secondly, by allowing the Council of Ministers to set the agenda for the transitional justice, the CPA makes the process more susceptible to politicisation. The CPA was signed during an environment of parity between the Maoists and the Government as the conflict had reached a stalemate. This enabled both parties to possess equal leverage in regard to formulating the document. By failing to outline a thorough transitional justice process and allowing the Council of Ministers to set this agenda, the parties risk the process succumbing to the future political climate. For example, if either of the parties were to dominate the future political landscape, they could use the transitional justice process as a means to incriminate those from rival parties in an attempt to weaken them. Simultaneously, they could disregard their own violations which further undermines the process. This is antithetical to the values of transitional justice which requires a fair judiciary in order to holistically address the human rights violations that occurred previously.

The inclusion of an independent third party, such as the UN, can be used to mitigate the issue of politicisation. However, unlike the DDR process, the role of this third party within transitional justice is minimal. Whilst the OHCHR have been mandated to monitor human rights, the CPA does not specify whether this includes the timeframe of the conflict era. This uncertainty is further exacerbated by the fact that the OHCHR has a conflicting mandate with the NHRC. As the NHRC is nationally led, it has an increased likelihood of being hijacked by political parties. The work of the OHCHR is also likely to be dismissed due to unfavourable findings and the whole process of transitional justice becomes tailor-made to suit the interests of the incumbent party. The CPA does not go far enough in detailing the process of transitional justice and what little is available is fraught with difficulties.

Root Causes of the Conflict

Socio-Political-Economic Reform

The end of the Cold War witnessed a surge in intra-state conflict as repressed hostilities surfaced within nations. Unlike interstate wars, which was the previous norm, a civil conflict resulted in warring parties having to be accommodated within the same nation. This was interpreted as a zero-sum game by warring parties as they committed genocide in an attempt to create a homogenous population as witnessed in the atrocities in Rwanda and the Balkans. Rising to this challenge, the Western nations along with the UN, formulated a doctrine of post-conflict reconstruction which would eventually be termed as "liberal peacebuilding". As the name suggests, the peacebuilding process was heavily influenced by Western norms and values based on democratisation, universal human rights, and neoliberal economics. This was facilitated by the fall of the Soviet Union and its satellite states as well as the fact that this era preceded the rise of China as a global superpower that could challenge the West. The West, uncontested in the Security Council, favoured humanitarian intervention over state sovereignty (Ryan, 2013). Seminal works such as Boutros-Ghali's (2015) "An Agenda for Peace" and the International Commission on Intervention and State Sovereignty's "The Responsibility to Protect" (2001) were vital in the conduct of UN and Western interventions in post-conflict nations. Whilst peacebuilding tackled the by-products of conflict through DDR and transitional justice mechanisms, it also aimed to transform the political, social, and economic landscape that motivated the conflict. To this end, the political, social, and economic reforms that constitute peacebuilding can be deemed as addressing the root causes of conflict.

The belief that democracy can create and consolidate peace is not new. It stretches back to Kantian philosophy which indicates that the general populace is likely to avoid war as they have to bear the brunt of the costs (Kant, 2008). Whilst this rationale was initially reserved for inter-state wars, recently it has been applied to the civil sphere. Democracies enable dispute settlement through non-violent means such as voting in elections or referendums. Moreover, whilst making negotiation and peaceful means feasible, democracies simultaneously make armed conflict more costly for dissatisfied actors. Alternatively, in other modes of government, peaceful means to settle differences such as protests may be restricted which would ultimately encourage violence. Additionally, the military possess the legitimacy to use violence but are under the control of democratic institutions in a liberal democratic nation. On the other hand, in a repressive state, the control of the army may be under a despot who could deploy it to squash peaceful protests which could increase the likelihood of a civil conflict.

This rationale has heavily influenced the liberal peacebuilding carried out by the UN and the West (Paris, 2004). Espoused within the liberal peace doctrine is the political transformation of states which sees the calls for free and fair elections, securing political rights for marginalised groups, democratisation of the military, as well as other forms of democratic institutions. By exporting the ideals of democracy to divided post-conflict societies, the interveners aspire to create conditions where armed violence is costly and peaceful negotiation is more attractive. Additionally, securing political rights for marginalised groups also aids in consolidating long-term peace.

The framework of liberal peace is perceived to be a synergy between peace, democracy, and the free market (Mandelbaum, 2002). Kant, yet again, draws the correlation between a liberalised market and peace by stating that the

Evaluating the Comprehensive Peace Agreement 37

nature of commerce is incompatible with conflict (Kant, 2008). Again, this was implied to the context of interstate wars as if nations were economically interdependent through trade, the cost of going to war would increase. The pacifying effect of a liberalised economy was further propagated by neo-liberal scholars (Keohane and Nye, 1987). The Marshal Plan which provided aid to post-conflict nations functioned under the rationale that market liberalisation and democracy are parallel to one another. Liberal peacebuilding also applies this logic to nations fresh off a civil war in order to strengthen democracy which ultimately leads to peace.

The International Monetary Fund (IMF), the World Bank, as well as regional banks such as the Asian Development Bank, have been heavily involved in post-conflict environments. These institutions along with the UN recommend market liberalisation in order to promote development and foster peace. Market liberalisation allows the inflow of Foreign Direct Investment (FDI) which in theory is followed by the inflow of capital, skills, and other expertise that are needed for the growth of the domestic market (Ganson and Wennmann, 2015). Along with FDI, privatisation and more liberal trade policies are also recommended. Private businesses are deemed to be more efficient and allow the government to focus on developmental objectives in a conflict situation whilst liberal trade policies make the market more competitive (Williamson, 1990). In short, the role of economic reform is to create prosperity and foster development in order to create conditions to make conflict less likely.

Political and economic reforms need to work in conjunction whilst considering the social context of a post-conflict nation. Social tensions in post-conflict nations are increasingly high, especially when the war has been fought along the lines of religion or ethnicity. A failure to address the social context may result in the peacebuilding process deepening the divides between groups in a nation. For example, the development community in Rwanda, following the failed Arusha Accords of 1993, acquired land to build offices for peacebuilding work (Uvin, 1998). Not only did this displace the Hutus, who were traditionally farmers, but the development community also disproportionately hired from the Tutsi community. This fostered resentment towards the Tutsis by the Hutus who eventually carried out an attempted genocide with astronomical death tolls. In addition to understanding the social context of the recipient nation, the social reform also needs to redress the grievances that marginalised groups have faced in the past. Liberal peacebuilding addresses and challenges this by introducing universal human rights as well as the protection of minority groups through the constitution.

The CPA acknowledges that social, political, and economic reform is conducive to long-lasting peace. The preamble itself commits to "keeping democracy, peace, prosperity, progressive socio-economic change . . . at the centre" (CPA, 2006, p. 1). The document particularly reinforces the democratic values that are enshrined in the liberal peace doctrine. Clause 3.4 outlines that political reform within the country will be of a democratic nature with periodic elections, transparency and accountability, constitutional balance, multiparty competition, and more. Clause 3.5 also hints at the devolution of power away from the central government and an introduction of a federal system as it states there is to be an ending of "the current centralised and unitary form of state". Additionally, the CPA also confirms the devotion of the political parties to conduct a restructuring and democratisation of the army as it was previously under the control of the monarchy. Social considerations are also addressed within the peace agreement. The devolution of the power of the central government is rationalised in order to address the problems related to the marginalised groups in Nepal.

The economic reform within the CPA is very ambiguous. There is a commitment to increasing employment, income generation, investment, and trade. However, the steps to be taken to ensure this has not been outlined. The peace agreement also intends to transform Nepal from a feudal system to a democratic country which has economic implications. To illustrate this, the document commits itself to land reforms within the country by introducing "scientific land reforms" and to end all forms of feudalism (CPA, 2006, p. 4). This also has social consequences as those victims of the feudal system in Nepal largely belonged to marginalised groups.

The CPA follows the general framework of peace agreements as it attempts conflict resolution by redefining the state, disaggregating power, and dislocating power (Bell, 2008). However, these are only outlined within the CPA and there is an inherent lack of detail. Nevertheless, the CPA through clause 2b does insinuate that the creation of a constituent assembly and the promulgation of a new constitution is an explicit goal of the signatories. The constitution, which was eventually announced in 2015, can be deemed to be part of the peace process as it was introduced to combat the root causes of the civil war. It attempts to addresses the lack of political representation of marginalised groups, to transform the feudal and monarchic state system, create a federal government to better meet the needs of citizens at a grassroots level, and more. These were all the grievances highlighted by the Maoist rebels prior to conducting their civil war (ICC, 2005). Scholars such as Ljiphart (2004) perceive constitutions as extensions of the peace process and propose constitutional designs to foster long-lasting peace within a nation. Despite this, there has been a lack of analysis of the 2015 constitution in regard to the Nepal peace process. To this end, this section will perceive the 2015 constitution as part of the peace process in Nepal by highlighting how it aimed to tackle the root causes of conflict.

Nepal has had different forms of government throughout its history. The kings have held absolute power as well as having a constitution role. A system of autocracy existed under the Rana Prime Ministers and the nation flirted with democracy in the 1950s and 1990s. However, a consistent feature amongst all of these governments was the centrality of the state. Despite geographical, ethnic, and regional constraints, power was always exercised by a central authority in Kathmandu. The grievances of this form of governance were

Evaluating the Comprehensive Peace Agreement   39

felt particularly at the local levels as their political representation was severely curtailed (Adhikari, 2014). This was influential in the promotion of the idea of a federal state which was seen in the Maoist demand prior to the war, the CPA, and the People's movement in 2006 (Adhikari, 2015).

The 2015 constitution seeks to mitigate the issues by adopting a federal framework (Constitution of Nepal, 2015). It restructures the state into a federal, provincial, and local entities each armed with a degree of autonomy. This autonomy at the local level includes tax collection, health service management, preservation of culture, control of local land, provincial police, and others. The central government has the power to conduct matters relating to national defence, diplomatic affairs, income tax, and more. The constitution also enshrines concurrent powers, which are powers that are to be enjoyed between the three levels. Additionally, the constitution also reinforces the democratic values included in the liberal peace doctrine such as the democratisation of the army, free and fair elections, a multiparty system, and more.

Additionally, the political reforms also have also addressed social grievances that led to the civil war. The legislature is bicameral in nature with the Federal Parliament consisting of the House of Representatives and the National assembly framework (Constitution of Nepal, 2015). A total of 110 of the 275 members of the House of Representatives will be elected by means of proportional representation which gives historically marginalised groups within the nation representation within the national legislature. The National Assembly, made up of 59 members, also guarantees representation of marginalised groups, albeit to a very limited level. The President and the Vice-President as well as the Speaker and Vice-Speaker of the parliament also have to be of different genders or parties. The constitution also ensures the human rights of marginalised groups within the country, a feature consistent with the CPA and liberal peacebuilding norms. The constitution also declared Nepal to be a secular nation and thereby ending its unique identity of being the only Hindu Kingdom in the world.

Feudalism and its negative effects on marginalised groups and the economy was stressed in the 40-point demand as well as the CPA. This along with the lack of economic infrastructure, corruption, and inadequate developmental policies had made Nepal one of the poorest nations on the planet. To address this, the constitution calls for an end to the feudal system and an introduction of scientific land reforms which is not developed within the constitution. The constitution also espouses neo-liberal values with the promotion of private enterprise, free and fair competitive market, import and export, and the encouraging of foreign capital and technology investment. Economic coordination between the different levels of government is also highlighted by the constitution so that the fruits of development can be obtained at all levels.

Economic reforms are also coupled with social considerations. The theoretical ending of the feudal system ends the serfdom of landless marginalised groups. The constitution also guarantees the right to employment and business for those from historically underprivileged groups.

Conclusion

Through the exploration of the CPA and its related documents, we can conclude whether there was an adequate framework in place for guiding the peace process in Nepal. A "good" peace agreement would include an implementation timetable, international monitoring, detailed intricacies within each mechanism, technical feasibility among others. From this perspective it is clear that the CPA fails to create the necessary framework and therefore can be deemed as being a "bad" agreement.

Firstly, the CPA and the 2015 constitutions can be credited for correctly addressing the needs of a comprehensive peace process. The parties correctly identify the mechanisms needed to tackle the by-products of the conflict such as a DDR and Transitional Justice process. Additionally, the CPA and the constitution does exceptionally well to recognise the underlying root causes of conflict. The need to introduce democracy, end the feudal system of state, and promote as well as protect the rights of the marginalised groups within the country is consistently reinforced between the documents. This is largely to do with the Maoists acquiring legitimacy and being involved in setting the agenda of the peace accords. Specific aspects of the CPA such as the ceasefire clause also has the level of detail required for success whilst clauses such as DDR attempt to outline a general framework.

However, largely the CPA does not go far enough to create a suitable framework for the peace process. DDR, despite being one of the most detailed mechanisms, still omits vital provisions related to the large number of child and women soldiers within the rebel army. Additionally, the reintegration aspect of the clause is also largely underdeveloped. The transitional justice mechanisms espoused within the CPA is wholly ineffective in creating the conditions for a holistic process. By leaving the workings of the transitional justice process to the Council of Ministers, the CPA allows for the process to be fragmented along political lines. Moreover, whilst the recognition of the OHCHR as a monitoring body is beneficial, they do not have an outlined mandate and their monitoring work clashes with the mandate of the NHRC. Finally, the social, political, and economic reform also has major shortcomings. The transition into a democracy is outlined well enough in the CPA and the 2015 constitution can be accurately labelled as a liberal democratic document. However, the socio-political reforms do not go far enough to address the disadvantages of marginalised groups in Nepal. The 48% of proportional seats within the House of Representatives is actually lower than the 58% in the pre-war 1990 constitution which mitigates the representation of marginalised groups. The 59-member National Assembly also aims to represent marginalised groups; however, the minimum number of women required is three and only one Dalit and one individual from a minority group. The CPA or the constitution also do not detail the transformation of the existing feudal system apart from guaranteeing "scientific" land reforms. There is also a glaring absence of implementation timetable

Evaluating the Comprehensive Peace Agreement 41

within the CPA enabling a lack of accountability to the progress of the peace process. These reforms are not detailed and severely undermines the social, political, and economic transformation of the country.

References

25-Point Code of Conduct. (2006), 25-Point Code of Conduct between the Government of Nepal and the Communist Party of Nepal (Maoist), 26 May 2006. https://pea cemaker.un.org/nepal-25pointceasefire2006]

8-Point Agreement. (2006), 8 Point Agreement between the Seven Party Alliance and the Communist Party of Nepal (Maoist), 16 June 2006. https://peacemaker.un.org/ sites/peacemaker.un.org/files/NP_060616_Eight%20Point%20Agreement.pdf

Adhikari, A. (2014). *The Bullet and the Ballot Box: The Story of Nepal's Maoist Revolution.* Verso.

Adhikari, I. (2015). *Military and Democracy in Nepal* (1st ed.). Routledge India.

Ansorg, N., & Strasheim, J. (2018). Veto Players in Post-Conflict DDR Programs: Evidence From Nepal and the DRC. *Journal Of Intervention and Statebuilding, 13*(1), 112–130. https://doi.org/10.1080/17502977.2018.1501981

Baldus, C. (2004). Vestigia pacis. The Roman Peace Treaty: Structure or Event?. *Historia, 3*(51), 103–146.

BBC. (2006). Nepal Maoist rebels declare truce. *News.bbc.co.uk.* Retrieved 15 February 2021, from http://news.bbc.co.uk/2/hi/south_asia/4949066.stm

Bell, C. (2008). *On the Law of Peace: Peace Agreements and the Lex Pacificatoria.* Oxford University Press.

Boutros-Ghali, B. (2015). *An Agenda for Peace: Preventive Diplomacy, Peacemaking and Peace-Keeping.* United Nations.

Constitution of Nepal. Lawcommission.gov.np. (2015). Retrieved 17 March 2021, from www.lawcommission.gov.np/en/archives/category/documents/prevailing-law/const itution/constitution-of-nepal

CPA. (2006). Contemporary Peace Agreement between the Government of Nepal and the Communist Party of Nepal (Maoist), 21 November 2006. https://peacemaker. un.org/nepal-comprehensiveagreement2006

De Greiff, P. (2012). Theorizing Transitional Justice. *NOMOS, 51,* 31–77.

Dixit, K. (2006). The Spring of Dissent: People's Movement in Nepal. *India International Centre Quarterly, 33*(1), 113–125.

DPKO. (2010). *Second Generation Disarmament, Demobilisation and Reintegration (DDR) Practices in Peace Operations.* United Nations.

Ganson, B., & Wennmann, A. (2015). Business and Conflict in Fragile States. *Adelphi Series, 55*(457–458), 11–34.

Galtung, J. (1969). Violence, Peace, and Peace Research. *Journal of Peace Research, 6*(3), 167–191. https://doi.org/10.1177/002234336900600301

Henshaw, A. (2019). Female Combatants in Post Conflict Processes: Understanding the Roots of Exclusion. *Journal Of Global Security Studies, 5*(1), 63–79. https://doi.org/ 10.1093/jogss/ogz050

Hutchinson, E., & Bleiker, R. (2013). Reconciliation. In R. Mac Ginty, *Routledge Handbook of Peacebuilding* (pp. 81–90). Routledge.

ICC. (2005). *Nepal's Maoists: Their Aims, Structure and Strategy.* International Crisis Group.

42 *Raunak Mainali*

International Commission on Intervention and State Sovereignty (2001). *The Responsibility to Protect*. International Development Research Centre.

Kaldor, M. (2012). *New and Old Wars* (3rd ed.). Polity Press.

Kant, I. (2008). *Toward Perpetual Peace and Other Writings on Politics, Peace, and History*. Yale University Press.

Kantha, P. (2012). Maoist-Madhesi Dynamics and Nepal's Peace Process. In M. Lawoti & A. Pahari, *The Maoist Insurgency in Nepal: Revolution in the Twenty-first Century*. Routledge.

Keohane, R., & Nye, J. (1987). Power and Interdependence Revisited. *International Organization, 41*(4), 725–753. https://doi.org/10.1017/s0020818300027661

Lawoti, M. (2012). Ethnic Dimensions of the Maoist Insurgencies: Indigenous Groups' Participation and Insurgency Trajectories in Nepal, Peru and India. In M. Lawoti & A. Pahari, *The Maoist Insurgency in Nepal: Revolution in the Twenty-first Century*. Routledge.

Lijphart, A. (2004). Constitutional Design for Divided Societies. *Journal Of Democracy, 15*(2), 96–109. https://doi.org/10.1353/jod.2004.0029

Mandelbaum, M. (2002). *The Ideas That Conquered The World*. Public Affairs.

Özerdem, A. (2013). Disarmament, Demobilisation and Reintegration. In R. Mac Ginty, *Routledge Handbook of Peace Building* (pp. 225–236). Routledge.

Paris, R. (2004). *At War's End: Building Peace after Civil Conflict*. Cambridge University Press.

Prachanda & Koirala, G.P. (2006). Letters to Kofi A. Annan, August 2006.

Rich, J., & Shipley, G. (1993). *War and Society in the Roman World*. Routledge.

Ryan, S. (2013). The Evolution in Peace Building. In R. Mac Ginty, *Routledge Handbook of Peace Building* (pp. 225–236). Routledge.

Shekhawat, S., & Pathak, B. (2015). Female Combatants, Peace Process and the Exclusion. In S. Shekhawat, *Female Combatants in Conflict and Peace* (1st ed., pp. 53–68). Palgrave Macmillan.

Sthapit, L., & Doneys, P. (2017). Female Maoist Combatants during and after the People's War. In Å. Kolås, *Women, Peace and Security in Nepal: From Civil War to Post-Conflict Reconstruction*. Routledge.

Swarbrick, P. (2007). *Avoiding Disarmament Failure: The Critical Link in DDR. An Operational Manual for Donors, Managers, and Practitioners*. The Small Arms Survey.

UN Secretary General's Report. (2004). *The Rule of Law and Transitional Justice in Conflict and Post-Conflict Societies*. United Nations Security Council.

UNSG. (2008). *Securing Peace and Development: The Role of the United Nations in Supporting Security Sector Reform. Report of the Secretary-General*. UN document no. A/62/659-S/2008/39. United Nations.

Uvin, P. (1998). *Aiding Violence: The Development Enterprise in Rwanda*. Kumarian Press.

Williamson, J. (1990). What Washington Means by Policy Reform. In J. Williamson, *Latin American Adjustment: How Much Has Happened?*, 2nd ed. Institute for International Economics.

Zartman, W. (1998). Putting Humpty-Dumpty Together Again. In D. Lake & D. Rothchild, *The International Spread of Ethnic Conflict: Fear, Diffusion, and Escalation*. Princeton University Press.

3 Rural Attitudes Towards the Peace Process in Nepal

Voice of the Villages

Raunak Mainali

Introduction

In Nepal, as in many other developing countries, there remains widespread disparities between urban centres and rural areas. Employment and education opportunities along with the wealth of the nation is often concentrated within these areas leading to internal migration from the villages to the cities. Schools, hospitals, and government presence is a scarcity and agriculture remains the primary means of survival. After centuries of centralised governance, Nepal's wealth and political power was concentrated mainly within Kathmandu Valley with other areas such as Pokhara, Rasuwa, and Chitwan also faring comparatively well. Developmental budgets and administrative appointments for rural areas were and are still largely orchestrated by the government in Kathmandu with little consideration for the needs of rural areas. Social media posts showing people having to cross fast-flowing rivers by zipline to get to school or a health point have gone viral even in recent years and many are familiar with their parents' stories about having to walk hours up and down hills to get to school. These posts and anecdotes are emblematic of a bigger issue in Nepal: the neglect and underdevelopment of the rural. Areas which now constitute the Far-Western and Mid-Western regions of Nepal had minimal state presence and performed the worst in terms of Human Development Index (HDI). Districts within these regions such as Mugu, Bajura, Kalikot, and Bajhang had the lowest HDI scored in the country in 2001 whereas Kathmandu, Bhaktapur, and Lalitpur, all within the Kathmandu Valley, had the highest (Devi Dulal, 2021). This is not to say that those living in urban areas are all elites as the levels of poverty in Nepali cities are still high when compared to more developed countries. However, as mentioned above, the concentration of wealth and opportunities in these cities has led to an existence of an elite class whose situations are vastly different from those in rural areas.

The Maoists, aware of the lack of state presence within the western regions of Nepal, launched their protracted civil war from the area, mainly the districts of Rukum and Rolpa. The negligence of the central government enabled Maoists to take over isolated police stations, recruit members through persuasion or coercion, and even create an alternative revolutionary governance

DOI: 10.4324/9781003289876-4

44 *Raunak Mainali*

in some areas (Lecomte-Tilouine, 2009). The fighting was primarily limited to the hilly regions of western Nepal which was optimal for guerrilla tactics as it included jungles for cover and a population that had been ostracised by the central government for centuries. However, violence sometimes did manifest itself, mainly in the form of bombings, in urban areas such as Kathmandu and Janakpur. The Maoists clearly outlined the need to develop rural Nepal and included it within their 40-point demand prior to the start of the conflict. They demanded that rural and urban areas be treated equally and that local bodies should be empowered, a precursor to the eventual adoption of the federal system in Nepal.

The aim of this chapter is to highlight the attitudes of the rural population of Nepal regarding the peace process. Theoretically, the main beneficiaries of any peace process are the citizens themselves and it is important to assess their attitudes to gain a comprehensive understanding of the process. Nepal's political discourse, despite the new federal structure, is so often dominated by voices in Kathmandu at the detriment of the rural population. Political analysis conducted by the intelligentsia of Kathmandu, international academics, or NGOs sometimes drown out the knowledge of the local population whose political awareness has increased since the civil war. The chapter is based on focus group discussions conducted in 2018 in districts affected by the conflict. These include: Jhapa, Bardiya, Sunsari, Dang, Morang, and Surkhet. Most of these discussions took place in village wards with the exception of Birtamode (Jhapa), Ghorahi (Dang), and Birendranagar (Surkhet) which took place in cities. However, these cities do not possess the same level of development as those within the Kathmandu Valley and fighting did take place during the civil war within the city and its surrounding areas. Additionally, interviews were also conducted in Kathmandu with senior bureaucrats, civil society leaders, and ex-combatants. This was done in order to account for any differences in perspectives between those in Kathmandu and those outside. The chapter hopes to challenge some common misconceptions held within Nepal relating to the civil war and post-war governance.

One Step Forward

From the focus group discussions, a clear positive of the civil war and the resulting peace process was the overall reduction of caste discrimination. As analysed by a previous chapter in this volume as well as a host of other texts, caste discrimination in Nepal had marginalised those who were not from the hill-Brahmin/Chettri castes. Caste discrimination was even more prevalent in rural Nepal where a lack of state presence meant that it was even more difficult to uphold the existing anti-discrimination laws. Rural Nepal also functioned in a feudal framework where the landowners mostly came from dominant castes whilst those from marginalised groups formed the peasantry. A Tharu participant from Dhadhwar in Bardiya stated that previously the Brahmins from the village would not eat food made by Tharus and other lower caste individuals.[1]

If they entered an upper-caste household, they would have had to clean it with cow dung before leaving in order to "purify" the house. However, they relayed that this was not the case anymore as caste discrimination had greatly reduced. A common view shared by individuals across these focus group discussions was that caste discrimination was less intense now than previously and any caste prejudice was mostly held by those from older generations. The participants also stated that arranged marriages, engineered by parents or older relatives, are mainly limited within their castes which reflects the reservations held by older generations. On the other hand, inter-caste marriages are mostly a result of love marriages where the individuals marry out of affection and therefore caste is not usually considered. Research conducted by Poudel (2018) and Basnet & Jha (2019) explore inter-caste marriages between Dalits and non-Dalits as well as between the Hill population and Madhesis. Both examples illustrate the difficulty of inter-caste marriage for the couples as they become alienated by their parents and other relatives. The rise in inter-caste marriages can partly be attributed to the Maoists who encouraged marriage between caste groups as a means of ending caste discrimination. After the conflict, the government of Nepal even offered grants to inter-caste couples recognising their financial vulnerability resulting from their ostracization from their families. However, there are still examples of instances in rural areas where couples are forced to split up due to caste incompatibility and, in extreme cases, violence is also used. Recently, a Dalit youth and five of his friends were stoned to death because he was in love with an upper-caste Chettri girl (Adhikari, 2020). The incident also took place in Rukum, an area that was and is still regarded as a Maoist stronghold. Therefore, whilst caste discrimination may have decreased overall, it has not been completely eradicated and still exists even in areas controlled by the anti-caste Maoists.

Another positive development that was mostly consistent between interviewees in the rural areas was the introduction of federal governance, particularly local. The 2015 constitution of Nepal introduced the federal framework in Nepal as an antidote to the failures of the long-established centralised system. The 2017 elections of Nepal were the first to encompass the federal framework and local governance bodies were created to induce more inclusive, efficient, and accountable development at the local level.

> Previously, it would take at least 10 days even to request an electricity pole from the district centre. Now it is much easier. But if we want even better service, there should be a better mechanism of leadership and governance. Apart from that, we are satisfied with the current local unit.[2]

There was similar praise for local governance across the interviews as the access to state mechanism itself was an achievement for many in rural areas who had found themselves excluded in previous administrations. Rural citizens were able to lobby their local politicians on developmental issues such as physical infrastructure, education, health, and more and had the knowledge that they could potentially vote them out in future elections if promises were not kept. The interviews also revealed other positive aspects that arose because of the new local governance. Villages that were "rivals" in previous governance mechanisms now found themselves within the same administrative unit which fostered cooperative relations and familial ties. Similarly, another participant provides an example of a Magar community and Dalit community coming together to celebrate each other's cultures during festivals.

The enthusiasm for local government can also clearly be seen from the turnout rate for the 2017 local elections. The first round saw a turnout rate of 73.81%, followed by 73.38% and 77% for the second and third round respectively. For comparison, the US presidential elections of 2020 saw a turnout rate of only 62% whilst the 2018 local council elections in England saw a meagre turnout rate of just 35%. The 2022 local elections of Nepal saw a decrease in turnout by about 10% but there were still positives to draw. The dissatisfaction with the Nepal Communist Party (NCP), who were in power for most of the electoral term, was displayed in the local election results as the share of local representatives for the Unified Marxist-Leninist faction of the NCP plummeted. This clearly shows that Nepali citizens were willing to use the ballot box to hold leaders accountable. Additionally, many were dissatisfied with the mainstream parties and their leaders who had largely remained the same since the start of the civil war in the mid 90s. This led to an increase of independent candidates elected at the local level including in rural areas as ward chairperson and members. Major cities such as Kathmandu, Dharan, Dhangadi, and Janakpur also elected independent mayors.

A clear distinction can be made here between the political elites of the mainstream parties in Kathmandu and the rural population. As mentioned previously, local governance was cited by many within the discussions as one of the main achievements of the peace process as it has the potential to address the concerns of populations that had been on the periphery of Kathmandu's elites. K.P. Oli, the first prime minister of Nepal under the framework of federalism, constantly undermined local and provincial governments and stated that they were not independent political units but were subordinate to the federal government (Kathmandu Post, 2019). Similarly, political elites within other mainstream parties, such as Nepali Congress as well as alternative parties such as Sajha Party, remain sceptical about federalism and have expressed their desire to call a referendum on the topic.

The increase in political consciousness within the rural population is also seen as a positive of the civil war by some. This changed the political dynamics in Nepal where previously the nation functioned under a framework that involved the "rulers" in Kathmandu and the "ruled" in rural areas. The empowerment of women, marginalised groups, and the rural population has led many from these groups to believe that they can be agents of change as opposed to just recipients of development. Issues that were previously taboo and left unengaged such as gender and caste became regular topics of conversation. This is essential for the transition of Nepal into a more democratic nation. As a Tharu woman from Dang puts it:

> Yesterday our thoughts were limited up to the works done for landlords like raising cattle and doing their household works but today our level of thinking is different. Today people think of how we spend our lives peacefully and how can we contribute for the development of society.[3]

Two Steps Back

Whilst the introduction of local elections have been viewed positively by the populace in regard to its potential, many stated their dissatisfaction with local governments in practice. The same pathogens found in earlier forms of Nepal's governance has infected local governance in Nepal, namely corruption and clientelism. Developmental project contracts are handed by local politicians to contractors who are usually a family member, friend, or party affiliate. In return, contractors fund the election campaigns for these politicians. This practice is so widespread in Nepal that the terms for contractor and middleman in Nepali (*thekedar* and *dalal*) carry negative connotations.

> When a candidate spends a fortune in election campaigns and wins the position, after the election he/she collects his/her expenses by creating channels among high positions to lower positions and profiting in the name of development. It is hard for low-earning people to run for local offices.[4]

As the quote states, the lucrative nature of development contracts in Nepal means that low-earning people are unable to win local offices. So just as the centralised government was previously run by national elites, the local and provincial government are now under local and provincial elites and their associates. The inefficiency and corruption of local governments is accepted to be the reality by many in Nepal. However, the solution is far more divisive. As mentioned previously, there are some elements within the country that want to be rid of federalism. On the other hand, a resounding number of participants within the rural area wanted to fix the system as opposed to getting rid of it. As of right now, the most effective way to take advantage of the local governance is to be affiliated with a party. As a citizen of Suddhodhan in Rupandehi says:

> In Nepal, if one does not have affiliation with a party then they would have to face difficulties even to solve their daily struggles. This is not a good aspect, but the public participates in political activities through political parties. This has politicised most areas of society. Independent people often try different ways, but they are unable to succeed in this highly politicised society[5].

48   *Raunak Mainali*

The benefits of the local governments have clearly not been equitably distributed amongst the local population as proximity to the ruling party seems to be a prerequisite for any state support. Some within the focus groups even stated that the Local Peace Committees (LPCs) were heavily politicised with compensation sometimes only given to those who have strong political or bureaucratic connections, a notion that has been put forward by other research (Tandukar et al., 2016).

There is an observable difference between those who are well connected and those who are not. Whilst conducting interviews for this chapter, I came across two ex-child combatants whose situation drastically differed. The first of these individuals now works as a full-time activist furthering the cause of former child soldiers and enjoys connections with politicians and NGOs.[6] Articles relating to them have been published frequently since they started their activism. They also frequently hold conferences and events in collaboration with NGOs in hotels around Kathmandu. On the other hand, the second former soldier is part of an organisation that does not have any connections with political parties or NGOs. He states that the Maoists had been actively dividing the ex-combatants in order to weaken them and their organisation wanted to remain independent of any other organisation to create a united former child soldier's organisation.[7] Evidence from Nepal has shown that donor organisations have led to less harmonious relations between organisations that ultimately possess the same aim; this is largely due to competition for funding (Bhattarai, 2015). This has meant that the organisation has very little financial support and is not able to pursue activism full-time as those with financial backing may. The second child soldier was part of Kathmandu's growing gig economy working as a driver for a ride-sharing mobile application. Whilst there may be other factors that have led to their disparate situations in the post-conflict era, political and organisational networks certainly pay a major role.

As stated before, one of the positives of the conflict was the empowerment of marginalised groups who felt more confident in demanding their rights and speaking on taboo subjects. As a result, women in rural areas have viewed gender progress in Nepal through a critical lens as displayed by this statement from a participant in Lamahi, Dang:[8]

> In reality, females should be taken to a place where they can make decisions. Women are only in those places where they are guided and where there is mandatory quota reservation which is also politically influenced. We women have not been able to reach that place freely. In legal terms, they fulfil the quota but in actual terms their place is just ceremonial.

Additionally, there are also other factors that have led to a lack of state support for the rural population. Women as well as some men in these discussions stated that they often felt reluctant to engage with state officials because many were subjected to violence at the hands of the state. This is consistent with the study conducted by Selim (2018) who found that women were hesitant to go to the police as they were victims of the police through torture and Sexual and Gender-Based Violence (SGBV) during the war. High-ranking administrative positions within each district such as Chief District Officer (CDO) are appointed by the federal government and many find this problematic due to the vast array of powers that are held by what they believe to be a "non-local" entity. CDOs were also in charge of district security during the civil war, and many gave orders that directly led to the killings of Maoists as well as violence against civilians. In regions with large numbers of ex-Maoist combatants and those who were abused at the hands of the state, there remains some resentment against them. The powers of the CDO have been curtailed since the introduction of federalism as jurisdiction related to dispute settlement, environment, and agriculture have been handed to local governments. Nevertheless, the conflict era seems to have eroded trust between forces of the state and some citizens from rural areas.

The decline in community trust within rural settings also warrants analysis. Participants pointed out that in their respective localities, those who were ex-combatants or Maoist sympathisers were stigmatised and labelled as violent. A woman from Pathari Shanishchare, Morang stated that in their village those who were involved with the Maoists were ostracised because they were perceived to have joined the conflict for selfish reasons.[9] Within the same discussion, the members pointed out that a local Maoist who had nothing before the revolution, now had four houses and that these types of selfish individuals should have action taken against them. Similar viewpoints were shared in other discussions as Maoists were involved in looting and confiscation of property and wealth in rural areas and therefore members were associated with self-aggrandizement.

The fact that those involved with the Maoists are perceived to be self-serving displays a clear failure of LPCs and other local peace efforts. The reality is that the decision to join the Maoists, for many, was far from a simple one based on selfish tendencies and greed. For example, a female ex-combatant from Magaragadi in Bardiya relayed that women in their locality faced violence at the hands of the state despite not being Maoists.[10] Hence, it made sense for them to join the Maoists and have the capability to defend themselves from further abuse from the state forces.

In some villages, men were targeted by the state forces due to being alleged Maoists so they ran away to the cities or to India.[11] This left many women being targeted by state forces and were forced to join the Maoists for security. Other recruits who joined as Maoists instigated a "one house, one Maoist" rule within areas where each household had to volunteer a recruit or provide financial help to the party (Sthapit & Doneys, 2017). This choice was not really a choice for those from poor rural areas and therefore they chose to provide a volunteer. Finally, there were people who joined the Maoists out of the real desire to improve their country and align themselves with the rebel group's agenda. A woman ex-combatant from Aurabarni, Sunsari mentioned that the reason she, along with other women from her village, joined the Maoists was

50 *Raunak Mainali*

because of their anti-patriarchal ideology which resonated with the women from the village.[12] Even in Thabang, an area considered to be the rebel ideological heartland, the local people were inclined to align with the Maoists mainly to foster community unity (Zharkevich, 2015). A participant from Birendrangar, Surkhet perfectly communicates this issue:

> Everyone has their own political thoughts, and I didn't participate in the war because of personal grudge or profit but totally with my political consciousness and understanding. But those who were affected by the armed conflict from the PLA won't accept us. The government should act as a mediator so that they can explain that it was anyone's fault and it happened in order to achieve a political change in the nation.[13]

The relationship between Maoist supporters during the civil war and the party itself is also revealed to be dynamic. Those who joined due to ideological sympathies stated that they felt that the party leaders had abandoned their initial path since joining mainstream politics. Since joining mainstream politics in Kathmandu, the Maoist leadership has been accused of being involved in corruption and other forms of kleptocracy, similar to other parties. This may also have contributed to the perception in rural areas of Maoist supporters, former and current, being corrupt and selfish. It can be argued that this issue could be solved with dialogue between different groups as it is clear that individuals joined the Maoists due to coercion or the need for security as opposed to greed. However, local peace initiatives in certain areas may have failed to do this.

It is also clear that this lack of trust occurred mainly in areas where there is a mixture of former or current Maoist sympathisers and those that did not identify themselves with the Maoist cause. Some members were ostracised from their own families due to their affiliation with the Maoists:

> After the conflict, if we fell sick and went to our relatives to ask for financial support, they would tell us to go and ask the Maoists for support. We were told "You voted for Maoist so they will help you".[14]

In these areas, members within the discussion stated that non-Maoists would often inform state forces on Maoist sympathisers leading to their persecution and eroding long-held community and families ties. This has worsened with the introduction of electoral politics in the local areas where people become more polarised due to political party affiliation. As a member from Gola, Bardiya explains the political polarisation that has occurred within his locality.

> They don't talk to each other even though they are childhood friends. They don't care for each other as they do their own groups. People still hold grudges so people still don't trust each other. The political parties help to boost that hatred to fulfil their own party interest. They don't speak with rival parties.[15]

Rural Attitudes Towards the Peace Process in Nepal   51

However, trust and community solidarity seem to have increased and reinforced in certain areas. Women from Dhadwar felt like trust within their own village, largely made up of ex-combatants, had increased and that no social stigmas existed due to their revolutionary past.[16] However, they do face discrimination if they visit other villages and they are recognised, as their village is known for having a large number of Maoists.

The focused group discussions also revealed that despite the Maoists' representation as an anti-caste/anti-feudal force, they may have hindered the cause of marginalised groups not explicitly aligned with them. It is also important to remember that not all marginalised groups chose to identify themselves with the Maoists and some even opposed them (Boquérat, 2006). For instance, the Kamaiya system in existence in Terai was a practice of bonded labour in which the landowners often came from a hill-Brahmin/Chettri background. These landowners gave loans to individuals, often from Tharu and Dalit communities, who in turn had to work in the fields of the landowner to repay their debt (Metzger, 2019). The labourers were often charged unjustifiable interest rates and were reduced to a state of slavery, sometimes across generations, to pay their debt. According to a participant who was involved in the Kamaiya movement in Terai, the Maoists would frequently kidnap Mukta Kamaiyas (free bonded labourers) and carry out extortion campaigns in the Mukta Kamaiya settlements.[17] Additionally, like many others, Kamaiyas also found themselves caught between the Maoists and the state forces.

> We used to get tortured for forming (independent) alliances or associations. We went to Dang, Banke, Bardiya, Kailali, and Kanchanpur during the emergency period. We weren't scared. At that time, we were advocating for land rights of freed labourers. The army and police used to show us bullets and guns, claiming us to be Maoist. At the same time, Maoists used to threaten us for forming alliances and claimed that we were causing displacement of poor freed labourers.[18]

On the one hand, because of their own independent battles against feudalism, the Kamaiya/Mukta Kamaiya movement were incorrectly assumed to be Maoists by the state security forces, leading to their abuse at their hands. Simultaneously, their choice of remaining independent to Maoists meant that they suffered at the hands of the rebels as well. Kamaiyas were evicted by the landlords during the civil war, leading to a loss of any limited livelihood they possessed. By choosing to remain independent of political parties, the Kamaiya movement has faced difficulties in fighting for their rights and in the past has looked towards NGOs for help in pressuring the government (Metzger, 2019). Bonded and freed labourers still face difficulties despite some support from the government and multiple leading politicians across parties have been alleged to take part in the system themselves.

It can also be suggested that the fact that the conflict was largely isolated within rural Nepal further worsened the divide between the rural and the urban.

52   *Raunak Mainali*

As mentioned previously, rural inhabitants often found themselves caught between the Maoists and the state security forces. Almost all participants in the discussions were affected by the war in some capacity. Many had lost a family member in the war and had to deal with the emotional side of the loss as well as the financial side as it was a loss of income, therefore pushing vulnerable people further into poverty. The Maoists would also force themselves inside rural households and demand to be fed which placed inhabitants in a precarious position. The participants stated that at times they would find their livestock butchered without permission by the Maoists to feed themselves. Business in rural areas were also highly disturbed as a consequence of the civil war.

> At that time, we had three night buses and in the conflict era they (Maoists) used to have programs in different places, so they used to ask us for our vehicles whenever they visited. When the army found out about this, about the fact that we gave them our vehicles, they used to harass us. Vehicles were used without pay and so business was affected. Eventually, a situation arose where we had to sell the buses.[19]

Many children lost years of education as they were either detained by the state, forced under suspicion of Maoist affiliation, or by the Maoists in order to recruit soldiers or extract ransom. A former child soldier believes that at least three generations were affected due to a lack of education and employment.[20] He claims that not only was education denied during the conflict years, but it was also heavily discouraged by the Maoist leadership when ex-combatants were held in cantonment sites. This, coupled with a virtually non-existent reintegration mechanism, meant that ex-combatants had very little means to survive after the conflict. Many ex-combatants within the discussions stated that a vast majority of other ex-combatants had gone abroad to find work. In Birtamod, Jhapa an ex-combatant stated that out of around 400 former soldiers within the area, only six or seven were able to secure employment within the country and that most of the others went abroad to secure employment.[21] According to another, most ex-combatants now live in poverty, work abroad in the Gulf, work in agriculture, or have resorted to prostitution.[22]

Many voiced their opinion that employment generation is key to long-term peace and that the peace process is not complete without socio-economic transformation. A social worker from Rolpa said that:

> Thousands of youths involved in the armed conflict have now gone abroad for foreign employment. We feel like there is peace when youths are not around. The situation might be out of control if those youths come back to the village after losing their jobs and have nothing to do here.[23]

The effect of migrant workers on peace in Nepal has not been explored in depth but these discussions have unearthed the importance of migrant workers to Nepal. Firstly, remittances from workers abroad play a major role in Nepal's economy especially in the rural areas where a lack of opportunities has led to many young men and women to seek employment abroad. The financial support provided by workers abroad to their relatives back home has been vital in tackling poverty in rural Nepal (The World Bank, 2017). A study by Regan & Frank (2014) also finds that remittances contribute to stability during times of economic constraint and lessens the risk of civil war. Secondly, as participants suggested, a lack of employment generation in post-war Nepal would lead to large numbers of dissatisfied youths that may lead to further outbreaks of violence. This is particularly the case in post-conflict societies where ex-combatants whose major skill is related to combat and warfare are left unemployed and disgruntled. Ex-combatants within the discussions stated that many of their formed comrades had engaged in criminal practices out of necessity due to a lack of employment. This is also reinforced by a study conducted by Subedi who concluded that unemployment, poverty, and a lacklustre reintegration process pushed many to crime (Subedi, 2014). The failure to address socio-economic issues such as employment proved to many participants that the peace process is far from complete. This was relayed by a school principal in Rolpa:

> The peace process is yet to be completed. A number of agendas, particularly the justice and socio-economic reform is yet to be resolved. On the surface, we feel peace around. But in reality, I feel that the country is slowly moving towards another conflict because the root cause of the previous conflict is yet to be resolved.[24]

There is some convergence in the perspectives of rural inhabitants and the senior civil servants interviewed for this study. Both groups have praised the introduction of local governments, despite their flaws, for their peace-making capability. However, whilst there is anxiety in rural areas in regard to a possible return to violence due to employment opportunities, those in Kathmandu from elite circles are less worried. A former secretary of Nepal stated that the country is unlikely to return to war due to the democratisation of the country that arose with the end of the conflict.[25] They stated that the constitution provided peaceful means of dispute settlement which discouraged large-scale conflict. In the post-war era, isolated instances of violence such as those that occurred in the Madhes movement and by Biplav (a splinter group split from the Maoists) were brought to a peaceful conclusion by negotiation. Another senior civil servant commented that conflict-sensitive development played a key role in the pacification of rural Nepal.[26] Here they referred to the increased connectivity of the rural areas through local government as well as through physical infrastructure such as roads which resulted in a decrease in isolation of rural Nepal.

Within the interviews and discussions, there was a clear understanding that the peace process was far from over. A member in Birendrangar, Surkhet expresses this sentiment:

54   *Raunak Mainali*

> It is said that conflict management has been completed after the army integration process but some here still say that it has not been managed. Though conflict management is going well in city areas, people still have not recovered in rural areas. There is still pain in rural areas. In Karnali, conflict management is not going well.[27]

There were differing thoughts on different aspects of the peace process. This is particularly the case for transitional justice. Some participants believed that those who committed crimes during the war should be persecuted and punished. There is an agreement that those who lost family members or were victims themselves should be compensated. However, there were also many who wanted to move on from the conflict era as transitional justice had the potential to reopen old wounds and grievances which may lead to another conflict. For many, the conflict era felt sacrificial as they lost family members, income, livelihood and education in the hope of a revolutionary transformation of this country. Loss of education means that many are not able to secure employment outside of agriculture or construction and they are accepting of this. However, the respondents' main concern was the creation of educational and employment opportunities for their children or younger siblings. Many are grateful for government educational scholarships provided to victims of the conflict but wish it was extended for higher education as well and not just primary and secondary. A failure to create more prospects, the respondents stated, would mean a repetition of history.

Conclusion

The conversation with rural inhabitants reveals several issues regarding the peace process in Nepal. Firstly, it can be argued that the conflict further worsened the situation in rural areas leading to an increase in disparity between them and the urban elites. The conflict taking place almost entirely in rural settings meant that those living in vulnerable situations were pushed further into precarity as a result of the civil war. In areas hosting former and current Maoists along with non-Maoists, tensions run high as there is a clear lack of trust between different groups. This situation seems to be intensified in some cases due to the introduction of federalism as local politics became increasingly uncompromising. However, despite their limitations, local governments were still viewed positively by most since rural Nepal had been neglected by the government for centuries. Federalism gave the opportunity to inhabitants to develop their area autonomously from the central government. The attitudes of political elites within the country regarding federalism is somewhat more divisive with former governments actively trying to centralise power to Kathmandu.

There is also a lingering feeling of anxiety within rural populations who display a concern that the country may revert to a state of war if socio-economic issues are not dealt with. This is mostly related to their fear that a lack of employment opportunities would push more youths towards violence. This also clearly insinuates the belief within rural Nepal that the peace process is far from complete, especially regarding the socio-economic transformation of the country. Transformative justice, especially in regard to victim justice in the form of compensation, was agreed as important by many. However, sentiments regarding punishment for perpetrators was more divisive – an argument that is reflected within transitional justice academia.

The discussions also reveal the nature of inconsistencies within the function of LPCs. The fact that there are still major misconceptions regarding the motivations of Maoist support clearly shows that the LPCs in some areas did not even carry out basic functions such as dialogue between groups to promote reconciliation. As a result, a situation exists where non-Maoists hold firm beliefs that those who joined the rebels did it out of greed and not due to coercion, security issues, or ideological affiliation. However, it is important not to generalise the work of LPCs as there were many across Nepal whose efficacy is influenced by a variety of factors. Currently, studies by Lundqvist & Öjendal (2018), Tandukar et al. (2016), and Upadhyaya & Miklian (2017) suggest that the main reason for the failure of LPCs was political polarisation but there may be more to unearth. Another area that could be developed with more research is the claim that migrant workers have had an overall contribution to peace in Nepal. The money they remit has led to a rise in living standards in rural areas and their occupation abroad means they are not in rural Nepal where disgruntlement may lead to organised political violence as it had done in the past.

As the participants have stated, the Maoists and their conflict was vital in raising the awareness of the marginalised in regard to their oppression. The importance of this should not be understated as increased political awareness means a better understanding of state mechanisms which ultimately leads to more peaceful means of furthering their agenda. Whilst Nepal's politics is riddled with corruption and polarisation, the constitution and laws remain largely progressive, a consequence of the conflict. This allows for potential peaceful movements to succeed in the future and the rural populations, now more politically consciousness than in the past, can use it to improve their situation.

Notes

1 Focused Group Discussion, February 2018, Dhadhwar, Bardiya.
2 Individual Interview, February 2018, Gurans, Dailekh.
3 Focus Group Discussion, February 2018, Lalmitiya, Dang.
4 Focus Group Discussion, February 2018, Birendranagar, Surkhet.
5 Individual Interview, February 2018, Suddhodhan, Rupandehi.
6 Individual Interview, November 2021, Kathmandu.
7 Individual Interview, January 2022, Kathmandu.
8 Focus Group Discussion, February 2018, Lamahi, Dang.
9 Focus Group Discussion, February 2018, Pathari Shanishchare, Morang.

10 Focus Group Discussion, February 2018, Magaragadi, Bardiya.
11 Focus Group Discussion, February 2018, Dhadhwar, Bardiya.
12 Focus Group Discussion, February 2018, Aurabarni, Sunsari.
13 Focus Group Discussion, February 2018, Birendranagar, Surkhet.
14 Focus Group Discussion, February 2018, Lalmitiya, Dang.
15 Focus Group Discussion, February 2018, Gola, Bardiya.
16 Focus Group Discussion, February 2018, Dhadhwar, Bardiya.
17 Focus Group Discussion, February 2018, Lalmitiya, Dang.
18 Focus Group Discussion, February 2018, Lalmitiya, Dang.
19 Focus Group Discussion, February 2018, Pathari, Shanishchare.
20 Individual Interview, November 2021, Kathmandu.
21 Focus Group Discussion, February 2018, Birtamod.
22 Individual Interview, January 2022, Kathmandu.
23 Individual Interview, February 2018, Rolpa.
24 Individual Interview, February 2018, Rolpa.
25 Individual Interview, November 2021, Kathmandu.
26 Individual Interview, November 2021, Kathmandu.
27 Focus Group Discussion, February 2018, Birendranagar, Surkhet.

References

Adhikari, A. (2020, June 10). Murder Case Sparks a Reckoning with Nepal's Caste Discrimination. *The Diplomat.* https://thediplomat.com/2020/06/murder-case-sparks-a-reckoning-with-nepals-caste-discrimination/

Basnet, C., & Jha, R. (2019). Crossing the Caste and Ethnic Boundaries: Love and Intermarriage between Madhesi Men and Pahadi Women in Southern Nepal. *South Asia Multidisciplinary Academic Journal.* https://doi.org/10.4000/samaj.5802

Bhattarai, P. (2015). The Impact of Relationship Dynamics on Third-Party Coordination: Perceptions of Third-Party Practitioners in Nepal and the Philippines. *International Negotiation, 21*(1), 43–74.

Boquérat, G. (2006). *Ethnicity and Maoism in Nepal. Strategic Studies, 26*(1), 79–99.

Devi Dulal, T. (2021Human Development in the Context of Nepal. *Journal of Population and Development, 2*(1),189–202.

Kathmandu Post. (2019). Oli makes Yet Another Remark that Contradicts the Spirit of Federalism. *Kathmandu Post.*

Lecomte-Tilouine, M. (2009). Political Change and Cultural Revolution in a Maoist Model Village, Mid-Western Nepal. In M. Lawoti & A. K. Pahari (Eds.), *The Maoist Insurgency in Nepal* (1st ed.). Routledge.

Lundqvist, M. O., & Öjendal, J. (2018). Atomised and Subordinated? Unpacking the role of International Involvement in 'The Local turn' of Peace Building in Nepal and Cambodia. *Journal of Peace Building & Development, 13*(2), 16–30. https://doi.org/10.1080/15423166.2018.1470023

Metzger, L. M. (2019). Modern Slavery: An Analysis of the Kamaiya System in Nepal Recommended Citation. *Orphans and Vulnerable Children Student Scholarship, 6.* https://pillars.taylor.edu/ovc-student/6

Poudel, T. M. (2018). Inter-caste Marriage in Eastern Nepal: Context and Its Consequences. *International Relations and Diplomacy, 6*(2). https://doi.org/10.17265/2328-2134/2018.02.003

Regan, P. M., & Frank, R. W. (2014). Migrant Remittances and the Onset of Civil War. *Conflict Management and Peace Science*, *31*(5), 502–520. https://doi.org/10.1177/0738894213520369

Selim, Y. (2018). *Transitional Justice in Nepal* (Y. Selim, Ed.). Routledge.

Sthapit, L., & Doneys, P. (2017). Female Maoist Combatants during and after the People's War. In Å. Kolås (Ed.), *Women, Peace and Security in Nepal* (1st ed.). Routledge.

Subedi, D. B. (2014). Ex-Combatants, Security and Post-Conflict Violence: Unpacking the Experience from Nepal. *Millennial Asia*, *5*(1), 41–65. https://doi.org/10.1177/0976399613518857

Tandukar, A., Upreti, B. R., Paudel, S. B., Acharya, G., & Harris, D. (2016). *The Effectiveness of Local Peace Committees in Nepal: A Study from Bardiya District Researching Livelihoods and Services Affected by Conflict Working Paper 40.* www.securelivelihoods.org

The World Bank. (2017). *Moving up the Ladder: Poverty Reduction and Social Mobility in Nepal.* The World Bank.

Upadhyaya, A. S., & Miklian, J. (2017). Does International Aid Help Women Peace Builders in Nepal? In Å. Kolås (Ed.), *Women, Peace and Security in Nepal* (1st ed.). Routledge.

Zharkevich, I. (2015). De-mythologizing "the Village of Resistance": How rebellious were the peasants in the Maoist base area of Nepal? *Dialectical Anthropology*, *39*(4), 353–379.

4 Transitional Justice in Nepal

An Insider's Perspective

Manchala Jha

Introduction

From 1996–2006, Nepal hosted a civil war between the Government of Nepal (GoN) and the Communist Part of Nepal- Maoists (CPN-M). The decade-long conflict encompassed grievances against the state which had resulted in the marginalisation of groups based on the intersections of gender, class, caste, ethnicity, and region. For the Maoists, the aim of the conflict was the social, political, and economic transformation of Nepal which would address these grievances. The conflict led to an estimated death toll of around 16,000 and a further 2,000 were reported as missing. Additionally, the conflict also witnessed grave human rights violations such as Sexual and Gender Based Violence (SGBV), torture, property damage, looting, and more.

With the conclusion of the conflict came the need to address wartime crimes and to investigate the whereabouts of those that were considered to be missing. The Comprehensive Peace Agreement (CPA) contained provisions which displayed an initial pledge from the warring parties to deal with past wartime crimes. Provision 5.2.5 commits the parties into setting up a High-Level Truth and Reconciliation Commission which would "investigate truth about people seriously violating human rights and involved crimes against humanity, and to create an environment of reconciliations in the society" (CPA, 2006). This was again reinforced in the Interim Constitution of 2007; however, neither document specified a date by which the commission would form. It was only in 2014, almost a decade after the end of the conflict, when the Truth and Reconciliation Commission (TRC) was formed in Nepal along with Commission of Investigation on Enforced Disappeared Persons (CIEDP). Although CIEDP was not guaranteed within the CPA or the Interim Constitution, there were clauses embedded which mentioned that the parties would disclose information on disappeared persons. By November 2021, the TRC had received 63,718 cases whilst CIEDP received 3,223. Nevertheless, a majority of the cases have not been investigated despite an extension of the original mandate, changing of the personnel within the commissions, international pressure, pressure from victim groups, and changes in government.

DOI: 10.4324/9781003289876-5

The transitional justice (TJ) process in Nepal has been well researched through contributions from Pasipanodya (2008), Robins (2011, 2012), and more recently Selim (2017a, 2017b, 2018). Selim (2018), in particular, provides the most comprehensive study of TJ in Nepal to date which encompasses research on participatory mechanisms, victim/perpetrator binary, TJ actors, and more. Additionally, comparative case studies of TJ in Nepal and other nations have also been drawn up such as with Afghanistan (Sajjad, 2013) and Timor-Leste (Robins, 2013). In a similar vein, Lundqvist and Öjendal (2018) compares the Local Peace Committees (LPCs) in Nepal with local efforts at reconciliation in Cambodia. LPCs in Nepal were mandated to collect data on conflict victims and therefore were very much a mechanism of the TJ process.

This chapter offers a unique lens into the TJ process of Nepal as the author herself was a member of the TRC between the years 2014 and 2018. By providing a practitioner's perspective, the aim is to capture the inner workings and hindrances faced by those involved within the TJ process in Nepal. However, there are limitations of this method which should also be outlined. Firstly, there were two main institutions created by the state that were a part of the formal TJ mechanisms in Nepal: the TRC and CIEDP. As the author was a member of the TRC and coordination between the two bodies was substandard, the insights will be limited to the former institution. Secondly, the author was a member of the TRC between the years 2014 to 2018. The mandate of the TRC had been extended and as of 2022 it is still active with a new commission and therefore the time range of the analysis is also limited. However, the lack of progress regarding TJ even in recent years suggests that some of the issues that plagued the commission previously are still pervasive. Finally, in any peace process the ultimate benefactors are the people of the nation and importantly the conflict-affected citizens; therefore, it is imperative that they are heard and empowered. This chapter, in relaying the experience of a TRC member, offers an elitist viewpoint of the TJ process which is especially problematic as elite discourse dominates Nepali political culture. However, this chapter still incorporates the voices of local actors and conflict-affected people as they were vital in the workings of the TRC. Additionally, a later chapter in this volume authored by Ram Kumar Bhandari, himself a victim of the conflict, captures the plight of victims in their fight for justice. An inclusion of both these perspectives is vital to understanding the dynamic process that is TJ in Nepal and offers an opportunity for comparative analysis.

This chapter begins by providing a brief introduction on the objectives and the mandate of the TRC. The second section is based on the experience of the author from the TRC visits to 72 districts after the formation of the commission. This section encompasses the views of those from rural conflict-affected areas and how this information was used by the TRC to formulate action plans. Finally, the last section aims to outline the experiences within the commission and the different factors that ultimately delayed and is still delaying the TJ process in Nepal today.

60 *Manchala Jha*

Formation of the TRC

After a long delay, the Commission on Investigation of Disappeared Persons, Truth and Reconciliation Act (better known as the TRC Act) of 2014 finally formed the dual transitional justice institutions of the TRC and CIEDP. The act outlined the objectives of the TRC as follows:

1. To find out and publish the incidents of the grave violation of human rights committed in the course of the armed conflict between the State Party and the then Communist Party of Nepal (Maoist) from 13 February 1996 to 21 November 2006 and of the persons involved in those incidents upon realising the essence and spirit of the Interim Constitution of Nepal, 2007 and the comprehensive peace accord;
2. To create an environment conducive for sustainable peace and reconciliation by enhancing the spirit of mutual good faith and tolerance in the society upon bringing about reconciliation;
3. To provide for reparation to the victims, and
4. To make recommendation for legal actions against those who were involved in the serious offences related with those incidents.

The grave human rights violations as outlined by the first objective are as follows:

1. Murder;
2. Abduction and physical captivity;
3. Disappearance;
4. Causing bodily harm to make disabled;
5. Physical or mental torture;
6. Rape and sexual violence;
7. Looting, capturing, destruction, or arson of personal or public property;
8. Forced eviction from property or displacement by any means, or
9. Any inhumane act or act against humanity committed against international human rights or humanitarian law.

The selection of the TRC members was also controversial as it was conducted without the consultation of victims' groups. The commission members had to possess at least a bachelor's degree, experience in relevant fields, and had to be at least 35. One of the members also had to be female and the members could not be a part of any political party. Names were nominated and shortlisted in national newspapers for public scrutiny. The public had five days to respond to the selection of members and any complaints were taken into account prior to the final decision.

Victims' groups expressed their displeasure at the government's unilateral decision which they felt was rushed and ignored the considerations of victims in regard to the selection process (R. Nepal, 2019). Whilst the selection process did not involve participation of victims, the TRC itself strove to ensure victim participation in its activities. The TRC decentralised the investigation process and set up offices in all seven provinces. It established a three-member investigation team headed by a joint attorney general which had a guarantee of at least one woman member. The provincial offices were active in taking statements from the victims and investigating their cases by making trips to rural areas to ascertain the truth. Interaction programs were held to ensure that the investigations were progressing and that the standards and practice as envisioned by the TRC Act was maintained. TRC members also made frequent field visits in order to better understand the difficulties of victims regarding TJ mechanisms and reports were made to the government in order to remove obstacles to investigations. Confidentiality of victims was of paramount importance and in cases relating to SGBV, women had the option to speak about their experiences in a separate room with female staff members. The sheer number of cases (61,000) speaks volumes of the work done by the TRC in gathering conflict data as well as the optimism of conflict-affected people in relation to the TJ process in its initial phase.

Insights from the Field

One of the major issues identified by the TRC early on was the fact that TJ was an entirely foreign concept in Nepal, both in terms of unfamiliarity and as a non-domestic concept. Whilst isolated political violence was frequent in Nepal, a statewide armed conflict had not taken place since the unification of the nation in the eighteenth century and to a lesser extent, the Nepali Congress armed democratic revolution in the 1950s. The latter was on a far smaller scale than the civil war that raged from 1996–2006. Neither of these earlier conflicts were succeeded by any TJ mechanism and therefore for much of the population, particularly those from rural areas, the concepts that are normally associated with TJ such as persecution, amnesty, and reconciliation were entirely alien. Even within elite circles TJ was unfamiliar and its inclusion was largely due to international pressure. Conversely, Nepal's involvement in peacekeeping operations abroad meant that there was preexisting domestic knowledge on Disarmament, Demobilisation, and Reintegration (DDR) especially amongst the Nepal Army (Ansorg & Strasheim, 2019). Eventually, experts such as Hannes Siebert and Gunther Baechler were contracted in order to help with the formation of TJ mechanisms. Parallels can be drawn between the TRC in Nepal and the Truth Commissions in South Africa which is a direct result of Siebert hailing from South Africa and being involved with the TJ process there. To address these concerns, the TRC visited 73 districts to disseminate information related to TJ in Nepal, raise awareness regarding the process as well as consulting with the local population in conflict-affected areas. In an effort to reach rural populations better, the TRC recommended creating local offices in conflict-affected villages. However, due to a lack of resources, only seven offices (one in each province) were established in 2017, nearly halfway through the mandated term of the TRC itself. The TRC members were then delegated to supervise these offices with myself in charge of Province 1 and Province 2 (now called Madhesh Province).

It is vital to mention that international NGOs as well as LPCs were active in some extent in carrying out similar campaigns. However, there is evidence supporting the fact that LPCs were inconsistent with their mandate as in some areas they interpreted their role as just collecting and verifying data on conflict victims (Lundqvist & Öjendal, 2018; Tandukar et al., 2016). Furthermore, international NGOs were also viewed in an unfavourable light particularly amongst those who were used to engaging with these organisations. For instance, in Karnali province, I was told by a participant in a consultation session that they often felt "used" by international NGOs as engagement with these actors had not resulted in any long-term benefits for them. For these participants, international NGOs were seen as self-serving as opposed to altruistic. They stated that interactions with NGOs and human rights workers almost followed a script as they would be invited to a program in a hotel or "party palace" where they would be fed, questions would be asked, and they would rarely hear from these individuals again. For these rural inhabitants, they perceived their relationship with these actors as exploitative. Similar dynamics between researcher and respondent have also been reported in Thailand and Kenya (Mackenzie et al., 2007).

This challenged harmful stereotypes prevalent within Nepal, especially in Kathmandu, in relation to Karnali as the habitants of the province are wrongly perceived to be uneducated and backwards. Centuries of centralised governance meant that those in remote districts were seen as subjects to be ruled by Kathmandu or villagers to be educated and informed by the international NGO community. However, from these trips it was clear that the rural and remote population of Nepal possesses the sagacity to be agents of change themselves rather than playing just a subordinate role within the affairs of the state. This could also have been as a result of the Maoists, who were vital in the empowerment of marginalised and rural communities.

During the initial trip to rural localities there was a noticeable atmosphere of optimism amongst the local populations. Participants were encouraged to air their grievances in public forums and many of them chose to do so, sometimes speaking for multiple hours. Participants relayed that it was reassuring to them they were able to engage directly with a government-mandated body such as the TRC. Significant to mention here is the fact that in previous centralised administrations, those from rural areas, particularly in Western Nepal, were ostracised from national-level politics and their development was largely ignored. Districts such as Rolpa, Rukum, and Kalikot, where the Maoist insurgency started and gained the most momentum, cited their exclusion and marginalisation by Kathmandu as a cause of the conflict. Consequently, in the post-war period, the rural population saw the presence of the TRC in their localities as a move away from the pre-conflict exclusion they had faced at the hands of the state. Nepal had witnessed major political changes since the end of the conflict with the removal of the monarchy, promulgation of an interim constitution as well as a planned constitution, and the establishment of the Maoists as a mainstream political party. This resonated within local populations in the form of optimism, and they stated that it felt like the nation had turned a new page. They also mentioned that there was a sense of national and personal pride to see domestic institutions take the lead in the formation of this new Nepal. Some stated that they felt personal pride or familial pride as many were involved in the conflict or the Second People's Movement. As a consequence, there was a general atmosphere of optimism during these rural consultations.

However, this atmosphere was not prevalent in all the consultations. In rural Rolpa, a young male injured ex-combatant expressed his displeasure at the commission's presence, stating that "you guys will not do anything, the commission is doing useless work" and that they had already reconciled amongst themselves. As mentioned earlier, government presence within rural communities was sub-standard prior to the civil war. Even in areas where governance existed, populations may have been excluded based on caste, gender, class, and political affiliation. Therefore, communities had learnt to deal with disputes amongst themselves. There are examples even in post-conflict Nepal where disputes were settled internally through monetary compensations or punishments such as *Uth-Bas*, whereby the alleged perpetrator holds their ears and squats up and down (Selim, 2018; Tandukar et al., 2016). At the end of this specific consultation, the male who had initially displayed his displeasure at our presence in the locality seemed to have changed his mind and apologised to the participants for his original hostility.

Nonetheless, the original comments made by this particular ex-combatant in Rolpa does provide a learning opportunity. The TJ process in Nepal was delayed and is still highly inefficient due to several factors. The TRC and CIEDP itself was formed nearly eight years after the conclusion of the conflict. This prolonged period meant that victims and conflict-affected people were unable to get the justice and closure that was promised to them and had to live with the wounds of the conflict for nearly a decade before a formal institution was formed to address this. This delay had several unintentional positive consequences. Firstly, communities took reconciliation into their own hands and in hindsight this was crucial as the TJ institutions had not been created and in hindsight, even after they were created, they have done very little in the way of reconciliation and justice. A participant in one of these consultation programs stated that if the "Maoists and Congress were able to reconcile when they were once enemies, we can do it as well". Once again, this is reflective of the optimism that existed due to the political changes in the country.

Furthermore, another unintended positive consequence of the delay in TJ mechanisms was the participatory approaches itself. These consultation sessions in rural localities included participants who were ex-combatants, victims of Maoists and the state, representatives of political parties, and more. In the immediate aftermath of the conflict, it would have been difficult

64 *Manchala Jha*

to assemble participants from these groups within a single program. Tensions lingering on from a polarising civil war and unhealed wounds of victims may lead to unwanted confrontation between victims and ex-combatants or Maoists and Nepali Congress representatives. In a highly sensitive immediate post-conflict context such as Nepal, a TJ process without domestic experts, as was the case in Nepal, may have done more harm than good. Research by Triantafilou (2005) suggests that revenge violence is more likely in states with a weak state authority such as Nepal and any immediate TJ process may have increased intergroup hostility and made post-conflict violent more likely. To further elaborate, findings from Tandukar et al. (2016) and Selim (2018) provide evidence of relief programs being highly politicised. If this practice was to take place in the immediate aftermath of the conflict, those members who may not have received relief due to the political affiliation would be hostile towards the process itself.

Due to the delay in the formation of the TRC, we were better able to assess the long-term and short-term needs of individuals and their communities. Our consultations supported the findings of other researchers that people wanted long-term socio-economic support in the form of access to health, education, and employment which had not been addressed by the Interim Relief Program (IRP) (Carranza, 2012; Selim, 2018). Participants, particularly ex-combatants, voiced their grievances stating that they felt as though they had lost formative years due to the civil war and wanted employment guarantees for themselves and educational scholarships for the children. Through these consultations, the TRC recommended the government to create employment guarantees to conflict-affected people such as through quotas in the Civil Service as well as providing educational scholarships to the children of conflict-affected people until undergraduate level. However, this was not heeded by the government, and they claimed scholarships were already provided by the IRP. However, these scholarships were in the jurisdiction of the District Education Office and the process to acquire them was time-intensive due to their overtly bureaucratic nature. Applicants from rural areas had to travel to district headquarters and had to be in possession of several hard-to-acquire documents (IOM, 2010).

Challenges

The process of TJ in Nepal was fraught with difficulties from the very beginning. One of the major issues that arose was the model of TJ that would be in place in the country. Selim (2018) suggests that the South African model of TJ was attractive to the political parties in Nepal due to its focus on amnesty. As a result, the issue of amnesty was at the forefront of TJ discourse in Nepal. After the promulgation of the TJ Act in 2014, the International Commission for Jurists (ICJ) released a report of amendments to the Act that would make it conform to international standards. Special attention was paid to section 26 which provided the possibilities for amnesties to be granted for gross human rights violations which would have breached Nepal's international legal obligations (ICJ, 2014). Domestic actors were also vocal in their opposition against granting amnesties for those who committed wartime atrocities. Victim groups, who saw amnesty provisions as an attempt by perpetrators in government to protect themselves and their political cadres, considered boycotting the process due to its flawed nature (I. Nepal, 2016). The TRC also viewed the provision as deeply problematic. The commission was tasked with investigation gross human rights violations that occurred during the war and none of the perpetrators of these violations could be granted amnesty: on a moral level and due to Nepal's obligations to international law. The TRC formally requested the government to amend this provision. The commission also received the support of the Supreme Court who deemed the granting of amnesties to be unconstitutional. However, the government refused to amend the act and the TRC faced the dilemma of deciding whether a case should be recommended for prosecution or for amnesty/reconciliation.

There were other glaring issues with the Act itself. Firstly, the statute of limitations in Nepal meant that rape victims had 35 days from the incident to report it to relevant authorities. Similarly, torture victims had six months to report to authorities. This framework was wholly inappropriate for the TRC as it was tasked to investigate abuses that may have occurred almost two decades earlier. Additionally, victims were wary of reporting their cases to relevant authorities such as the police as the police themselves had been committing these atrocities during the conflict. The statute of limitation for rape was increased in 2018 to one year, still an unjustifiable time limit not only for wartime cases but also during peace. The case of *Fulmati Nyaya vs Nepal* exemplifies this as her rape case was not registered by local authorities as she did not report it within 35 days. Furthermore, the statute of limitation for torture remains at six months. Torture cases such as *Prashanta Kumar Pandey vs Nepal* and *Bholi Pharaka vs Nepal* which occurred in the post-conflict period did not progress as it had been reported after the sixth-month period. Another issue raised was in relation to section 28.4 of the TRC Act which mandated the creation of a "Special Court". There seems to be confusion as the exact role of the court was not outlined and the court never materialised (Bisset, 2014). This TRC recommended that the court should be mandated to oversee cases relating to the conflict as opposed to traditional courts since conflict-era crimes needed specialised knowledge. However, this recommendation was not heeded by the government and even the Supreme Court which had sided with the TRC on other issues did not support this as they believed another judiciary body would "dilute" their power.

Another obstacle that hindered the TJ process in Nepal was the lack of international support. As mentioned earlier, the lack of domestic expertise within TJ meant that international support was vital, and their inclusion would have provided much-needed expertise. The UN in the form of United Nations Mission in Nepal played an integral supporting role in the DDR process and their observer role in monitoring the elections to the first Constituent elections should also not be understated. However, their exclusion as well as that of other international institutions within the TJ process was largely due to the TRC Act's amnesty clause. Organisations such as the Office of the High Commissioner for Human Rights (OHCHR), International Center for Transitional Justice (ICTJ), Amnesty International, amongst others, had detailed their displeasure of the potential for grand amnesty for serious abuses. However, in the initial stages, the UN did display their interest in being involved in the process. During the first meeting between the TRC and CIEDP, the chairman of the NHRC and a former Chief Justice relayed that the UN had sought representation within the TRC and NHRC, which they felt was deserved due to their advocacy of TJ in Nepal as well as their earlier role with the United Nations Mission in Nepal (UNMIN). This was rejected by the government of Nepal which felt that the peace process in Nepal had been nationally led thus far and wanted to continue in the same manner. The fact that other aspects of the peace process were nationally led also put pressure on the TRC to function without direct international support. The inclusion of the UN within TJ mechanisms may have led to more accountability for wartime crimes which was unfavourable to the government as it had the potential to implicate high-ranking party members. With just national actors in the process, it becomes far easier for any ruling party to manipulate the process of justice. The lack of coordination between international and domestic institutions was also harmful in other ways. Donor organisations conducted projects independently and therefore knowledge could not be diffused to domestic actors. Donor organisations usually provide more lucrative opportunities when compared to domestic institutions and therefore they attract more qualified and capable personnel leading to a drain in talent (Acharya et al., 2006). The Ministry of Peace and Reconstruction (MoPR) was not an attractive destination to many civil servants as the Home, Finance or Foreign ministries would be. It is common in Nepal for civil servants without political connections to be sent to undesirable locations and ministries and therefore the personnel within the ministry have low morale and would not possess the political clout necessary to make substantial changes. Chief District Officers (CDOs), part of the Home Ministry, often took charge of district-level peace efforts despite not being part of the MoPR. In Bardiya, the poor relationship between the CDO and LPC may have led to the freezing of funds which reflects the asymmetry of power that exists within Nepal's governance (Tandukar et al., 2016).

Arguably, the main hindrance to the TJ process was its politicisation. As Mohna Ansari, a member of the NHRC, puts it: "The state is, in some ways, almost nervous. If transitional justice is fully practiced, a great number of people will be brought to the book" (Humagain & Ghimire, 2017). This quote clearly encapsulates why political parties are so reluctant to move the TJ process forward and to allow TRC and CIEDP to function according to their mandates. The political will to carry out the TJ process was cloudy from the start as Nepal chose to adopt the South African model that was based on truth telling, reconciliation, and amnesty which suggests prosecution for human rights violations was never a priority. With the Maoists and Congress parties forming governments in the post-conflict period, it was never in their interest to see a thorough implementation of the process as both were belligerents of the conflict and implicated in human rights abuses. The leaders of both parties during the conflict, Pushpa Kamal Dahal alias *Prachanda* (Maoist) and Sher Bahadur Deuba (Nepali Congress), are still the leaders of their respective parties and are currently part of a government coalition. These individuals, as well as several of their high-ranking contemporaries, have cases submitted against them for their wartime conduct. As Ansari correctly points out, a strong TJ process would lead to prosecution against the top-ranking leaders of the government and therefore it is not in their best interest to pursue it. Both parties had been instrumental in ensuring amnesty provisions within the first TJ Act which has still not been ratified when the TRC and CIEDP commission terms were extended. Furthermore, the new commission comprising new members, is still functioning under the same limitation as the Act has not been amended despite calls from the TRC, Supreme Court, victims' groups, and the international community.

Whilst the Nepali Congress and the Maoists are hindering the TJ process with amnesty provisions, another mainstream party, United Marxist-Leninists (UML), are weaponising it for their political gain. For instance, after entering an electoral coalition UML and Maoists released a 9-point plan in May 2016 which included several provisions that addressed the needs of conflict victims. These include providing reparations and to "initiate amendment and other procedures within 15 days with a time-bound plan on transitional justice as per the spirit of the Comprehensive Peace Agreement" (Nine Point Agreement between the CPN-UML and UCPN (Maoist, 2016). However, this did not come into fruition despite the fact that the UML-Maoist formed the largest majority government in the post-conflict period giving the party complete power to enact these amendments. As mentioned earlier, a strong TJ process would severely hamper the Maoists due to prosecution of high-ranking members and cadres and therefore serious changes were very unlikely. Throughout the coalition, the leader of the UML, K.P. Oli, often employed the language of TJ to pressure Prachanda and his Maoists during times of disputes. In an effort to threaten Prachanda, Oli was reported to have said "Don't make the mistake of taking it (transitional justice) lightly" (Ghimire, 2020). Oli would then follow this up with deciding to provide free treatment for those injured in the conflict at government hospitals. These thinly veiled attempts in weaponising TJ and victims was criticised by victim's groups who stated that the party could have given these treatments whenever they wanted but only chose to do so in a game of political upmanship (ibid.). The appointment of members in the commission has also been heavily influenced by political leaders preferring to select those who are close to their respective parties. This has led to the stalling of many decisions within the TRC as some members prioritised pleasing their political patrons over progressing TJ. The government also continued to delay the TRC process by not designating the appropriate financial and human resources

68   Manchala Jha

required to fulfil its mandate which then led to the then chair, Surya Kiran Gurung, threatening to quit (Pandey, 2016).

Internal disputes were also common within the TRC. For instance, there were members who opted to classify victims as either victims of the state or of the rebels. This limited classification meant that those who were forced to join the Maoists under the "one house, one Maoist" and child soldiers would not be perceived as victims but more as perpetrators. As Selim (2017a, 2018) correctly points out, the victim/perpetrator binary is too limited to explain societal dyamics in a post-conflict context as research has shown that the term "victim" in Nepal is more closely associated with state support. Within the first year of my term, there were many cases which had completed the stage of preliminary investigation and needed to be passed on to the detailed investigation stage. I drew the attention of the commission to this and submitted a written request of resources to the secretariat to progress these cases. However, the petition took weeks to register, and a senior member requested a detailed investigation procedure from the TRC. This never came to fruition as a meeting between the TRC could not be convened and some members displayed clear displeasure at having to draw up a detailed investigation plan. The Nepal Army also placed roadblocks for the TRC as they did not allow the TRC to conduct investigations into cases that were being handled by the military court. This was clearly problematic as the army was also a party to the conflict who had committed atrocities.

There have also been disputes between the TRC and CIEDP more recently. As per the law, those who were arrested during the conflict but were not brought to a court for a trial are classified as disappeared. The TRC claims to have 7,000 of these cases which they believe should be in the jurisdiction of the CIEDP (Ghimire, 2021). The CIEDP has claimed that it is considering what to do with these case and officials within the commission stated they are unlikely to tackle these cases due to an increase in their workload (ibid.). Furthermore, the CIEDP has also forwarded 250 cases to the TRC as they claim it does not fall under their mandate.

TJ in any post-conflict context is extremely zero-sum where a party assumes that their loss is a gain for their rival. A proper functioning mechanism would lead to the prosecution of many leading politicians in the country and therefore they aim to turn the odds in their favour. They are doing this by weaponising the process, not providing adequate resources, weakening the mandate, and putting party loyalists within the mechanism. This has ensured their impunity despite almost seven years since the formation of the TRC and CIEDP. TRC also got off to a rough start due to a lack of international support, domestic expertise, and internal division within and between TJ bodies. Not mentioned in this chapter was also the adverse effect of the unforeseen disasters of the 2015 earthquake and the recent Covid-19 pandemic, both of which wreaked havoc on an already fragile economy. However, there are still some positive aspects worth mentioning and some reasons to be hopeful for the future of TJ in Nepal. Despite facing many roadblocks, many conflict-affected people were still able to receive relief in the form of monetary aid or educational scholarship for their children. Despite a deeply flawed process, victims' groups in Nepal have been incredibly active in their campaigning and therefore still able to exert pressure on the government not to completely dismantle the TJ institutions. After my term ended, a new commission was formed which still means an opportunity for justice exists along the road. As recently as June 2022, the TRC was still conducting consultations amongst victims and looking to further progress TJ. Victims are also pleased with the conduct of Govinda Sharma Bandi, the Minister for Law and Justice, who they say has been proactive in reaching out to them (Ghimire, 2022). The recent local elections have also led to the success of independent candidates throughout the country including the capital. It could be an encouraging sign as this may be a sign that the nation is moving away from the mainstream parties of Nepali Congress, UML, and the Maoists. Despite transitional justice not being mentioned in any recent agendas, moving away from these mainstream parties may lead to development in Nepal that brings healthcare, employment, and education – necessities that martyrs fought for and what victims are fighting for now.

References

Acharya, A., de Lima, A. T. F., & Moore, M. (2006). Proliferation and Fragmentation: Transactions Costs and the Value of Aid. *Journal of Development Studies*, *42*(1), 1–21. https://doi.org/10.1080/00220380500356225

Ansorg, N., & Strasheim, J. (2019). Veto Players in Post-Conflict DDR Programs: Evidence from Nepal and the DRC. *Journal of Intervention and Statebuilding*, *13*(1), 112–130. https://doi.org/10.1080/17502977.2018.1501981

Bisset, A. (2014). Transitional Justice in Nepal: The Commission on Investigation of Disappeared Persons, Truth and Reconciliation Act 2014 (Bingham Centre Working Paper 2014/07). In *BIICL*. www.binghamcentre.biicl.org

Carranza, R. (2012). *Relief, Reparations, and the Root Causes of Conflict in Nepal*. www.ictj.org/publication/relief-reparations-and-root-causes-conflict-nepal

CPA. (2006). Contemporary Peace Agreement between the Government of Nepal and the Communist Party of Nepal (Maoist), 21 November 2006. https://peacemaker.un.org/nepal-comprehensiveagreement2006.

Ghimire, B. (2020). Transitional Justice is Once Again Being Used as a Tool for Political One-Upmanship, Conflict Victims Say. *The Kathmandu Post*. Retrieved March 17, 2022, from https://kathmandupost.com/national/2020/12/03/transitional-justice-is-once-again-being-used-as-a-tool-for-political-one-upmanship-conflict-victims-say

Ghimire, B. (2021). Transitional Justice Bodies Spar over Who Should Look into Which Cases. *The Kathmandu Post*. Retrieved March 17, 2022, from https://kathmandupost.com/national/2021/11/23/transitional-justice-bodies-spar-over-who-should-look-into-which-cases

Ghimire, B. (2022). Conflict Victims have High Hopes Amid Fresh Bid to Deliver Transitional Justice. *The Kathmandu Post*. Retrieved June 2, 2022, from https://kathmandupost.com/national/2022/06/01/conflict-victims-have-high-hopes-amid-fresh-bid-to-deliver-transitional-justice

70 *Manchala Jha*

Humagain, M., & Ghimire, B. (2017). If Parties Allow Human Rights Problems to Fester, New Issues Will Crop Up. *The Kathmandu Post*. Retrieved March 17, 2022, from https://kathmandupost.com/interviews/2017/10/23/if-parties-allow-human-rights-problems-to-fester-new-issues-will-crop-up

ICJ. (2014). Justice Denied: The 2014 Commission on Investigation of Disappeared Persons, Truth and Reconciliation Act. International Commission of Jurists. www.ohchr.org/Documents/Countries/NP/OHCHR_Nepal_Conflict_Report2012.pdf

IOM. (2010). *Report on Mapping Exercise and Preliminary Gap Analysis of the Interim Relief and Rehabilitation Programme: Interim Relief and Rehabilitation to the Victims of Nepal's Armed Conflict*. International Commission of Jurists.

Lundqvist, M. O., & Öjendal, J. (2018). Atomised and Subordinated? Unpacking the Role of International Involvement in 'The Local turn' of Peace Building in Nepal and Cambodia. *Journal of Peacebuilding & Development*, *13*(2), 16–30. https://doi.org/10.1080/15423166.2018.1470023

Mackenzie, C., McDowell, C., & Pittaway, E. (2007). Beyond "do no harm": The Challenge of Constructing Ethical Relationships in Refugee Research. *Journal of Refugee Studies*, *20*(2), 299–319. https://doi.org/10.1093/jrs/fem008

Nepal, I. (2016). Nepal's Botched Truth and Reconciliation Program – The Record. *The Record*. Retrieved March 17, 2022, from www.recordnepal.com/nepals-botched-truth-and-reconciliation-program

Nepal, R. (2019). Process of Selecting TRC, CIEDP Members Okayed. *The Himalayan Times*. Retrieved March 17, 2022, from https://thehimalayantimes.com/kathmandu/process-of-selecting-trc-ciedp-members-okayed

Nine Point Agreement between the CPN-UML and UCPN (Maoist). (2016, May). Retrieved March 3, 2022, from www.satp.org/satporgtp/countries/nepal/document/papers/Nine_Point_Agreement_between_CPN-UML_and_UCPN-M.pdf

Pandey, L. (2016). TRC Chair Threatens to Quit. *The Himalayan Times*. Retrieved March 27, 2022, from https://thehimalayantimes.com/nepal/truth-and-reconciliation-commission-chairman-surya-kiran-gurung-threatens-quit

Pasipanodya, T. (2008). A Deeper Justice: Economic and Social Justice as Transitional Justice in Nepal. *International Journal of Transitional Justice*, *2*(3), 378–397. https://doi.org/10.1093/ijtj/ijn032

Robins, S. (2011). Towards Victim-Centred Transitional Justice: Understanding the Needs of Families of the Disappeared in Post Conflict Nepal. *International Journal of Transitional Justice*, *5*(1), 75–98. https://doi.org/10.1093/ijtj/ijq027

Robins, S. (2012). Transitional Justice as an Elite Discourse: Human Rights Practice Where the Global Meets the Local in Post-Conflict Nepal. *Critical Asian Studies*, *44*(1), 3–30. https://doi.org/10.1080/14672715.2012.644885

Robins, S. (2013). *Families of the Missing: A Test for Contemporary Approaches to Transitional Justice* (S. Robins, Ed.). Routledge. https://doi.org/10.4324/9780203517079

Sajjad, T. (2013). *Transitional Justice in South Asia* (T. Sajjad, Ed.). Routledge. https://doi.org/10.4324/9780203431375

Selim, Y. (2017a). Examining Victims and Perpetrators in Post-Conflict Nepal. *International Review of Victimology*, *23*(3), 275–301. https://doi.org/10.1177/0269758017710818

Selim, Y. (2017b). The Opportunities and Challenges of Participation in Transitional Justice: Examples from Nepal. *Journal of International Development*, *29*(8), 1123–1148. https://doi.org/10.1002/jid.3001

Selim, Y. (2018). *Transitional Justice in Nepal* (Y. Selim, Ed.). Routledge.
Tandukar, A., Upreti, B. R., Paudel, S. B., Acharya, G., & Harris, D. (2016). *The Effectiveness of Local Peace Committees in Nepal: A Study from Bardiya District Researching Livelihoods and Services Affected by Conflict Working Paper 40*. www.securelivelihoods.org
Triantafilou, E. (2005). In Aid of Transitional Justice: Eroding Norms of Revenge in Countries with Weak State Authority. *UCLA Journal of International Law and Foreign Affairs, 10*(2), 541–575.

5 Governing Conflict Victims in Nepal

Ram Kumar Bhandari

Introduction

Nepal's Maoist 'People's War' created thousands of victims as a result of the myriad of violations of human rights that the conflict inspired. Their victimhood at the hands of both the state and the rebels gave them an identity and a set of needs with which the state had never before been confronted on such a scale, and in so doing gave a new lens on governance in Nepal. Victims include the families of the dead and the disappeared, those displaced or who saw their livelihoods destroyed by the conflict, and the children mobilised as part of the Maoist armed forces, among others. Here, the chapter will examine how conflict victims have articulated their demands of the state, and how these have been addressed by the political class, with victims' experiences encompassing being ignored, harassed, and threatened, instrumentalised as a tool of politics, and eulogised as positive examples of sacrifice.

A first observation is the extent to which victims of the conflict over-represent the historically marginalised groups of Nepal. The Maoists successfully mobilised those marginalised by caste, ethnicity, gender, and geography. Whilst not emphasised in post-conflict Maoist rhetoric, this has been integral to the genesis of an ethnic politics that has seen identity and political mobilisation linked in ways that has created myriad new narratives around victimhood in the last decade or so. At the local level, discourses of victimhood in the conflict and claims making on that basis have catalysed and intersected with an increased awareness of historic structural violence and its positioning as an issue of national politics. A second lens that conflict victims provide is one on how governance has sought to manage them in the framework of a political elite linked to the commission of conflict-era violations—and thus the creation of victims—on all sides, while rhetorically acknowledging human rights and the nation's international obligations. Whilst major parties, notably the Maoists, as well as the United Marxist-Leninists (UML) and Nepali Congress, have cultivated conflict victims as representing both the history and the conscience of their respective movements, parties have had to find a balance between using victims as a tool of mobilisation and their need to ensure that there is no substantive accounting for the crimes of the conflict. After years

DOI: 10.4324/9781003289876-6

of resisting international entreaties to initiate transitional justice mechanisms, politicians appear to have chosen to create bodies that offer no challenge to the position of highly placed perpetrators, but that can be claimed to have addressed the state's obligations.

Addressing the legacies of the conflict has ensured the state has had to confront international norms, notably around accountability for rights violations, that clash with the traditional prioritisation by political parties of their own interests. That the conflict ended with a negotiated settlement has led to parties on both sides of the conflict that collectively dominate contemporary politics driving an elite consensus – encompassing all major political parties as well as the security forces – around impunity, with the limited efforts that are made to address victims' agendas driven by narratives of 'relief' and 'compensation'. Whilst this is to be expected of parties that had long been a part of the establishment it is remarkable that the Maoists were so quick to adopt such an approach, given their close identification with victims of the state. This reflects the broader accommodation of the Maoist party with many of the agendas of traditional elites, and the incorporation of their leaders into a predominantly upper-caste hill ruling class.

Victims have become a constituency in their own right, justifying and spoken for by the human rights community and both championed and pilloried by political leaders. An effort has been made for victims to themselves become collective social actors, with mobilisation around both particular violations and around the identity of 'victim' itself. This victims' movement has begun to make links between the marginalisation that drove the Maoist insurgency, and how government has ignored and challenged victims fighting for justice, and that has seen victimhood become an essential part of a new politics of ethnicity that has emerged in the post-conflict era.

The Maoist Conflict and the Production of Victims

Cycles of victimisation and consequent radicalisation underpin the origin of the Maoist People's War, with the conflict fed by the production of victims. The Maoists' bases in civilian areas and among certain populations were countered by security forces in ways that led to casualties of civilians and those not linked to the CPN-M (Jha, 2014). As a result, escalations of the conflict were consciously driven by the Maoists, most notably the drawing in of the Royal Nepal Army (RNA) in 2001, through an audacious attack on a barracks in Dang. This drove the declaration of a state of emergency and legislation, the *Terrorist and Disruptive Activities (Control and Punishment) Ordinance* (known as TADO), which gave sweeping powers to the security forces, including the ability to detain in protective custody for up to one year without trial. This in turn drove further violations, most notably disappearances. The majority of casualties in the conflict, including a spike in disappearances that have driven the post-war victims' movement, followed this period. This reflects a pattern of a significant number of violations and killings being committed by state forces.

74   *Ram Kumar Bhandari*

Furthermore, in the areas they controlled, the Maoists were similarly ruthless in asserting their authority, but using more targeted violence.

The apparent disdain of the security forces for both human rights and the laws of war was accompanied by the CPN-M seeing the People's War as fed by sacrifice, and a culture of martyrdom developed as a political tool. A Maoist publication elaborated: "The people who commemorate the martyrs have developed a new culture in which martyrs' doors and pillars are created, martyrs' photos are exhibited and villages, hamlets, companies, battalions and brigades are named with martyrs' names" (Lecomte-Tilouine, 2006, p. 69). As such, state violence and Maoist eulogisation of victims reinforced each other in a cycle of escalation.

After ten years of conflict, when the Comprehensive Peace Accord (CPA) was signed in 2006, more than 17,800 people had died, and more than 1,300 were missing, their fate unknown. Countless others had been displaced, mostly chased out of communities by the Maoists, while others had been victims of the violence meted out by both sides of the conflict in communities caught between them. This included those held in state detention and tortured, as well as those subject to the routine violence that enforced Maoist authority in rural areas. Sexual violence has been widely referred to, but cultural taboos have prevented any comprehensive reckoning with the issue or with its victims.

The Truth and Reconciliation Commission has received 58,052 complaints, which include 10, 582 related to extra judicial killings, 15,129 cases of torture, 278 of rape, 4,513 related to disablement, 3,325 of abduction, and 15,321 of seizure of property. The Commission for the Investigation of Enforced Disappeared Persons (CIEDP) has received 3,093 complaints of victims of enforced disappearance during the armed conflict, where this includes disappearances that have already been resolved. ICRC has listed 1,347 cases of persons missing linked to the conflict.

The Politics of Victimhood

In principle, a victim is defined as such by what has been done to them, with this codified in the violations defined by various bodies of law. In practice victimhood does not emerge naturally from the experience of being harmed, but is constructed socially and subjectively, with a range of factors determining who will be accorded victim status. Most formally, bodies established to deal with victims, such as Truth Commissions or prosecutorial bodies, will determine who is considered a victim, while the Nepalese authorities have attempted a comprehensive count.

The language of victimisation remains potentially problematic, reinforcing an imbalance of power between strong, powerful victimiser and weak, helpless victim. As a result, the passive implications of the term 'victim' have been increasingly challenged through the use of terms perceived as positive and empowering, such as 'survivor', although this appears to have rarely been done on the terms of those being so renamed. In Nepal, however, victims of

Governing Conflict Victims in Nepal   75

conflict-era violations see the status and label of 'victim' as one which serves to support their claims making, particularly of the state and political parties. This challenges liberal discourse which implies that being a victim and being an agent are mutually exclusive: indeed, political mobilisation has been precisely on the basis of their victimhood. Despite efforts of rights activists to use the term 'survivor', victims largely reject this as reducing their apparent needs. Victimhood is claimed as a permanent status, which would remain even if all their demands were met. Whilst this challenges transitional justice discourses that embrace the idea that violations can be 'repaired', it confirms that victims have suffered traumas that will mark them for life.

In Nepal, as elsewhere, political agendas have privileged particular conceptions of victimhood, and in this sense victims constitute a part of the contested terrain of the memory of the conflict, at both national and local levels, often creating a hierarchy of victimhood. Victims have inevitably been drawn into Nepal's patronage-driven politics, perceived as constituencies to be managed and cultivated and as repositories of conflict-era values, particularly for the Maoists who have been reluctant to abandon the rhetoric of heroes and martyrs of the People's War even as the concrete achievements of the conflict have visibly shrunk. Given the elite consensus on avoiding accountability, the efforts of the state to recognise and reward victims have been driven by compensation approaches, albeit typically wrapped in the language of 'relief'.

The Interim Relief Programme (IRP), initiated in 2008 and a substantial effort to address victims' needs, demonstrated the challenges of approaching support to victims in a context both of state efforts to deflect accountability for crimes committed and where governance remains so flawed. The IRP was focused on material support, and so excluded the addressing of many of the greatest needs of victims, including the truth about the disappeared, acknowledgement of their victimhood, and formal memorialisation or commemoration, as well as prosecutions (Carranza, 2012). Suspicions about the politicisation of the process begin with the recipients, dominated as they are by the internally displaced, who are known to be largely linked to the NC and UML. Remaining IRP recipients, including families of the dead and missing, are dominated by those who were victimised by the state and assumed to be close to the Maoists. Both identification and implementation of the IRP was supported by Local Peace Committees (LPCs) in each district, composed of local political party cadres, giving a central role to the politically affiliated. As such, the IRP can be seen as an example of how addressing the legacies of the conflict has been pressed to serve the system of patronage that dominates politics, with widespread accusations of 'fake' victims benefitting from assistance through the informal use of quotas for each party at district level, whether or not people are genuine victims.

Beyond the IRP there has been a number of initiatives to provide support to victims, usually in terms of cash payments, and often to constituencies that are perceived as serving one party's interests. This is most clearly seen in the series of payments made to the families of the disappeared: in the absence of a willingness or capacity of government to address their broader demands for truth, families—the majority of whom are poor—have received a number of significant payments from Maoist-led governments. The families of the disappeared remain a salient symbol of the People's War for the Maoists and have achieved a level of mobilisation and activism that has maintained their visibility and taken families outside the orbit of the Maoist party.

The interaction between politics and the idea of victimhood emerges most clearly when considering child recruitment by the Maoists. Following the signing of the CPA, People's Liberation Army (PLA) fighters were cantoned and over the next years the fate of the thousands of PLA fighters became a central issue of dispute between the Maoists and the other parties. At the time the issue of the large fraction of those troops that had been recruited as children was considered one of legitimacy in the demobilisation process, but not one of criminality and victimhood, largely because Maoist participation in the process would be threatened by the pursuit of such issues. Those determined to have been under 18 at the time of the signing of the CPA, regardless of the length of their service in the PLA, were 'disqualified' from the demobilisation process and sent home. The fact that the recruitment of minors constituted a war crime was never mentioned while the Maoists were negotiating their return to constitutional politics, barely even by Nepal's human rights activists. Similarly, the fact that child soldiers were victims has only been acknowledged following a remarkable mobilisation by ex-PLA, following a process where they received less recognition and less support than those adults formally demobilised.

A number of studies have been made of the status and needs of conflict victims and most paint a picture of those who were always poor having been further impoverished by their victimhood (IOM, 2010). This sees many victims emphasise economic issues including access to education and healthcare as well as sustainable livelihood. This contrasts with an agenda of addressing acts of violence through prosecutions that has dominated civil society demands. Whilst victims would welcome prosecutions of perpetrators, this is not their priority, when so many of their daily lives remain highly constrained by the impacts of what they have experienced. Transitional justice in Nepal, in the legalist model that has been advocated most widely, promises to return poor victims to the poverty they have always suffered, rather than to transform their lives, reflecting a politics of rights that privileges civil and political rights over the social and economic. This, reflecting a refusal to engage with the issues of marginalisation and social exclusion that drove the conflict—as rights issues— represents the limits for addressing victims' needs of the liberal discourse of transitional justice in Nepal that presents itself as an apolitical and technical approach to the past.

The valorisation of victims as a tool of politics led inevitably to their being seen as epitomising the values of the concerned parties to the conflict, either as symbols of righteous struggle or of valiant resistance against terrorism. As such, while conflict raged, in Maoist base areas memorials to martyrs were

Governing Conflict Victims in Nepal   77

erected and families of the dead and missing at the hands of the state were financially supported by the Maoist party. At this stage victims of the conflict were seen as heroes of the struggle and caring for them was a duty of the party, not least to ensure loyalty of cadres and the communities who supported them. Similarly, the state and political parties sought to make victims of the Maoists visible to demonstrate the cruelty of their enemy, while offering support to those displaced from Maoist-dominated areas, largely as a result of their links to the ruling parties.

In the post-conflict period, it would seem necessary for a shared perspective on the conflict to emerge, in which truth would be used to overcome past propaganda, and to allow a narrative sanctioned by the new state, and reflecting a national consensus, to emerge. Interestingly, this has not happened, with no effort—formal or otherwise—to triangulate between the opposing views of the conflict held by the Maoists and the other parties, even as they shared power, and—for the Maoists and their erstwhile enemies in UML—now share a political party. Whilst the People's Movement of 2006 that toppled the King has been embraced across the political spectrum as worthy of commemoration, and its victims declared martyrs, the meaning given to the conflict is still contested. A vacuum remains where such official narrative should be, perhaps linked to the official amnesia that is required to maintain an approach to the conflict that denies accountability. As a result, there has been little official commemoration or memorialisation of the victims of the conflict at the national level, with divergent understandings of the past being approached only through an apparent effort at formal forgetting.

At the local level, where the history of the conflict continues to have political and social repercussions, contestation over the meanings of the past endures. Those who must live with the consequence of what neighbours did to each other and how victims continue to suffer are constantly reminded of the relevance of the conflict's legacies. For political parties at the national level, however, victims are rarely used any longer as political symbols that can serve their interests. Parties have understood the political limits of the use of the past, particularly where they are unable to engage with issues of responsibility for creating victims. This again demonstrates the challenges for governance and the addressing of the legacies of the past, where the state is subservient to political parties with particular interests. The consequence for the victims is that they must represent themselves and their own interests, and this has been the goal of the victims' movement.

State Engagement with Histories of Violence

The response of the political establishment in Nepal to a demand that violations of the conflict be addressed has been consistent across the political spectrum, despite the commitments made in the CPA. It seems clear that at the time actors on both sides of the conflict committed themselves to a Truth and Reconciliation Commission (TRC), they had little idea what this entailed, with

78   *Ram Kumar Bhandari*

the transitional justice elements of the Accord representing a wish list of the international community more than anything else. As a result, for many years after the signing of the CPA, whilst important donors, the UN, and national NGOs repeated the mantra of the need for a comprehensive process to address histories of violations, the political parties deflected this by referencing the need to entrench the peace process and finalise the political transition.

Only in March 2013 did the Government eventually pass an Ordinance creating a TRC and the Commission for the Investigation of Enforced Disappeared Persons (CIEDP). This highlighted the strategy the political class would use to protect themselves, not least the fact that the legislation allowed for amnesty for perpetrators. Shortly afterwards, instigated by a petition from victims' groups and civil society, the Supreme Court negated the provisions concerning amnesties, limitations on criminal prosecution, and forced reconciliation,[1] beginning a contest that demonstrated the Court as one of the last non-politicised institutions in the country. In April 2014, ignoring the Supreme Court ruling, Parliament endorsed a bill that would again provide for amnesty to perpetrators of serious human rights violations, and in February 2015 the two Commissions were created with a two-year mandate and one year of possible extension.

The two Commissions represent the only institutional efforts at transitional justice in Nepal. The work of the commissions has provoked concern not just over the atmosphere of impunity in which they operate but in the failure of government to provide them with sufficient resources to do their job in the limited time available to them. It seems clear that the government decided to create bodies that would be unable to do their job, that can constitute an empty ritual but not address the impunity of political leaders and the security forces. Because of the politicisation that infects all state activities, commissioners were selected at least partially on the basis of their party affiliations, such that the (then) three major political parties are all seen to be represented. At the local level, limited resources meant there was no dedicated presence of the commissions to engage with victims. Rather, complaints from victims were collected by Local Peace Committees at the district level, themselves representing political parties, and thus raising the possibility that a statement about a killing or disappearance would have to be made to the perpetrators of that crime. The Commission process also unfolded in an environment where the security forces remain unreformed and unconstrained. The army and police — constituting the alleged perpetrators in a majority of violations — have been seen to be destroying evidence and continuing to threaten activists in the absence of any witness protection policy.

Civil Society and Its Limits

At the time of writing, the global transitional justice industry, as represented by major donors, the UN and the national rights agencies they fund, have boycotted the commission process as a result of the accountability failures the

Governing Conflict Victims in Nepal 79

process incarnates. One consequence of this strategy is the removal of routes to making the commissions more effective, through technical and financial support, and of using them as a site to contest the political failure they articulate. Victims' organisations have in contrast sought a relationship of 'critical engagement' with the two Commissions and encouraged and supported victims to share their experiences with the commissions (Billingsley, 2019). This has ensured that the two bodies received a large number of complaints from victims.

Whilst it was very often political activism that led to their victimisation, where victims were not previously politically affiliated their experience often led them to become so—most often in terms of building a relationship with the Maoist movement. Victims have however seen traditional loyalties to the parties they served challenged by the visible neglect of their issues in the decade since the end of conflict, and many have distanced themselves from their party affiliations to identify and mobilise as conflict victims. This has seen the emergence of a conflict victims' movement as a civil society actor that seeks to challenge both traditional party-political understandings of how change is driven in Nepal, and the civil society model of liberal advocacy and primarily legal challenge to the authorities.

The relationship between conflict victims and human rights NGOs has evolved since the time of the conflict, when agencies did extraordinary work in difficult circumstances to identify violations and support victims. As the conflict ended, and political space to discuss past violence increased, rights NGOs were able to access the significant donor funds that became available. Such resources were however used in a particular way, with NGOs seeing their role as primarily collecting testimony from victims for use in legal or other formal processes and supporting victims to understand their rights and how transitional justice could guarantee them. This model reproduced many of the power relationships that had driven the conflict, with Kathmandu-based agencies, led largely by caste and ethnic elites, using a legal basis to work on behalf of victims in institutional spaces in the capital in ways that were defined by NGOs. This had the effect of denying any role for victims, beyond sharing their testimony, and restricting the interest of transitional justice to addressing acts of violence, reflecting a global discourse that prioritises both legalism and civil and political rights. This modality served to deny as a justice issue the social exclusion by caste, ethnicity, gender, and region that underlay the conflict: not only were social and economic rights violations ignored,[2] but it was denied that marginalisation and horizontal inequalities were human rights issues. It also had the effect of denying the links between such inequalities and the acts of violence that were acknowledged as violations. The most extreme demonstration of this is the 'exemplary' case of the torture and murder of Maina Sunuwar, a 15-year-old girl, that has been the subject of a large number of NGO reports, but where the fact Maina was Dalit is rarely even referenced, even though this was a driving factor in her being targeted by Royal Nepal Army troops (Advocacy Forum, 2010; OHCHR, 2006).[3] It is also demonstrated in the hundreds of

80 *Ram Kumar Bhandari*

disappearances of Tharu men in Bardiya, arising from the instrumentalisation of the Maoist conflict by local high-caste landlords as a way to blunt Tharu land rights activism.

The politics of human rights in Nepal has been moulded by the emergence of the rights movement alongside the first People's Movement of 1990. One result of this has been that rights NGOs are closely aligned with the UML, with some leading activists also having explicit political roles in the party. As such, NGOs have been seen to have perspectives on some issues, particularly around ethnic rights and federalism, that reflect the narrow nationalism that has emerged in UML and the narrow base of activists' ethnic and caste origins, rather than a broader rights-based perspective. As a result, transitional justice practice in Nepal restricts victim status to those who have suffered physical violence, and denies it to communities who are struggling for social inclusion. The result has been that Kathmandu-based civil society has seen itself as having little role to play in the struggles of minorities, such as the Janajatis and Madeshis, seeking a place in the post-conflict dispensation of Nepal and the new federal republic. The consequence of this has been that new civil society organisations have had to emerge from these struggles, indigenous to those regions and communities.

Similarly, the response of conflict victims to the failure of others' agendas to resonate with their own has been to create their own movements. In a context such as Nepal, victims' groups at the local level do not form from a desire to impact a transitional justice process; indeed prior to their mobilisation, most victims were unaware of the concept (Robins, 2015). Victims come together to address their immediate needs: to express solidarity and to create structures that can offer emotional, psychological, and social support, as well as to advocate for action to address the impacts of violations. The victims' movement in Nepal has its roots in such initiatives, with the first such group— beyond the confines of the Maoist movement—being the Conflict Victims' Committee (CVC) established in 2006 in Bardiya, the district most affected by disappearances, by a local teacher (ibid.). Similar groups were established elsewhere, largely in districts where the conflict had been fiercest, and where the success of Maoist mobilisation during the conflict reflected poverty and exclusion.

Victims' groups represent an alternative form of action to that of the human rights NGO, not only in the sense of having a constituency beyond donors, but in the forms of action in which they engage. As social movements they are identity-based, serving as a source of solidarity among victims with the capacity to create as well as mobilise a victim community, redefining understandings of who is a victim and how victimhood is perceived (Gready & Robins, 2017). As identity-based movements, they encompass the complexity of identities people bring to them, which has meant in Nepal that such movements cannot ignore marginality arising from gender, caste, and ethnicity, as rights NGOs typically do. Whilst the original victims' groups were firmly rooted in political attachment to one or other side of the conflict, the victims' movement

Governing Conflict Victims in Nepal 81

has successfully challenged this polarisation and enabled a cross-cutting victim identity that carries a different political salience.

Whilst a part of civil society, the victims' movement in Nepal is best characterised as a social movement and as such has engaged in contentious politics, with modes of action often characterised by demonstrations and occupations, rather than the production of reports and international advocacy. The victims' movement however has remained very much human rights focused but seeking to contextualise rights in the lives of those who constitute it. This has broadened the nature of its advocacy to include demands for livelihood, for employment, and for acknowledgement of victims. One of the most remarkable mobilisations has been that of the PLA fighters discharged for being recruited as minors. They have made themselves visible as victims, and labelled themselves as 'child soldiers', abandoned by their political masters once they accessed power, in ways that both demand an accounting for the past and challenge particular narratives of the conflict. Their mobilisation has always, perhaps unsurprisingly, used tactics that diverge from that of traditional civil society, ranging from vandalising United Nations vehicles in protest against the perceived role of the UN in their demobilisation, to *gheraoing* (picketing) the Maoist HQ in Kathmandu.[4] Their activities have successfully put the experience and needs of ex-minor combatants on the agenda in Kathmandu and they have successfully built a relationship with broader actors, including NGOs and donors, and in so doing have adopted a human rights framing of their issue.

Victim movements also articulate a prefigurative politics that implicitly critiques the undemocratic practices and patronage networks of both governance and civil society in Nepal. Victims' movements are built on a coming together of peers, who will choose representatives to speak for them when required, but whose logic is one of victims acting together, whether petitioning the local school to offer fee reductions for children of victims, or marching in Kathmandu (Robins, 2015). Social movements are also tools of personal transformation through conscience, and there are many cases of the caricature of the passive victim—reinforced by Nepali stereotypes of women and deferential lower castes—being radically altered by engagement with victims' groups. For most this will not mean gaining national profile or engaging in formal activism, but a challenging of isolation by networking with other victims, and the development of solidarities that create meanings that can enlarge the lives victims lead, and in turn allow victims to act together in their communities to change how they are perceived and listened to.

In Nepal, however, such radical democratic practice has faced great challenges, with the rural women who are over-represented among victims unable to play a full role in the movement through poverty and a need to work, through deference to the idea of always having been spoken for, or simply because they live too far from the capital and regional centres (Robins & Bhandari, 2012). The victims' movement remains led largely by high-caste men, despite its success in empowering women and other marginalised groups. One great success of the movement has been the emergence of a new generation

82   *Ram Kumar Bhandari*

of young activists, who see the victims' movement and their identity as victims as a way of fighting for justice that circumvents the manifest recent failures of both politics and civil society.

The failure of transitional justice in Nepal and of the substantial spending of major donors, appears to be a natural result of a Western advocacy model in a political context poorly suited to it. While the global model understands liberal democracies as susceptible to pressure from citizens as a natural consequence of electoral democracy, in practice Nepal operates very differently. Political parties have usurped much of the role of the state in constructing machines of patronage, and political change is driven largely through efforts to influence these. As long as political parties are insensitive to both popular advocacy and able to resist the demands of foreign donors, the classic advocacy model will be ineffective. The rise of the victims' movement however offers a view of a potential alternative, through the creation of grassroots-driven groups that can contest both the politics of patronage that has driven the impunity-focused post-conflict agenda, and the narrow civil society agenda of judicial accountability. Seeing such actors successfully drive change is a huge challenge, but an investment in supporting such actors can create a capacity in the long term to support both justice—as understood by victims—and a different form of politics.

Conclusions: Governing Conflict Victims

I have tried here to show how victims, and their relationship to the state—as well as to other actors—offer a broader lens on governance in Nepal. Victims and their treatment have made existing hierarchies more visible, with conflict victims a new category of the marginal to be managed by the state, political parties that have largely captured it, and civil society, all actors beholden to traditional Nepalese elites. This demonstrates that governance concerns not only the direct engagement of victims with the state and its institutions, but also the crucial social role of civil society and the international community who sustain certain approaches to governance. This encourages an understanding of power not only in terms of the hierarchical, top-down power of the state, but a wider perspective that also includes the forms of social control in all (highly politicised) institutions of the state, as well as the non-state apparatus where unequal relationships, political values and forms of knowledge are disseminated and reproduced. Victimhood as it is lived by victims emerges not only from a relationship with the state and other perpetrators, but from other local hierarchical relationships, which in turn determine how post-conflict efforts to address the legacies of violence and violations are perceived, enacted, and communicated.

Conflict victims have their origins largely in the poorest and most marginal groups of citizens and the failure of the state to address victims' needs echoes its broader failure and intrinsic incapacity to articulate political and social approaches that are focussed on the marginal. Despite the federal agenda, politics remains a Kathmandu-centred, elite preoccupation, driven not by accountability to citizens, but by a need to maintain patronage networks and ensure that state resources enable this. The one institution of the state that has sought to challenge the agenda of the political class to ensure there is no legal accountability for the crimes of the conflict has been the judiciary, but this has been ignored and bypassed by politicians. As long as the state remains captured by parties with an interest in forgetting the war and the victims it created, there is little hope of any state-centred approach that can serve victims.

More than a decade after the end of the conflict one route to challenging both how the marginal are represented and how routes to political change are perceived has been the emergence of dedicated victims' organisations. The limits of these must be acknowledged: these are currently small organisations with some visibility in dialogues around the conflict and victims' issues in Kathmandu and a capacity to link to and provide solidarity with victims where they are, but that themselves struggle against the constraints on effectively representing the most marginalised. They have however created routes to engaging state institutions, most notably the two transitional justice commissions, that permit an unprecedented access of the excluded to some of the machinery of governance. Victims' organisations have also shown that the human rights NGO sector, whilst using victims to legitimate their calls for transitional justice, are embedded in power structures and certain political frames that lead them to strictly limit the influence they allow victims to wield over their activities. The very existence of conflict victims' groups, paralleled by the growth of what might be called an alternative civil society in the Terai to represent victims of systematic social exclusion, shows that the marginalised can self-organise and represent both a threat and an example to traditional Kathmandu civil society.

Such radical and emancipatory practice potentially represents an approach to escaping and thus challenging governance in Nepal, both in terms of the state and social institutions that articulate the same power relationships. It is, however, far from clear that such an approach can be enabled on the scale necessary that such actors can have sufficient influence to concretely advance their agenda.

Notes

1 Ram Kumar Bhandari vs Government of Nepal, 2 January 2014, Supreme Court Verdict.
2 Nepalese human rights agencies have produced a huge number of reports on transitional justice, but not one to date that addresses issues of social or economic rights violations.
3 It is also interesting to note that her family name — actually the common Dalit surname, Sunar – has been consistently misrepresented as 'Sunuwar', apparently an error made in the initial engagement with her family by human rights workers that has been perpetuated ever since.

84 *Ram Kumar Bhandari*

4 While the mobilisation of ex-combatants in Nepal is largely undocumented, Nepalese media have reported their action: http://thehimalayantimes.com/nepal/disqualified-peoplesliberation-army-fighters-padlock-cpn-maoist-centre-headquarters/

References

Advocacy Forum. (2010). *Maina Sunuwar: Separating Fact from Fiction.* Advocacy Forum, Nepal.

Billingsley, K. (2019). Making Them Accountable: Victim-Activists' Critical Engagement with Truth Commissions in Nepal. *Journal of Human Rights Practice*, *11*(1), 190–208. https://doi.org/10.1093/jhuman/huz015

Carranza, R. (2012). *Relief, Reparations, and the Root Causes of Conflict in Nepal.* International Center for Transitional Justice.

Gready, P., & Robins, S. (2017). Rethinking Civil Society and Transitional Justice: Lessons from Social Movements and 'new' Civil Society. *The International Journal of Human Rights*, *21*(7), 956–975. https://doi.org/10.1080/13642987.2017.1313237

IOM. (2010). *Report on Mapping Exercise and Preliminary Gap Analysis of the Interim Relief and Rehabilitation Programme: Interim Relief and Rehabilitation to the Victims of Nepal's Armed Conflict December 2010.* International Organisation for Migration.

Jha, P. (2014). *Battles of the New Republic: A Contemporary History of Nepal.* Hurst and Company.

Lecomte-Tilouine, M. (2006). "Kill one, he becomes one hundred": Martyrdom as Generative Sacrifice in the Nepal People's War. *Social Analysis: The International Journal of Anthropology*, *50*(1), 51–72.

OHCHR. (2006). *The Torture and Death in Custody Maina Sunuwar.* Office of the High Commissioner of Human Rights in Nepal.

Robins, S. (2015). *Families of the Missing: A Test for Contemporary Approaches to Transitional Justice.* Routledge.

Robins, S., & Bhandari, R. K. (2012). *From Victims to Actors: Mobilising Victims to Drive Transitional Justice Process.* National Network of Families of Disappeared & Missing Nepal.

6 Reflection on Past Assumptions Vs Present Realities of Social Reintegration in Nepal

Chiranjibi Bhandari

Context

A decade-long conflict formally ended with the signing of the Comprehensive Peace Accord (CPA) in November 2006 between Government of Nepal and then Communist Party of Nepal (Maoist). Since then, disarming, containing, rehabilitating, and reintegrating of People's Liberation Army (PLA) emerged as a pertinent issue in the post-conflict peace-building process (Bhandari, 2017). Right from the signing of the CPA in 2006, protracted discussions to resolve the differences concerning the process of integration and reintegration of combatants prevailed until the next milestone, the 7 Point Agreement in November 2011 (Bhandari, 2017). Another major agreement signed during this period include the Agreement on the Monitoring of the Management of Arms and Armies (AMMAA) in 2006. Additionally, the Interim Constitution of Nepal 2007 was also a major guiding document to facilitate supervision, integration, and rehabilitation of combatants. The process took a long period due to the actors associated with the conflict being divided on major issues of integration and reintegration.[1] As per the commitment expressed in these aforementioned documents and the letter sent to the United Nations on behalf of the Government of Nepal and the CPN (Maoist) on 9 August 2006, United Nations Mission in Nepal (UNMIN) took charge of the process of confining ex-combatants within designated cantonments.[2] UNMIN verified combatants in the designated cantonments and monitored the management of arms and armed personnel of the Nepali Army and the Maoist army from the period of 2007 to January 2011. Moreover, UNMIN was responsible in assisting the parties through a Joint Monitoring Coordination Committee (JMCC), which was set up to implement their agreement on the management of arms and armed personnel.

In the same way, the Special Committee for Supervision, Integration and Rehabilitation of Maoist Army Combatants (Special Committee) was established in 2008 as per constitutional provisions mentioned in article 146 and 147 of the Interim Constitution of Nepal 2007 and other subsequent decisions made by Nepal's Council of Ministers. The committee was entrusted to prepare the guidelines relating to the implementation of supervision, integration,

DOI: 10.4324/9781003289876-7

86 *Chiranjibi Bhandari*

Table 6.1 Statistics relating to PLA combatants post-2006

S.N.	Registration and verification process by UNMIN	Total	Male	Female
1	Total number of registered combatants	32,250		
2	Total number of combatants verified by UNMIN	19,602	15756	3846
3	Total number of weapons registered and stored in the containers	3,475		
4	Absentees, automatically considered as disqualified combatants, during the verification process	8,640		
5	Disqualified combatants			
6	Under the age of 18 as of 25 May 2006 (considered minors)	2,973	1,987	986
7	Late recruits	1,035	804	231
8	Total disqualified (minors + late recruits) Number of Combatants in 2011, after verification by Special Committee	4,008		
9	Number of combatants absent in the regrouping process	2,456		
10	Total number of combatants present in the categorisation process	17,052	13,494	3,558
11	Dead, suspended and deserters	94		
12	Total number of combatants selected for integration	1422	1318	104
13	Total number of combatants opting for voluntary retirement	15,624	12,170	3,454
14	Total number of combatants opting for rehabilitation	6	6	0

Source: Secretariat of Special Committee for Supervision, Integration and Rehabilitation of Maoist Army Combatants (Bhandari 2017).

and rehabilitation activities. Likewise, on 22 January 2011, all the combatants came under the Special Committee through the declaration ceremony and the committee became the sole authority to continue the activities accomplished by UNMIN. Finally, the process concluded in three options; integration, rehabilitation, and voluntary retirement as per the provisions mentioned in the 7-Point Agreement signed between four major party leaders in November 2011. Based on this agreement, regrouping, integration, and rehabilitation-related activities were conducted. A much celebrated success within Nepal and internationally was the fact that 1422 ex-combatants were integrated into the Nepal Army and 15,630 ex-combatants were returned into society, which clearly marked a great achievement in the peace process. In the process, the total number of combatants was significantly less than the UNMIN verified 19,602 ex-combatants from 2007; accounting for 94 deaths as well as a total of 2456 ex-combatants who were and remain unaccounted for in the process.

The number of 'missing' ex-combatants created a tension among the politicians, on a political level, including regarding the potential misuse of allowances that were provided to Maoist commanders based on the number of combatants housed in the cantonments (Bhandari, 2017). In this context,

Assumptions and Realities: Social Reintegration in Nepal 87

this chapter highlights the expectation and realities of the ex-combatants, as well as explicitly describing the process of reintegration in one aspect and the expectation and realities of social reintegration in other ways.

Methodology

The method this chapter employs is twofold. There is an element of auto-ethnography as the author was directly involved in the management of arms and armies process at the Secretariat of Special Committee for Supervision, Integration and Rehabilitation of Maoist Army Combatants as an officer. Additionally, the author also worked closely with ex-combatants in other research projects and programmatic initiatives and therefore was able to closely observe their long-term realities from the period of 2011 to 2020. The chapter is also based on the testimonies of the experiences of ex-combatants who were interviewed as primary sources for this chapter. Apart from the primary sources, secondary information including national broadsheets, research articles, journals, and book chapters were also consulted to complement the findings of the primary sources.

This study is limited in its scope since it depends on personal observation. The term 'ex-combatant' is not homogenous term. The study doesn't concentrate on the combatants, who participated with the Young Communist League (YCL) and any other outfit of the Nepal Communist Party (Maoist) after the signing of Peace Agreements. Also, this chapter doesn't focus on the combatants, who were discharged from the cantonment as verified late minor recruits in 2009. The chapter strictly focuses on those who joined the conflict from 1996 to 2006 in the capacity of a soldier and who went through the process of registration and verification conducted by UNMIN in 2007 and the Secretariat of Special Committee in 2011.

Social Reintegration

Social reintegration is conceptualised as a process in DDR theory by which ex-combatants convert their identity from soldiers to civilians and transform themselves into society; both transforming themselves and the views of the surrounding civilian society. It indicates the multiple processes, of which ex-combatants go through the various stages, re-connecting with family, friends, and various communities. The global practice of reintegration of ex-combatants has however been seen largely as a challenge of managing a group who can pose potential threats to a fragile peace, rather than understanding and addressing their needs and those of communities receiving them (Robins et al., 2016).

These complex processes help to rebuild trust in the community and increase a confidence in ex-combatants as co-citizens who can be fully included into the civilian society (Özerdem, 2013). The United Nations, in 2006, defined social reintegration as a process that takes place mainly in local communities where reintegration has largely been interpreted in terms of former combatants

88 *Chiranjibi Bhandari*

gaining acceptance by their families and local communities (Gomes Porto et al., 2007; Humphreys & Weinstein, 2007) or in terms of their capacity to participate in civic and community life (Buxton, 2008; Kaplan & Nussio, 2012). The study of social reintegration is very important in many aspects of post-conflict peace-building. Kaplan and Nussio (2012) also highlight that social reintegration may help to limit the recurrence of civil war.

A greater access to political participation has significant negative effects in the likelihood of renewed war (Walter, 2004). In the case of Nepal, a number of research articles have been published in the theme of social reintegration of ex-combatants. Some of the empirical studies include Bhandari, 2017, 2019; Bhatt, 2016; Martin Chautari, 2013; Upreti & Shivakoti, 2018. However, comprehensive study in comparison to their past assumptions and realities of reintegration of ex-combatants into society has not been studied in depth.

A participatory action research carried out by Simon Robins, Ram Kumar Bhandari, and the ex-PLA research group entitled 'Poverty, Stigma and Alienation: Reintegration Challenges of Ex-Maoist Combatants in Nepal' briefly evaluates the success of the reintegration process from the perspective of ex-combatants; assesses the challenges faced by ex-combatants in the communities where they are residing and engage with groups of ex-combatants in their communities – and mobilise such groups where they do not already exist — in order to both create a support structure for ex-fighters, and to create a forum for dialogue (Robins et al., 2016).

Observation

The author's interaction with the ex-combatants of the PLA was very limited in the initial phases of the peace process. However, intensive interaction and close communication and personal touch with ex-combatants became possible from 2011, after the author joined the Secretariat of Special Committee for Supervision, Integration and Rehabilitation of Maoist Army Combatants as an officer. The work at the secretariat was helpful in understanding the political and technical aspect of integration and reintegration of ex-combatants. That was the first gateway to getting to know ex-combatants in their personal and professional life. In order to make the context clear, observations over different periods of time are summarised as different scenes.

An important landmark to the peace process of Nepal was the departure of the UNMIN on 15 January 2011 and handover of the Maoist army combatants and arms to the Special Committee on 22 January 2011. With the end of term for UNMIN, the Government of Nepal was performing the role of monitoring the cantoned arms and armies, previously being carried out by UNMIN. The work was to be taken over by the government before the end of 15 January 2011. For the supervision, rehabilitation, and integration of combatants of Maoist army, the Government of Nepal had formed a Special Committee. Under the Special Committee (SC), the Secretariat

Assumptions and Realities: Social Reintegration in Nepal   89

was given the task to undertake functions of Integration and Rehabilitation. Thus the government has left the Secretariat with all these communicating and coordinating tasks. Integration and Rehabilitation was the priority issue. The gradual development of integration and rehabilitation proceeded forward with the deployment of a monitoring team, recruitment process of survey teams, and extensive discussions by the political parties at different levels. The issue of Integration and rehabilitation was discussed a number of times among and between the secretariat members and political leaders.

> (Personal Observation, June 2011, at Secretariat of Special Committee for Supervision, Integration and Rehabilitation of Maoist Army Combatants)

Despite a wide range of meetings and discussions at both political and technical level, there was a disconcertment among the ex-combatants regarding their destiny until November 2011. The ex-combatants, cantoned in various locations, were uncertain about their fate. A clear understanding of process and clarity on their personal decision had not been made. The Maoists' landslide victory in the first constituent assembly election of 2008 was a major morale booster for those cantoned during this period. They saw themselves as agents of change who had been the responsible force for major social and political change in the country and many were enthusiastic for their 'dignified' adjustment into the state security forces.[3] At the same time, the discourse at political leadership was centred on finalising four major issues; norms, modality, numbers, and rank harmonisation (Bhandari, 2015). As a pinpointing voice, an ex-combatant working at the Secretariat shared his opinion with regards to PLA integration in 2011:

> I am a Battalion Commander in PLA with direct experiences of around twenty battles during the Maoist War. My position is equivalent to a Colonel in the Nepal Army. Immediately after the decision at political level for integration and reintegration, I will hope to join the state security force as a Battalion commander with my PLA team and will serve as a professional security officer in the National Army.[4]

The statement shared by a Battalion Commander indicates that even someone who had been serving as a battalion commander was not clear on his fate and a possible way out of integration and reintegration. The issue remained contentious among the major actors for a longer time than expected when the CPA was signed, since it took six years and numerous other agreements to finalise the details regarding the arms and armies management process. The 7-Point Agreement guided several activities such as the regrouping of ex-combatants, facilitation of voluntary retirement, rehabilitation, and integration. The agreement remained controversial within the Maoist leadership; however, it provided a ground for prolonged issue of integration and reintegration of ex-combatants.

90 *Chiranjibi Bhandari*

The activity of updating and regrouping began on 17 November 2011 and successfully ended on 2 December 2011.[5] The number of combatants verified by UNMIN in 2007 was 19,602; however, the number of combatants that participated in November and December 2011 at the time of regrouping facilitated by secretariat was only 1705. Ninety-four combatants were reported as dead. Out of 17,052 combatants, 9702 combatants decided to go for integration, 7344 chose voluntary retirement, and 6 chose the rehabilitation option. The 7344 combatants who opted for voluntary retirement in the first round of regrouping received their first instalment cheque in January 2012. After the first phase of regrouping, the number of ex-combatants in the cantonment sites was reduced by 7344, therefore leaving 9708 personnel. As a result of this reduction, 13 satellite cantonment sites were closed.

The activity of re-grouping was carried out simultaneously in seven main cantonments. The process was led by the secretariat, and it was noticeable that ex-combatants were mainly polarised into two groups: those opting for integration and those for the voluntary retirement process. Despite being offered more than three dozen options and alternatives as part of the package of rehabilitation, it was to be the most neglected option by the combatants. The decision of ex-combatants on the various alternatives offered by the Special Committee was determinant with the guidance provided by party leadership, family, and peer pressure, as well as their own free will.

In order to adjust the number of Maoist Army combatants from 9702 to maximum 6500, as agreed on Seven Point Agreement, the Special Committee decided to regroup combatants into those who opted for integration. In this phase, 6578 combatants opted for voluntary retirement. This was done in April 2011.

The conversation with ex-combatants in April 2012 still resonates in my mind. Ex-combatants shared that the underlying hesitation towards the integration process and attractive package of voluntary retirement motivated them to choose voluntary retirement. At the political level, Maoist leaders were strongly divided into two major groups: a group led by Chairman Puspa Kamal Dahal (Prachanda) and another group led by Mohan Baidya. The former group initially suggested supporting combatants to favour choosing alternatives to integration and later directed them to follow voluntary retirement. As mentioned by Subedi (2014), the option of voluntary retirement would likely keep the ex-combatants more politically engaged and therefore they would aid the Maoists as a mainstream political party.

Following the decision made by the Special Committee on 27 August 2012, the secretariat provided a third opportunity to opt for voluntary retirement. In the period of August to September 2012, 1664 combatants chose voluntary retirement leaving 1460 for integration.

Assumptions and Realities: Social Reintegration in Nepal 91

Consensus was made at the political level to provide flexibility in education, age and marital status and integrate a maximum of 6500 combatants in Nepal Army. However, the number of combatants declined to 1460 on final round. Out of them, 71 combatants were selected for officer ranks and 1389 for rank and file. Throughout the process of rank harmonisation and training, 38 ex-combatants including 1 officer and 37 rank and files decided to quit the process and finally 1422 ex-combatants integrated into Nepal Army.

First instalment cheque was distributed from seven main cantonments in two rounds in the period of January to April 2012, and cantonments were officially closed in September 2012. When cantonments were closed, there was no possibility to distribute cheques on the same procedures adopted in the first instalment. Hence, the secretariat established temporary offices within District Administration Offices in Jhapa, Sindhuli, Chitwan, Nawalparashi, Dang, Surkhet, and Kailali and distributed cheques from 31 October to 10 November 2012.

After the closure of cantonment sites between the period of September 2012 and April 2013, ex-combatants were resettled into society. The satisfaction level among the ex-combatants was high for their decision of opting for voluntary retirement with cash packages.

In the period of July 2013 to September 2013, I was associated as a conflict expert in the work of vertical monitoring of the Nepal Peace Trust Fund (NPTF) projects. Out of a number of questions associated with their satisfaction level to facilities available at cantonments, a specific question was asked to ex-combatants expecting their genuine voice on the reintegration process. A total of 897 ex-combatants representing 30 different districts participated in the research. In that study, a majority of the ex-combatants expressed their satisfaction on reintegration, which took place between July and August 2013.

'Do you think that it is difficult for (you) ex-combatants to integrate into the society/community?' Little less than two thirds (65%) thought that it was not difficult for ex-combatants to integrate into the society/community. Proportion of those who thought very difficult is 4% followed by difficult (9%). Around one out of five respondents stated that it felt somewhat difficult (23%).

In October 2015, I joined an initiative program 'From Combatants to Peacemakers' as the training, monitoring, and evaluation coordinator. My role in this project was to prepare training manuals for basic, advanced, and refresher training on dialogue facilitation and mediation and train the ex-combatants and community people for promotion of social harmony and peace in their communities. Around 750 individuals, 50% ex-combatants and 50% community people along with local government bodies and other stakeholders

92 *Chiranjibi Bhandari*

in 16 communities of 12 districts, directly participated in this program (Pro Public, 2017).

As per earlier observation, a majority of the ex-combatants were excited to depart from cantonments with cash packages. They aspired for better livelihood options by utilising this cash package that was provided as part of voluntary retirement. Despite their excitement, social interaction among the ex-combatants and community people was a problem at one level and therefore was not perceived as a complete barrier of social reintegration. It was the main barrier of communities in development activities. During the work with ex-combatants in the period of 2013 to 2016, it was clearly observed that a majority of ex-combatants was struggling for their livelihood options, and they were expecting a program to support their livelihood in addition to initiatives regarding dialogue and mediation.

Mostly, ex-combatants were sharing their struggle for securing employment in their places of settlement, employable skill for future prospects, medical support for injured and needy, as well as long-term livelihood opportunities for female and wounded ex-combatants. They also wanted opportunities for education and access to health facilities for their children and family members. Also, a limited number of female ex-combatants shared their problems of family disputes, psychological issues such as trauma, as well as social and cultural discrimination in their communities. As a representative voice, an ex-combatant shared her experience of social discrimination and cultural deviation accordingly:[6]

> I was originally from Kalikot and settled in Kailali. We had an inter-caste marriage during the cantonment life and are settled in this area. We joined the PLA for political change as well as to overcome the discriminatory social and cultural norms and practices in society. However, we ourselves suffered through various problems. Some of our friends who also took part in inter-caste marriages during the war and cantonment, got divorced after leaving the sites. Cultural deviation and family tension is visible in our area, which is common among other ex-combatants too.

After the three tiers of election in 2017, I visited Rolpa, Bardiya, Gorkha, Parbat, Achham and Kailali district for restorative dialogue and transitional justice research work. The experience during that period is different in terms of social reintegration of ex-combatants.[7] It was commonly heard that a significant number, around 200, of the ex-combatants secured their leadership position and were serving as elected representatives in local, provincial, and federal parliament.

> A combatant reported that including both federal and provincial governments, around 40–45 ex-PLA are serving as a Member of Parliament. Mahendra Bahadur Shahi, an ex-combatant, was serving as the Chief Minister of Karnali Province. Some other former ex-combatants are

Assumptions and Realities: Social Reintegration in Nepal 93

working as ministers in provincial governments and head of local government bodies. In the case of Rolpa, out of 11 local government bodies, seven local bodies are headed by ex-combatants including head of district coordination office.

Mostly, ex-combatants started their own business usually by investing the cash package that they received for choosing to voluntarily retire. A limited number of ex-combatants saw themselves go out of business due to their own inefficiency in personal and professional management. It can be argued that this issue may have been averted with rehabilitation packages that focused on providing ex-combatants with education and professional skills. The Covid-19 pandemic is also likely to have pushed more of them out of business but that remains to be studied.

An ex-combatant and PLA battalion commander from Kailali opted for voluntary retirement in 2012 and started a business along with social work in his new settlement. In the period of five to six years, his social and financial status was completely ruined, he sold his hardware business and is now working as a cart puller, with a small mobile shop selling biscuits and noodles for schoolchildren. His health is deteriorating as a result of a regular drinking habit.

Assumption on Social Reintegration

A single factor is not sufficient to justify the underlying causes for war. Social discrimination, poverty, unemployment, unequal distribution of resources throughout the countryside, a personal interest to transform society, better livelihood opportunities, the political ideology of Marxism, Leninism, and Maoism motivated people to join the war (Thapa & Sijapati, 2004). The conflict spread throughout the country and people from all caste and ethnic groups including three geographic regions and almost all districts (74 districts out of 75 districts) were attracted towards the PLA. Significant number of youths joined the war after being attracted to the radical ideology of Maoism as well as for their own aspirations of a better society and nation. They were handed various responsibilities as messengers, intelligence operatives, and even as members of an assault group. It was also apparent that one third of the combatants were female in the PLA (Bhandari 2016).

Unlike senior commanders, most of the foot soldiers aspired for a better life, a dignified life, and recognition for their contribution in the war. Combatants were hopeful to be in the patronage of party leadership after the voluntary retirement process. This assumption vanished with the deviation of party leadership behaviour as there was a new sense of elitism with the higher ranks of the party. Ex-combatants were also side-lined as a consequence of factionalism within the party which saw prominent leaders such as Baburam Bhattarai, Netra Bikram Chand, and Mohan Baidya, and others leave the party. The

94   *Chiranjibi Bhandari*

aspirations of the ex-combatants were furthered dampened when the Maoists merged with their long-time rivals Communist Party of Nepal-United Marxist Leninist (CPN-UML) to form a united Nepal Communist Party (NCP).[8]

Realities of Social Reintegration

Previous studies concluded that a significant number of ex-combatants had resettled in a cluster basis in the nearby areas of East-West highway (Bhandari, 2015, 2019).The rationale for resettlement of ex-combatants in nearby areas of cantonments is the familiarity with the places and people, better facilities and livelihood options compared to their villages or places of origin (Robins et al., 2016). In terms of social and political reintegration, despite the successful closure of the cantonments, the questions over continued discrimination against ex-combatants and the problem of integrating into the very social order dominated by exclusion on the basis of caste, class and gender, which the ex-combatants as Maoists fought to fundamentally transform and dismantle was as it is (Bhandari, 2016). The preliminary assumption of senior commanders was to get integrated into mainstream party politics.

The election of all three tiers of government in 2017 provided a major gateway for ex-combatants for their political participation and majority of ex-combatants are being engaged in various political, social, and economic activities at the level of their community. Not all of them are politically engaged as Maoists as some of them joined the splinter political groups formed by Mohan Baidhya Kiran, Gopal Kiranti, Netra Bikram Chand, and Baburam Bhattarai. In addition, large numbers of ex-combatants are frustrated with politicians and mainstream party politics. The reasons they shared include corrupt behaviour of party leadership, frequent split in Maoist Party, Party unification with CPN-UML. Successful conversion of ex-combatants into civilian life by addressing their social, political, and economic aspects was a major concern of social reintegration, which proved challenging in Nepal.

The interviews with ex-combatants and their families confirms that significant numbers, roughly 10–15%, of ex-combatants are now working overseas as migrant workers due to a lack of employment opportunities within the country coupled with the fact that many chose to sacrifice their education in order to fight for the Maoists which left them at a disadvantage.[9]

At some point, the issue of identity transformation amongst ex-combatants is an important aspect that warrants discussion. The lives of ex-combatants have seen dramatic and polarising changes as they went from being revolutionary soldiers to cantonment and finally reintegration. For many youths who joined the conflict, a majority of their lifetime was that of a solider and a Maoist and the post-conflict phase has seen a rapid disintegration of that identity. Ex-combatants went from being politically engaged and fighting for a social, political, and economic transformation of their country to civilians who realised that these aspirations were not being met. After ten years of war

Assumptions and Realities: Social Reintegration in Nepal 95

and around six years of cantoned life, most of the combatants are focused on securing their livelihoods as opposed to politics. For many, the conflict and cantonment period were periods of social cohesion and camaraderie amongst their fellow combatants. They supported one another and were further supported by party leadership at this time. With the conclusion of the war, this camaraderie came to an end for many who returned to their homes and faced social stigma whilst being isolated from their comrades. This is also true for those who have gone abroad to seek opportunities as they too find themselves isolated. Ex-combatants were also largely let down by party leadership and many have completely severed their ties to the party. As mentioned in a previous chapter, ex-child soldiers who felt aggrieved even picketed the Maoist headquarters. This drastic change in situation and identity has led to a proliferation of psychological issues within the ex-combatant community. This has also been worsened due to the economic challenges they are facing in social reintegration. Similarly, ex-combatants stress a lack of medical support and their mother party itself as a major challenge for them in the post-conflict era. Currently, ex-combatants opine that financial security and skills development training were desirable for a secure life.

I had contested the elections for the post of deputy mayor in my municipality and I realised that a lack of financial security is a major threat for the social and political reintegration of female ex-combatants like me. Being a candidate for the local elections, I realised importance of financial security for politics and dignified reintegration. Social awareness and consciousness by itself can't generate better results without regular income, skills. and financial arrangement.[10]

Political reintegration of ex-combatants is directly related with the current trend of politics, social norms, and practices, as well as broader discourse of women's participation in politics. Both male and female ex-combatants are active in politics at local, district, province, and central level. Several female ex-combatants, who are serving as deputy mayors and vice-chairpersons of rural municipalities as well as member of municipalities, are also experiencing challenges in their new role. Lacking the knowledge on legal issues and governance, elected representatives from the ex-combatant community are having problems working effectively in their current roles. As underlying challenges, ex-combatants reported weak social security and insurance systems for ex-combatants as also being problematic. In the study area, ex-combatants shared that mental health is one of the serious problems that they experienced in their surroundings. Also, the problems induced by inter-caste marriage such as social stigma are also reported by ex-combatants as difficulties in study areas. The experience of social reintegration of ex-combatants in Nepal is no exception to such pronounced post-war governance challenges, faced in other post-conflict societies.

96 *Chiranjibi Bhandari*

As their immediate needs, ex-combatants are also demanding improved support in the areas of healing, counselling, and psychological support to various groups of war-affected people. Observation proved that former guerrillas are getting benefits extremely unequally from transitions towards peace. Some ex-combatants are established as prominent political leaders, other battlefield comrades are returning to pre-war occupations as farmers and street vendors. Even the combatants who are seriously injured and experiencing mental distress, they may or may not receive some medical and financial support for treatments, most often for major physical injuries, illness, and impairments, often at the expense of psychological challenges. Moreover, the visibility, public recognition as heroes or traitors, support systems and treatments extended to former combatants and civilians (the latter have often equally serious needs for treatments and aids) may differ substantially. Such unequal treatments are being identified as new humiliations and grievances.

So, it can be argued that a clear difference on expectations and realities of ex-combatants is visible. Collected testimonies of ex-combatants need to be dealt separately to figure out the group-wide expectations and reality. Those who were verified minors and late recruits are completely dissatisfied with the Government of Nepal and their party leadership for neglecting their issues. Some of the ex-combatants, who chose not to integrate into the Nepal Army are now currently regretting their past decision and their blind trust towards their party leadership. Also, the ex-combatants who invested their cash amount for everyday consumption related activities are now expecting proper job-related skills in their present life.

It can clearly be observed that political integration of foot soldiers and the senior level of ex-combatants are completely different. High-ranking commanders are well-integrated in politics either as elected representatives in local bodies or in party portfolio from local to district to province to central committee. Their political position is considered helpful for them to regain social status in their communities. There is no systematic inquiry on integration of ex-combatants into the Nepal Army. However, some of the ex-combatants, who integrated into the Nepal Army, expressed their satisfaction towards the integration in Nepal Army. They said that the Nepal Army is a professional army and the role of ex-combatants in the Nepal Army is no different than other individuals in their profession.

Conclusion

To generalise, the social reintegration process of ex-combatants has been recognised as a unique, homegrown, and successful model both in the domestic and international arena. Despite this fact, the situation regarding verified late minor recruits and ex-combatants who opted for voluntary retirement is unsettled and contentious in social, political, and economic aspects of reintegration. The reintegration of ex-combatants was led by political imperatives rather than social imperatives. The initial perception of ex-combatants on the concept of reintegration and rehabilitation also added more complication for ex-combatants in the later phase.

The study shows that initially ex-combatants expressed a strong sense of dissatisfaction with the word 'rehabilitation', and this is clearly witnessed with the few numbers of combatants who chose the rehabilitation option. Even observing the current situation, top tier leaders and middle-range leaders who were above the rank of company commanders during the verification process facilitated by UNMIN are doing relatively better in comparison to the rank and file of the PLA. As immediate concerns, those soldiers are living in difficult situations and expecting support in the areas of healing, counselling, and psychological support in their everyday life. With reference to their past assumptions and present realities, the degree of satisfaction among the foot solders was high in the period of war and cantonment, where they enjoyed the equality and freedom. However, they are struggling for their everyday life after the social reintegration and satisfaction level towards the decision and process of reintegration is gradually declining.

Contrary to the rank and file, senior commanders of PLA are found happy right now with their public roles in various levels of government agencies. The satisfaction level is not determined by a single reason of social reintegration, wide ranges of incidents or circumstances including internal party politics and polarisation among the leaders in Maoist, party splits into various groups, neglect of the conflict victims and verified late and minor recruits, party unification with CPN (UML) as well as the prolonged process and uncertainty of transitional justice playing a pivotal role in their frustration. Apart from the broader political change, the common assumption of ex-combatants, at the personal level, during the war and cantonment period was to achieve equality in society, end discrimination, create employment within the country, and adopt the best practices in society and state along with a dignified life and integration into society, politics, and economic activities.

Notes

1 The number of ex-combatants to be integrated into security agencies along with finalising the norms, modality, rank, and process of arms handover appeared as divisive issues throughout the process.
2 Seven main and twenty-one satellite cantonments in seven different locations.
3 Interview with ex-combatants in Kathmandu and MCS-3, Chitwan.
4 Testimony of a combatant, recorded in October 2011 at Secretariat of Special Committee for Supervision, Integration and Rehabilitation of Maoist Army combatants.
5 Seven teams were deployed in the field under the leadership of secretariat members, altogether 210 surveyors were deployed at seven main and twenty-one satellite cantonments.
6 Lamki Chuha, Kailali in October 2015.

98 *Chiranjibi Bhandari*

7 Mainly the opportunities ex-combatants noticed during the work include their participation in political parties and mainstream government. It shows that a majority of ex-combatants are integrated into the society in one or other ways. A significant number of ex-combatants integrated into mainstream politics from central to provincial to local-level politics as well as represented their electoral constituencies and society as MP in federation, province, and local bodies, municipalities, and rural municipalities.
8 This party has since been dissolved due to strategic and personal disputes between K.P. Oli (UML faction) and Prachanda (Maoist faction).
9 Individuals are working overseas and their family members.
10 Testimony of a female ex-combatant, contested for the position of Deputy Mayor in local election of 2017.

References

Bhandari, C. (2015). The Reintegration of Maoist Ex-Combatants in Nepal. *Economic and Political Weekly, 50*(9), 63–68.
Bhandari, C. (2016). Social Realities of War and Peace: Expectation and Realities of Female Ex-Combatants in Nepal. In P. Adhikari, S. Ghimire, & V. Mallik (Eds.), *Nepal Transition to Peace: A Decade of the Comprehensive Peace Accord 2006-2016* (pp. 242–259). NTTP-I.
Bhandari, C. (2017). People's Liberation Army Post-2006: Integration, Rehabilitation or Retirement?. In A. Ramsbotham, & D. Thapa (Eds.), *Two Steps Forward, One Step Back: The Nepal Peace Process.* Conciliation Resources.
Bhandari, C. (2019). Social Dialogue: A Tool of Social Reintegration and Post-Conflict Peace Building in Nepal. *Asian Journal of Peace Building, 7*(1), 143–160.
Bhatt, D. P. (2016). Nepal's Homegrown Model: Integration and Rehabilitation of Maoist Combatants. In P. Adhikari, S. Ghimire, & V. Mallik (Eds.), *Nepal Transition to Peace A Decade of Comprehensive Peace Accord 2006-2016* (pp. 354–365). NTTP-I.
Buxton, J. (2008). Reintegration and Long-Term Development: Linkages and Challenges. *Thematic Working Paper 5.* Centre for International Cooperation and Security.
Gomes Porto, J., Parsons, I., & Alden, C. (2007). *From Soldiers to Citizens The Social, Economic and Political Reintegration of Unita Ex Combatants.*
Humphreys, M., & Weinstein, J. M. (2007). Demobilization and Reintegration. *Journal of Conflict Resolution, 51*(4), 531–567. https://doi.org/10.1177/0022002707302790
Kaplan, O., & Nussio, E. (2012). Community Counts: The Social Reintegration of Ex-Combatants in Colombia. *SSRN Electronic Journal.* https://doi.org/10.2139/ssrn.2138188
Martin Chautari. (2013). *Political Risk and Ex-Combatants. Policy Brief, 9.*
Özerdem, A. (2013). Disarmament, Demobilisation and Reintegration. In R. Mac Ginty (Ed.), *Routledge Handbook of Peace Building* (pp. 225–236). Routledge.
Pro Public. (2017). Community Envisioning Report of 10 Communities. *Combatants to Peacemakers Program Annual Report.* Pro Public.
Robins, S., Bhandari, R. K., & Ex-PLA Research Group. (2016). *Poverty, Stigma and Alienation: Reintegration Challenges of Ex-Maoist Combatants in Nepal.* Berghof Foundation.

Subedi, D. B. (2014). Dealing with Ex-Combatants in a Negotiated Peace Process: Impacts of Transitional Politics on the Disarmament, Demobilization and Reintegration Programme in Nepal. *Journal of Asian and African Studies*, *49*(6), 672–689. https://doi.org/10.1177/0021909613507537

Thapa, D., & Sijapati, B. (2004). *A Kingdom under Siege: Nepal's Maoist Insurgency, 1996 to 2004*. Zed Books.

Upreti, B. R., & Shivakoti, S. (2018). The Struggle of Female Ex-Combatants in Nepal. *Peace Review*, *30*(1), 78–86. https://doi.org/10.1080/10402659.2017.1419937

Walter, B. F. (2004). Does Conflict Beget Conflict? Explaining Recurring Civil War. *Journal of Peace Research*, *41*(3), 371–388. https://doi.org/10.1177/0022343304043775

7 The Post-Conflict Context of Marginalised Groups in Nepal

Unmet Expectations

Ram Prasad Mainali

Introduction

Inequality has remained a central debate in academia and practice due to its relevancy across disciplines and its global applicability. The ideals of Marx and Engels are still discussed in classes today and the popularity of economists such as Thomas Piketty and Joseph Stiglitz has led to further work on inequality within the field of economics. The recent Covid-19 pandemic has made previously unengaged areas of inequality more prominent such as in access to health resources. Likewise, within the peace and conflict discipline, inequality has longstanding credence. Inequalities between ethnic groups, religions, regions, gender, and more have been a major contributor to civil wars. Grievance, actual or perceived, of a certain marginalised group or groups in relation to others is often cited to have been a factor in the onset of civil wars as seen in the cases of Northern Ireland, El Salvador, and more.

Nepal is not an outlier in this case as historical inequalities, as well as a host of other factors, ignited a conflict in 1996. Inequality occurs through various interactions in Nepal. The historical adoption of the caste system meant that Nepali society hosted inequalities based on caste on top of other more common forms of inequality such as those based on ethnicity, gender, region, and religion. The Maoists, who portrayed themselves as an anti-caste, anti-patriarchal, anti-feudal force, appealed to the marginalised groups of Nepal who saw Nepali society and politics dominated by the so-called dominant castes of Brahmin and Chettri. Furthermore, they also coopted the concerns of the Terai and remote western regions, whose inhabitants often felt ignored by the central government in Kathmandu. By successfully relaying the grievances of the marginalised in Nepal, the Maoists were able to recruit heavily from these groups into their fighting force as well as their leadership.

The conflict and the subsequent peace process was successful in raising and addressing the concerns of marginalised groups in the country. Clause 3.5 of the CPA committed the signatories to the restructuring of the state and to "address the problems related to women, Dalit, indigenous people, Janajatis, Madhesi, oppressed, neglected and minority communities and backward regions by ending discrimination based on class, caste, language,

DOI: 10.4324/9781003289876-8

Post-Conflict Context of Marginalised Groups in Nepal 101

gender, culture, religion, and region". Additionally, other provisions codified the intention of the signatories to introduce policies aimed to provide land and end all forms of feudalism. Similar provisions were also included in the Interim Constitution of Nepal as well as the Constitution of Nepal that was promulgated in 2015. This chapter posits that despite constitutional guarantees, the progress in addressing socio-economic inequality in Nepal has not been satisfactory. To do this, the chapter will briefly introduce the causes of inequality within Nepal. Following this, the second section contains a quantitative analysis of the effects of marginalisation on Socio-Economic Status (SES) on different groups in the country. The subsequent section will explore government initiatives introduced since 2015 in order to address inequality in the country and its overall impact. The final section will outline the current challenges and shortcomings of the government in transforming Nepal into a more egalitarian society.

There are certain issues that need clarification. Firstly, the analysis of this chapter does not explore inequality related to gender and region in depth. It is impossible to conduct intersectional analysis in regard to inequality in Nepal without addressing gender and region but both these topics require more nuanced analysis which is conducted elsewhere in the book. Federalism was introduced as the antidote to regional inequalities in Nepal and therefore an entire chapter written by Shuvam Rizal is devoted to the analysis of federalism and post-2017 governance in Nepal. Similarly, gender inequalities in Nepal also require nuanced analysis and this is accomplished by Susan Risal in the following chapter. Another issue that requires clarification is the methodology of the chapter. Initially, the idea was to conduct a quantitative-focused analysis related to SES inequalities within the country. However, due to the Covid-19 pandemic, national-level surveys such as the 2021 Census and Nepal Living Standards Survey (NLSS) were unable to be conducted. This setback means a more representative national-level analysis is not possible. However, there is a silver lining as due to the vast number of NGOs in operation within Nepal, there is an abundance of qualitative material available for analysis and which has been consulted in the formation of this chapter.

Context

"Casteism is an ideology, in fact 'dominant ideology', established and mobilised by the dominant classes (and thus dominant castes) to establish and maintain relations of domination with the lower classes (castes)" (J. Gurung, 2005). The so-called dominant castes as indicated in this quotation refers to the Brahmin and Chettri groups of Nepal, more specifically Hill-Brahmin and Chettris that have monopolised the roles relating to the administration of the country. Armed with the Hindu mandate, Nepal's society was structured with the Brahmins at the top followed by Chettris. Whilst Brahmins were traditionally priests and educators, Chettris were the ruling class and both the Shah and Rana families who were de facto rulers for most of Nepal's history belonged

102   *Ram Prasad Mainali*

to that caste group. Due to Nepal's cultural heterogeneity, indigenous groups were also incorporated within the caste system. Most indigenous groups found themselves labelled as either non-enslavable alcohol drinkers (Rai, Gurung, Limbu, Magar, etc.) or as enslavable alcohol drinkers (Tharu, Tamang, Sherpa, Chepang, etc.). Mulsims and foreigners were ranked below these groups as water-unacceptable but touchable, meaning that these groups were not allowed to drink water from the same source as those of so-called 'higher' castes but they were allowed to come into contact with them. Finally, at the base of the pyramid were Dalits who were classed as water-unacceptable and untouchable. It is important to remember that the Newars, an ethnic group indigenous to the Kathmandu Valley, already had their own caste system and this was also incorporated within the wider Nepali caste system. Similarly, the Tarai region, which sees a lot of cultural exchanges with neighbouring India, also had their own caste system.

The caste system was institutionalised in 1854 with the introduction of Muluki Ain by then prime minister, Jung Bahadur Rana. Whilst the caste system was practiced throughout the country, the Muluki Ain provided it with legal and state legitimacy and anyone who defied the system would be punished. With the rigid caste system in place, social mobility was virtually impossible. Occupation was predetermined by caste so there was no option of improving your situation by finding different means of survival. Inter-caste marriage was, and still is, considered to be taboo so marrying someone from a higher caste was also not feasible. The livelihood of marginalised groups was further diminished due to dwindling land ownership within their population. Hill Brahmins-Chettris were accorded several advantages that allowed them to acquire plentiful lands to the detriment of marginalised indigenous groups. They were better educated, had a better understanding of the legal realm, had connections with ruling classes or the bureaucracy and a better knowledge of the Nepali language which was the official language of the country. Weaponising these advantages and through duplicity they were able to amass huge amounts of land whilst those from marginalised groups had barely enough land for sustenance. Communal lands were now in private hands and many had to resort to working as labourers in the farms with meagre pay (O. Gurung, 2009). When land became scarce in the hill region, many hill groups such as Brahmin-Chettri as well as hill-indigenous groups made their way to Tarai. Forests were cleared to make way for agricultural land displacing indigenous groups who were reliant on the forest for their livelihoods (Gellner, 2007). Tharus, an indigenous landowning group from Tarai, were adversely affected as their land was taken by those from hill groups using coercion or manipulation.

The introduction of the party-less *panchayat* system of governance introduced by King Mahendra in 1960 further entrenched these caste divides. Under Mahendra, a harmful Nepali nationalism was promoted which emphasised the unity of the country under one language, religion, dress, and policy. This initiative further fortified the privilege of the existing

Post-Conflict Context of Marginalised Groups in Nepal 103

so-called dominant castes by placing the Nepali language and the Hindu religion at the forefront whilst simultaneously sidelining those groups who did not adhere to these customs. Indigenous and ethnic-based organisations were also allowed to exist on a limited mandate relating to culture and were not allowed to advance social and political causes. Those from the Terai regions of Nepal also found themselves discriminated against despite the majority being Hindus themselves. Madhesis, the inhabitants of Terai with an Indian background, are perceived to be less Nepali by their hill counterparts due to their cross-border lineage and activities. Nepal's nationalism, which is so often anti-Indian in its nature, is extremely harmful towards Madhesi groups and has led to violent disputes in the past (Deysarkar, 2015). Muslims, who constitute around 4.5% of Nepal's population, are often excluded in the analysis of inequalities in Nepal despite ranking similarly, or worse, when compared to Dalit groups across several indicators (The World Bank, 2017). Educational opportunities in the Panchayat era were also limited to well-connected Brahmins, Chettris, and high-caste Newars further cementing socio-economic disparities (Gellner, 2007; Koirala, 1996). It is important to state that not all indigenous groups are marginalised to the same extent and some such as the high-caste Newars are even advantaged. A classification was created by Nepal Association of Indegenous Nationalities (NEFIN) and Nepal Foundation for Indigenous Nationalities (NFDIN) which categories groups in terms of their status as endangered, highly marginalised, marginalised, disadvantaged, and advantaged (Gellner, 2007).

The introduction of multi-party democracy and constitutional monarchy in 1990 was met with optimism within those from marginalised communities. However, the inability of the government to address these inequalities along with poor governance, corruption, and political instability eventually paved the way for the Maoists and the civil war. The Maoists, in their 40-point demand, proposed equality of languages, ending of discrimination between hill and Terai, decentralisation of governance, and even alluded to ethnic federalism. Although the support for Maoists was strong amongst marginalised groups, it was not a universal support as the security forces of Nepal contain a large amount of indigenous groups. The leadership of the Maoists was also dominated by Brahmins and prominent indigenous leaders chose not to be affiliated with the Maoists (Boquérat, 2006).

Effects of Marginalisation

Despite caste-based discrimination being outlawed in 1963 and the introduction of other legal protections of marginalised groups since then, there remains a need to put forward and implement policies that empower these groups. The caste system has ensured disparities in human capital endowment between caste groups in Nepal which is a major hindrance on the road to equality in Nepal. Human capital refers to factors such as education and health which has a direct effect on the productivity of an individual and therefore their wealth

104 *Ram Prasad Mainali*

(Mincer, 1958). Therefore, human capital endowment refers to human capital that is inherited across generations which can take the form of inequalities that are passed down in the case of marginalised groups (Menchik, 1979). For example, the human capital endowment inherited by the children of a rural Dalit labourer is far inferior compared to the children of a Brahmin civil servant based in Kathmandu. The former will likely attend public schools and receive treatment at government health posts which vastly limits future occupational choices and leads to poorer health conditions making them less productive than more privileged individuals. Therefore, inequality, if there is no policy intervention, is likely to continue the pre-existing trend and in many cases may even worsen.

A study conducted by Mainali (2014) indicates not only the vast inequalities between castes pertaining to human capital endowment but also how it has worsened from the conflict year of 2001 to the post-conflict year of 2010. By deploying a nationally representative dataset, the NLSS, it is clear that there are wide inequalities concerning human capital endowment between the so-called dominant castes and those from lower castes. This has a direct effect on their labour outcome which has an adverse effect on social mobility. The study categorises the population into three distinct groups: the so-called dominant castes of Brahmin-Chettri and high-caste Newars; the intermediate group comprising the enslaveable/non-enslaveable indigenous groups; and finally the lower-caste group which includes the water-nonacceptable and untouchable groups.

The study found that despite only making up around 30% of the total population of Nepal, the so-called dominant castes made up 70.7% of total employees in 2003 which increased to 71.3% in 2010. The intermediate group also saw their share increase from 19.2% in 2003 to 21.4% in 2010. Conversely, the lower-caste group saw their share decrease from 9.9% to 7.03% in those years. Not only did the so-called dominant castes have a large monopoly on employment, they also had better-paying jobs as they earned 30% more than the other groups in 2003 and 49% more in 2010. For instance, jobs in the civil service within this timeframe were largely in the hands of hill-Brahmin and Chettris. Indigenous peoples made up 12% of the jobs within the civil service followed by Madhesis at 5%, Dalits with 1.3%, and religious minorities at 1.1% (O. Gurung, 2009). A career as a civil servant is highly sought after in Nepal due to benefits such as jobs security, pension, free lodging, personal connections, and unfortunately also due to avenues for corruption. The reasons for low representation of marginalised groups in the civil service are twofold. Firstly, the criminalisation of caste-based discrimination has not eradicated this form of prejudice within the country. Inter-marriage is still taboo and even as recently as 2022 there were numerous cases of caste-based discrimination and violence being reported throughout the country (INSEC, 2022). Additionally, in the Terai region there is evidence of Dalits working as bonded labourers to pay off their debts that were burdened upon them in the forms of predatory loans by the so-called dominant castes (Castelier & Muller, 2022). Caste-based discrimination is also likely to occur within recruitment for the civil service and

Post-Conflict Context of Marginalised Groups in Nepal 105

other white-collar jobs, limiting the earning potential of more marginalised groups and reinforcing inequality. This is referred to within the literature as taste discrimination (Becker, 1971). The second reason for low representation of marginalised groups within the bureaucracy is due to inequalities related to human capital endowment. Even in an instance where discrimination is not taking place during the recruitment phase, a higher-caste individual is more likely to be offered a role due to inherited advantages when compared to those from more marginalised groups. This necessitates a framework for positive discrimination within recruitment for the civil service.

The caste system also has a direct effect on health outcomes (Mainali, 2014). Due to access to better-paying jobs as well as inherited wealth, so-called dominant groups have access to better healthcare when compared to marginalised groups. They are also discouraged from pursuing education which in turn could lead to poor health outcomes as a result of income effect (Lenhart, 2019). Those from lower castes were involved in manual labour and were therefore more susceptible to injuries and ailments also referred to as occupational effects on health outcomes. However, this does not imply that only marginalised people take in part manual labour as there is still a large number or Brahmin-Chettris who engage in agriculture and other physically intensive labour. This is emblematic of a greater urban/rural divide in Nepal.

The NLSS data reports four types of categorical Self-Assessed Health status (SAH), namely: Very poor, Poor, Fair, and Good.[1] Mainali (2014) carried out a scientific study to assess the impact of caste on SAH by employing an ordered probit model. Therefore, categorical variable SAH is regressed on a set of explanatory variables that includes ratio of out-of-pocket expenses, income proxied by monetary value of land holding, rural urban categories, age interval, level of schooling, marital status, and so on. The model includes regional and low Human Development Index (HDI) variables to capture the effect of access to health facilities and the impact of development on health outcome so that the estimation of caste impact on health outcomes becomes unbiased. This study concludes that historically discriminated against castes utilise fewer healthcare services as an outcome of financial constraints. This in turn ends up resulting in relatively inferior health outcomes for the intermediate and lower-caste groups.

Overall, these studies illustrate the fact that historically discriminated groups earn less in wages and have lower levels of human capital endowment in comparison to the dominant castes. It provides strong quantitative evidence that caste is one of the key factors that contribute to social inequality in Nepal. Moreover, the longitudinal study shows that there has been no improvements over time and this trend is likely to continue without policy intervention.

Policy Intervention

The immediate post-war period showed that not only was inequality still persistent, it was also increasing. The findings suggested that even if discrimination

106 *Ram Prasad Mainali*

was removed at an institutional level, inequality was still pervasive due to the inferior human capital of the marginalised groups. One of the antidotes for this issue was the introduction of the reservation policy in 2007 which amended the 1993 Civil Service Act. The act reserved 45% of all bureaucratic vacancies to those from historically disadvantaged groups: 33% is reserved for women, 27% for ethnic and indigenous nationalities (Adivasi-Janajati), 22% for Madhesis, 9% for Dalits, 5% for people with disabilities, and 4% for "backward" regions. Reservation policy within the bureaucracy has had a substantial impact on the overall composition of civil servants. Women's representation within the civil service rose from 11% in 2007 to over 20% in 2018 (Khadka & Sunam, 2018). Additionally, reservation policies have also had a positive impact on the representation of indigenous groups whose representation rose from 12% to 19.5%, Dalits from 1.3% to 2.5%, and Madhesis from 5% to 15.40% (Bhul, 2021). Around 15,000 civil servants that make up the civil service are from targeted groups, a testament to the effectiveness of the policy. However, reservation polices have been the point of critical debate within Nepali policy circles. As with India, the reservation policies of Nepal are said to not account for merit and that they only select a privileged 'creamy layer' of those from marginalised groups. The first point of criticism can be undermined by the fact that even those who applied under reservation have to pass a general test and interviews just as the rest of the candidates and minimum requirements are still expected to be met by all candidates regardless of whether they are applying through open competition or reservation. Additionally, a study carried out by Sunam, Pariyar, and Shrestha finds that most non-Dalit civil servants thought that their colleagues performed excellently or satisfactorily (Sunam et al., 2022). Recently, the first Dalit Chief District Officer (CDO) who is also a woman was appointed to Humla after making their way through the open category. The second criticism may have more credence and will be discussed further in the next section; however, there are studies that show that Dalits who have entered the civil service are mostly from rural areas who attended public schools and therefore they do not represent the 'creamy layer' (Sunam & Shrestha, 2019). The increasingly diverse bureaucracy also leads to more efficient governance as there is a better understanding of ground realities, better engagement with citizens, and a more multicultural understanding, a necessity for a heterogenous nation like Nepal (Sunam & Shrestha, 2019).

Along with representation within the bureaucracy, the government also included several constitutional candidates to include the representation of marginalised groups. According to the 2015 constitution, Village Executives are meant to include four women members and two members from the Dalit or minority communities. Similarly, the Municipal Executive should include five women members and three members from the Dalit or minority communities. The National Assembly, which is the upper house of the federal government, includes 59 elected members from who at least three have to be women, one Dalit, and one from a minority group or a representative with disabilities. Nepal also has a dual-electoral mechanism where 165 members of the House of Representatives (HoR) are elected through the first-past-the-post system (FPTP) and 110 are elected through proportional representation (PR) which considers the whole country and a constituency. The percentage for PR reflects the national population composition as 28.7% of the candidates have to be from indigenous backgrounds (Adivasi-janajati), 13.8% for Dalits, 15.3% for Madhesis, 6.6% for Tharu, and 4.4% for Muslims. Likewise, there is also a 60/40 split between first-past-the-post and proportional representation seats within the Provincial Assemblies. Either the Speaker or Deputy speaker of the HoR must be a woman and the same provision is also consistent with the Chairperson or Deputy Chairperson of the National Assembly. Political parties also must ensure that 33% of the Federal Parliament members are women and 50% of the candidates for proportional representation candidates also have to be women.

These mandates have led to an increase in overall representation of marginalised groups within Nepali politics. In 1999, a conflict year, the representation of the so-called dominant castes in parliament was around 59.5% (O. Gurung, 2009). This has decreased to 45.21% in the recent 2017 elections. Madhesi representation has increased from 14.1% in 1999 to 16.47% in 2017. Indigenous groups, who had a 18.4% share within the parliament in 1999 now constitute closer to 30%. Between the years 1991 to 1999 no more than 5% of women were represented in parliament whereas in 2017 this number increased to almost 34%. Finally, Dalits who had no representation in parliament in 1994 and 1999 now constitute around 8%. During the local elections of 2022, a panel of independent Dalits also managed to win in their rural municipality by defeating other candidates from mainstream parties. This increase in the overall numbers of marginalised groups has been a direct result of government policy intervention.

Along with policies related to inclusion within the state administration, the government also introduced policies to improve the overall socio-economic conditions of marginalised groups. Dalits, along with people from the far-west region of Nepal and Karnali, are entitled to their old age pension from the age of 60 whilst others receive it at 70 (Adhikari et al., 2021). In 2010, then Prime Minister Madav Kumar Nepal introduced a grant for inter-caste and other grants that were targeted at Dalit children up to the age of five to improve their nutritional status. Since the introduction of federalism, provincial governments have also introduced initiatives to improve the socio-economic conditions of marginalised groups. For example, Province 2, now named Madhes province, introduced higher-education scholarships for low-income Dalits and Muslims. This extends the existing scholarship program offered by the Ministry of Education for women, Dalits, indigenous persons, as well as those who are victims or related to a victim of the civil war. Health initiatives such as the Aama Program was also introduced by the government which provided financial support for mothers to give birth at medical facilities (Subedi, 2016). This was instrumental in reducing home births which have a higher mortality rate and disproportionately affect those from marginalised

108 *Ram Prasad Mainali*

groups as they are often from lower socio-economic backgrounds. A recent study by the Government of Nepal shows that between the period of 2014 to 2019, 12.7% of Nepal, or about 3 million people left poverty (GoN, 2021). The study, which was conducted in collaboration with UNICEF, UNDP, and Oxford Poverty and Human Development Initiative gives a more holistic analysis of poverty as it analyses socio-economic indicators related to health, education, and living standards such as child mortality, school attendance, years of schooling, and access to water, sanitation, housing, and more. The post-conflict era of Nepal shows a desire to address the inequalities embedded in the country that was highlighted by the Maoists. There has also been a clear quantitative improvement in terms of representation of marginalised groups and overall socio-economic indicators.

Shortcomings and Challenges

Whilst Nepal's post-conflict transformation can be lauded for increasing overall representation of marginalised groups, numbers do not tell the complete story. For instance, with the introduction of reservations within the civil service, the previously Brahmin-Chettri dominated civil service is slowly altering in order to better reflect the demographic composition of the country. However, the civil service is still monopolised by the dominant castes who make up 63.5% of the bureaucracy whilst making up only around 30% of the population. More concerningly, despite the influx of personnel from marginalised groups, the senior positions within the civil service were still under the control of Brahmin and Chettris. Gurungs, Rais, and Sunuwars were the only marginalised groups represented at the senior level and most other disadvantaged groups made up the junior ranks (Rai, 2022). Women from marginalised groups were better represented at the senior levels than men but this is likely due to some senior positions such as Women's Development Officer and Women's Assistance being open to women only. There is likely to be an increase in senior officials of marginalised backgrounds in the future as many have just begun to utilise the reservation policies and therefore are not as experienced as those from the upper castes. However, promotion within the bureaucracy is not guided entirely by merit as there exists a culture of sycophancy and deploying personal connections which is less available for those from marginalised backgrounds.

As the reservation policy failed to distinguish between different indigenous groups, it has led to the overrepresentation of certain groups and the under-representation of others. Most glaringly, Newars have been categorised as an indigenous group despite the fact that high-caste Newars are seen to be an advantaged group (Gellner, 2007). Data from the Public Service Commission shows that despite making up around 15% of the total indigenous population, they make up around 30% of the civil servants from indigenous groups. Rais and Sunuwars were also overrepresented in the bureaucracy in comparison to their population but they are regarded to be disadvantaged and marginalised respectively according to the NEFIN/NDFIN classification. Tharus, Tamangs, and Gurungs, who make up a large number of the indigenous population of Nepal, are underrepresented and "endangered" groups such as Kisan, Raji, Bankariya are not even represented albeit they make up a very small number of the population. Reservation is also very limited in understanding Nepali inequality through an intersectional lens. For example, the quotas for women have largely been used by women from Brahmin-Chettri backgrounds leading to an intensification of caste inequalities. The Dalit quota has been largely used by hill-dalits as opposed to Terai Dalits leading to an intensification of regional inequalities. The Madhesi quota has largely been used by Terai Brahmins widening the gap between them and other marginalised groups from Terai such as Muslims.

Another shortcoming of the civil service to create a truly representative administrative body is the recruitment method itself. The reservation policies adhere to what Harrison et al. (2006) refer to as weak preference policy whereby preferential treatment is given to disadvantaged groups only when they have the same qualifications as those from advantaged backgrounds. The entry to Nepali bureaucracy is made up of two phases: a centralised written examination and an interview. As both open field candidates and reservation candidates must meet a minimum requirement to pass these phases, those who are better educated and well connected are likely to pass. This favours the argument that only the 'creamy layer' or elites of marginalised groups would be favoured by the reservation policy, further increasing inequality within caste groups. In fact, a study found that nearly 75% of applicants received help in some form in order to secure their first job (Sunam et al., 2022). The disadvantaged elements within indigenous and other marginalised groups are less likely to have these connections and coupled with their inferior education means that their chances of entering the civil service is lower than their more elite counterparts. Furthermore, the examination and the interviews are primarily conducted in Nepali,[2] ignoring the linguistic diversity of the country and enforcing the limited sense of nationhood from previous eras. This particularly effects those from the Madhes region who speak Maithili, Bhojpuri, and Tharu.

Similar issues have also arisen within the political sphere as a consequence of attempting to make the political body more representative. Whilst the number of total representatives from marginalised backgrounds has increased, a more in-depth analysis reveals pressing issues. Firstly, elections in Nepal are extremely expensive especially as a developing nation. A study conducted by the Election Observation Committee Nepal (EOC Nepal) found that winning candidates spend an average of 21.3 million rupees (US$160,000).[3] This spending completely disregards the government mandate of 2.5 million rupees (US$19,000) for FTTP candidates. This means that candidates either have to possess that wealth themselves or be close to the party in order to access the party fund which is usually made up of donations from their support base consisting of businessmen, bureaucrats, and sometimes even criminal elements. This limits the representation of marginalised groups to the socio-economic elites of their group or those who are willing to be loyal to the party as opposed to their own caste/ethnic community. Nepal's only dollar billionaire, a Madhesi, used the Madhesi election quota to be elected to parliament. Similarly, whilst Nepal boasts one of the highest percentages of women's representation within parliament, a sizeable number were related to a senior male politician in one way or another. The relatives of former prime ministers Prachanda, Baburam Bhattari, and Sher Bahadur Deuba have all held political office of some capacity including as minister and mayor. The very nature of reservation, which intends to represent and address the grievances of disadvantaged groups, has been undermined in Nepal due to elite capture and patronage politics; a feature that is also common in other aspects of Nepali society. Staying on the topic of intersectional representation, Tarai Dalits are virtually non-present in Nepali politics and representation of Dalits has largely been limited to Hill-Dalits.

The attitudes of political parties towards marginalised groups, particularly Dalits, means that they have limited effective representation. Discouragement from higher-caste counterparts is common and parties do not adhere to implementing representation quotas. The increase in marginalised group representation in 2017 local elections declined slightly in 2022 as only 6,620 Dalit women were elected on to local bodies instead of the required 6,743 (Pradhan, 2022). Leading Dalit politicians have even stated that political parties only encourage Dalits to contest in PR seats and do not promote them in direct FTTP seats despite their ability to win elections (Bishwakarma, 2017). Nepal also does not have any rules regarding whether a candidate has to have lived in their contesting constituency for a prolonged amount of time. This has led to political parties fielding candidates from marginalised groups in areas where there is no party stronghold and they are likely to lose, therefore maintaining the image that they are fielding marginalised candidates without jeopardising their electoral chances. Bishwakarma (2017) adds that the PR candidates are nominated by the central committee of the party and not the local bodies. This means that not only are parties nominating relatives and those close to their circle, but they are also nominating individuals who are not knowledgeable about the local issues. This means that the chosen candidates are less likely to represent their own caste/ethnic group grievances and the localities undermining the spirit and aims of PR and federalism simultaneously. Dalits are viewed by party elites as supporters or cadres or an electorate who need to be engaged for votes but do not view them as leaders. A lack of policy implementation, political will, and immoral practices has largely undermined representation of marginalised groups in Nepal.

Finally, the effectiveness of policies introduced to improve socio-economic conditions for marginalised groups is questionable. The Government of Nepal established the Landless Problem Resolution Commission in order to address land-related issues which disproportionately affects those from marginalised backgrounds. The commission recognised landless citizens and gave them a temporary land entitlement certificate which is a good initial step to combat landlessness within the country (Biswakarma, 2018). However, even this was

Post-Conflict Context of Marginalised Groups in Nepal   111

fraught with setbacks. Marginalised groups, particularly Dalits, Madhesis, women, and those from rural areas do not possess citizenship certificates along with other documentation which may be required for state benefits and therefore excluding them from any state services. A study by Biswakarma (2018) states that almost 35% of the Dalit population do not have citizenship certificates, although this has not stopped the government from collecting tax from them. Those from low socio-economic backgrounds are also less likely to have government connections or the money to bribe officials which is almost a prerequisite due to widespread corruption within the country. Dalits, along with Madhesis, due to their lack of documentation have to pursue work in the informal sector and many face wage discrimination and food deficiency. Their exclusion from the state apparatus coupled with the contractor-politician nexus in Nepal means that construction workers from marginalised groups are discouraged from reporting bad labour practices. The introduction of new technologies has also meant that Dalits who engage in traditional occupations are struggling to make a living. The taboo related to caste occupation has also been lifted but it seems as though this is only the case for higher-caste individuals occupying the traditional roles of Dalits. For example, it is common to see high-caste tailors and jewellers when this was the occupation of Pariyar and Sunar castes. However, an ex-child soldier belonging to the Dalit caste, who was trained as a chef by reintegration programs, was refused jobs at restaurants due to their status as an "untouchable".[4]

Data relating to Nepal's poverty rate paints a positive picture due to its decline. One of the major reasons for the decline in poverty, especially amongst marginalised groups, is not due to any specific government intervention, but rather to individuals seeking opportunities abroad. Remittance is a major source of income for rural households and is said to account for 33% of poverty reduction in rural areas and 27% overall (The World Bank, 2017). Whilst migrant workers derive from all caste groups and regions, those from marginalised groups are more likely to seek opportunities abroad. A study of six adjacent villages of Kaski district shows that 89.3% of Bishwakarma, 86.2% of Pariyar, and 85% of Nepali households have someone who is or has been abroad to work (Adhikari et al., 2021). All three are Dalit castes. The figure for Gurung households, an indigenous group, stands at 88.3% whilst the high-caste priestly Brahmin have a figure of 50.8%. The data provided by the Ministry of Labour, Employment and Social Security also reinforces the fact that marginalised groups are more likely to pursue employment opportunities abroad. The districts with the highest number of migrant workers tend to be those from the Madhes such as Dhanusa, Siraha, Jhapa, Morang, and Sunsari (GoN, 2020). Districts with a large number of indigenous groups such as Taplejung also have high rates of migration compared to their smaller total population. It is important to note that the data does not consider all the migrant workers who are based in India as the open border between the two nations makes data collection difficult. Marginalised groups, with a history of exclusion from the state, still struggle to find opportunities within post-war

112   *Ram Prasad Mainali*

Nepal as a consequence of discrimination, inferior human capital, failure of policy, and a lack of political will.

Conclusion and Future Considerations

The Maoists were successful in highlighting the discriminatory nature of the Nepali state towards those from lower castes, indigenous groups, women, and rural people. It is with this rhetoric that they were able to attract large elements of these marginalised groups into their rank and file as they hoped to be the agents of positive change within their country. The Maoists were also clearly successful in lobbying for a more inclusionary Nepal. Their transformation into a mainstream party led them to a resounding victory in the 2008 constituent assembly elections and they remained a major party in subsequent elections. Their highlighting of issues pertaining to marginalised groups has led to the creation of a secular and federal democratic republic, a far cry of the centralised Hindu monarchy or autocracy of the past. Inclusion was made a priority in the transformation of the state apparatus and policies directly targeting marginalised groups were formulated. There have certainly been success stories. The percentage of marginalised groups within both the civil service and the parliament have increased significantly, albeit not proportional to the population. Nepal boasts one of the highest representations of women in parliament of anywhere in the world.

However, any progress made seems to be symbolic and superficial. As with other aspects of the country, corruption and patronage-based politics has severely limited what could have been an exemplary case of post-war transformation. Senior positions within the government and civil service are held exclusively by high-caste men. Gender representation has been undermined by the selection of relatives and close associates as candidates. Additionally, any progress made in the improvement of socio-economic conditions of marginalised groups is largely due to migrant workers and their remittances.

Setbacks were always bound to occur in a complicated peace process that had to deal with inequalities that were cemented for centuries based on so many cleavages. However, it is a failure to address these setbacks which is concerning for the future. The government is planning to introduce reservations for Khas-Arya groups in the state mechanisms even though these groups have dominated the social, political, and economic landscape of the country. Additionally, a lack of political will to enforce existing representation mechanisms as seen in the recent local elections is also likely to do further damage to marginalised groups.

Pragmatic problem solving is required to deal with such issues. Inequality needs to be viewed through a more intersectional lens and an individual's' identity shouldn't be defined by a single characteristic such as caste, gender, and region. A failure to do so has led to an elite capture of reservation quotas and only token candidates are selected as party representatives. Within the civil service, a different mechanism of affirmative action can be adopted. Stronger

Post-Conflict Context of Marginalised Groups in Nepal 113

positive discrimination in recruitment, as referred to as strong preference policies by Harrison et al. (2006), may be more suitable in order to avoid only recruiting elites from each marginalised group. This method offers preferential treatment to applicants even if they do not possess the same qualifications as their advantaged counterparts. Detractors may argue that this may lead to weak governance but a large majority of training for the civil service job is done in the post-recruitment phase so there are ample opportunities to "learn on the job". Applications should also be optional in all the major languages of Nepal to better reflect the linguistic diversity of the country. Finally, there needs to be more work done to combat inequalities between different indigenous and marginalised groups. Indigenous groups such as high-caste Newars enjoy a far superior socio-economic status than other groups such as Tarai Dalits or Muslims who are some of the poorest in the country. A failure to tackle these issues means the continuation of the status quo which has supposedly been addressed in the country.

Notes

1 These categories have been slightly changed in the latter survey (2010) as Poor, Fair, Good, and Excellent.
2 Some ministries such as the Ministry of Foreign Affairs offer examinations in English and Nepali.
3 Around £140,000 sterling as of 2022.
4 Personal interview with editor.

References

Adhikari, K., Gellner, D., & Bahadur Karki, M. (2021). Dalits in Search of Inclusion: Comparing Nepal with India In A. S. Rathore (Ed.), *B R Ambedkar: The Quest for Justice* (Vol. 2). Oxford University Press.
Becker, G. (1971). *The Economics of Discrimination*. The University of Chicago Press.
Bhul, B. (2021). Representative Bureaucracy: The Nepalese Perspective. *Prashasan*, *52*(134), 198–216. https://mofaga.gov.np/news-notice/2549
Bishwakarma, M. (2017). Democratic Politics in Nepal: Dalit Political Inequality and Representation. *Asian Journal of Comparative Politics*, *2*(3), 261–272. https://doi.org/10.1177/2057891116660633
Biswakarma, T. (2018). Citizenship and Social Security of Landless Dalits in Nepal. *Globe: A Journal of Language*, *6*, 52–65.
Boquérat, G. (2006). *Ethnicity and Maoism in Nepal. Strategic Studies*, *26*(1), 79–99.
Castelier, S., & Muller, Q. (2022). *Nepal Workers Look to Gulf to Escape Forced-Labour System*. Al Jazeera.
Deysarkar, S. (2015). The Madesi Citizenship and the New Constitution: Emerging Questions . *Proceedings of the Indian History Congress*, *76*(2015), 686–692.
Gellner, D. N. (2007). Caste, Ethnicity and Inequality in Nepal. *Economic and Political Weekly*, *42*(20), 1823–1828.
GoN. (2020). *Nepal Labour Migration Report 2020*. Ministry of Labour, Employment and Social Security, Government of Nepal.

114 *Ram Prasad Mainali*

GoN. (2021). *Nepal Multidimensional Poverty Index: Analysis Towards Action 2021.* National Planning Commission, Government of Nepal.

Gurung, J. (2005). Empirical Glimpses of the Situation of the Dalits in Nepal. In D. Pramodh (Ed.), *Dalits of Nepal Issue & Challenges* (pp. 53–64). Feminist Dalit Organization.

Gurung, O. (2009). Social Inclusion: Policies and Practices in Nepal. *Occasional Papers in Sociology and Anthropology, 11*, 1–15. https://doi.org/https://doi.org/10.3126/opsa.v11i0.3027

Harrison, D. A., Kravitz, D. A., Mayer, D. M., Leslie, L. M., & Lev-Arey, D. (2006). Understanding Attitudes toward Affirmative Action Programs in Employment: Summary and Meta-Analysis of 35 Years of Research. *Journal of Applied Psychology, 91*(5), 1013–1036. https://doi.org/10.1037/0021-9010.91.5.1013

INSEC. (2022). *Nepal Human Rights Year Book 2022.* www.insec.org.np

Khadka, M., & Sunam, R. (2018). *Workforce Diversity and Reservation Policy in Nepal: A Strategic Approach to Strengthening Women's Voice and Visibility in Formal Employment Sector.* A research paper for the regional conference on Women and the Future of Work in Asia and the Pacific' Conference, Jan 31–1 Feb 2018 Bangkok, ILO and DFAT. 10.13140/RG.2.2.31927.04000

Koirala, B. N. (1996). *Schooling and Dalits of Nepal: A Case Study of Bungkot Dalit Community* [Unpublished PhD Thesis]. University of Alberta.

Lenhart, O. (2019). The Effects of Income on Health: New Evidence from the Earned Income Tax Credit. *Review of Economics of the Household, 17*(2), 377–410. https://doi.org/10.1007/s11150-018-9429-x

Mainali, R. (2014). *The Economics of Inequality and Human Capital Development: Evidence from Nepal* [PhD Thesis]. City University of London.

Menchik, P. L. (1979). Inter-Generational Transmission of Inequality: An Empirical Study of Wealth Mobility. *Economica, 46*(184), 349–362. https://doi.org/10.2307/2553676

Mincer, J. (1958). Investment in Human Capital and Personal Income Distribution. *Journal of Political Economy, 66*(4), 281–302.

Pradhan, T. (2022). Despite Law, Nepal Fails to Achieve Dalit Women Representation in Wards. *The Kathmandu Post.*

Rai, P. R. (2022). Reservation for Janajati in Nepal's Civil Service: Analysis from Intersectional Lens. *American Journal of Arts and Human Science, 1*(1), 1–10. https://doi.org/10.54536/ajahs.v1i1.257

Subedi, M. (2016). Caste/Ethnic Dimensions of Change and Inequality: Implications for Inclusive and Affirmative Agendas in Nepal. *Nepali Journal of Contemporary Studies, XVI*(1–2), 1–16.

Sunam, R., Pariyar, B., & Shrestha, K. K. (2022). Does Affirmative Action Undermine Meritocracy? "Meritocratic Inclusion" of the Marginalized in Nepal's Bureaucracy. *Development Policy Review, 40*(1). https://doi.org/10.1111/dpr.12554

Sunam, R., & Shrestha, K. (2019). Failing the Most Excluded: A Critical Analysis of Nepal's Affirmative Action Policy. *Contributions to Nepalese Studies, 46*(2), 283–305

The World Bank. (2017). *Moving up the Ladder: Poverty Reduction and Social Mobility in Nepal.* The World Bank.

8 Analysing the Peace Process of Nepal through a Gender Lens

Susan Risal

Introduction

Addressing the gender dimension of an armed conflict has emerged as a key component of contemporary peace agreements. Some peace agreements have incorporated gender element extensively such as the Juba Agreement of 2020 which contains references to sexual violence, widows, and even commitment to prioritising education for girls. On the other hand, most peace agreements can still be classified as being gender blind with only 6 out of 21 peace agreements in 2020 mentioning women, girls, and gender. In principle, three important elements should be taken into consideration to evaluate whether a peace agreement has incorporated a gender perspective. Firstly, whether the peace agreement has kept the agenda of conflict victim women in high priority and has clearly articulated their concerns and needs. Secondly, how the issue of women ex-combatants is dealt with in the peace agreement. Finally, whether a peace agreement is progressive enough to bring several structural reforms to ensure the social, economic, and political rights of women in the post-conflict period.

With the assumptions mentioned above, this chapter mainly focuses on explaining whether the implementation aspects of the Comprehensive Peace Agreement (CPA) have addressed the issue of conflict victim women, ex-combatant women, and women in general in the post-conflict and post-constitution environment. Despite many opportunities to use the promises of the CPA to bring about a real impact in the lives of the women who were severely affected by the conflict, it has never been implemented by the state in the peace process. The social grievances of women and other marginalised communities – such as discrimination, inequality, power division, poverty, and subjugation – were factors that contributed to the armed conflict. These were the same issues that were used by the Maoist rebels to gain the momentum for their movement. These factors remain unaddressed in the post-conflict and post-constitution period. Exploring socio-cultural factors that have marginalised conflict-affected women, ex-combatants, and other women, this chapter aims to convey the current difficulties women in Nepal are facing in achieving their promised rights.

DOI: 10.4324/9781003289876-9

Women During the Period of Armed Conflict

The twenty-first century has witnessed a greater appreciation for gender-specific experiences of war thanks to the work of academics across various fields as well as organisations such as the UN. In fact, the century began with the UN adopting resolution 1325 which specifically acknowledged the unique experience of women and girls during conflict periods. This has led to an increase in the stories of women from conflict zones being amplified, leading to a more nuanced understanding of the disparate effects conflict can have between genders.

Traditionally, women's involvement in conflict was limited to logistical and support roles whilst men occupied the combat roles. However, the anti-patriarchal stance of the Maoists sought to challenge these very notions of tradition, and women were recruited into the rebel force as combatants. Women were glorified for being agents of change and standing up to their oppressors which attracted more of them to join the Maoists (Riley, Ketola and Yadav, 2022). It is important to note that many women were also coerced to join the Maoists as part of their "One Household, One Maoist" strategy or because they wanted to ensure their security against the state forces or the Maoists themselves (Lawoti and Pahari, 2010). Additionally, women who joined the Maoists also were given traditional gender roles and had to prove their bravery before being promoted as combatants, something the men did not have to do (Sthapit and Doneys, 2017) .The exact proportion of women combatants are unknown and there are differing claims. The Maoists claimed that around a third of their combatants were women, whereas UNMIN data shows only 19% of registered combatants were women (Tamang, 2009). From 2004 onwards, the National Army also began recruiting women, meaning there were now women combatants on both sides. This warranted gender-specific mechanisms for ex-combatants in the post-conflict processes.

The civil war also resulted in the victimisation of women throughout the country. The large amounts of women recruited as combatants meant that women were killed, injured, or disappeared during the war. Women were also victimised during conflict through loss of property and the loss of their husbands. The patriarchal nature of Nepal meant that the loss of their husband was not only an emotional burden but also pushed women and families into further economic marginalisation through the loss of the breadwinner. Displaced women migrated from rural areas to cities which made them more vulnerable. Additionally, civilian women were also victims of sexual violence at the hands of the Maoists and the state security forces. During conflict, women's bodies are targeted, and violating women from the enemy's side is seen as damaging their honour. As a family member of a deceased rape victim from Nepal puts it: "Raping women was an act of victory" (Rayamajhi and Shrestha, 2022).

To summarise, the peace process needed to address the issues of women ex-combatants, women victims of war, as well as the wider gender discrimination faced by women that was a significant motivator of the conflict.

Situation of Women During the Active Post-Conflict Phase (2006–2015)

The armed conflict of Nepal ended with the signing of the CPA in November 2006 between the GoN and the Maoists. However, Nepal's peacebuilding process, in many senses, has failed to acknowledge women's contribution towards systemic change and has excluded them from peacebuilding processes. A gender lens was never seriously considered within the negotiation phase which is reflected in the subsequent peace agreement and in the implementation of the peace process. The UN Security Council (UNSC) Resolutions 1325 and 1820 are considered as revolutionary documents that envisioned changing the nature of peacebuilding. It has been perceived to provide women with the necessary political framework by allowing and encouraging their participation in formal peace processes (Cohn, 2004). Alongside other nation states, Nepal also formulated a first National Action Plan (NAP) on Security Council Resolutions in February 2011. NAPs were seen as the primary vehicles to implement the aforementioned UNSC resolutions, but scholars have argued that they are ineffective in doing so in states with weak internal institutions (Basini and Ryan, 2016). Nepal's NAP was limited and failed to proactively engage with women who were affected by the conflict. Yadav (2020) posits that Nepal's lack of gender expertise meant that they were largely influenced by international actors and there was limited consultation with conflict-affected women. The NAP also did not include any implementation plans or accountability measures and there was a distinct lack of coordination between the actors. This meant that the primary mechanism through which gender was to be considered in the peacebuilding process in Nepal was severely limited, leading to detrimental consequences.

The impact of conflict on women has been explained from both positive and negative aspects. Studies conducted in Africa and the Balkans suggest that post-conflict countries show more progress towards women's empowerment than non-conflict countries (Tripp, 2015; Berry, 2018) . Armed conflict also creates an enabling environment to allow women to take on social and economic duties that were previously reserved for men in both family and community life (Arostegui, 2013; Shekhawat, 2015). This case has also been made for Nepal as some scholars argue that post-conflict political, social, and economic achievements that women have made in Nepal were possible so quickly only because of armed conflict (K.C., Van Der Haar and Hilhorst, 2017; Yadav, 2020). Increased participation of women in community decision-making processes such as during consumer committees, forest management initiatives, and cooperative meetings, has been possible due to changes in government policies with the provision of mandatory participation of women from the local to national level decision-making bodies. It was also made possible due to the empowerment of women through their active involvements in different political struggles, including armed conflict, to claim their rights (K.C., Van Der Haar and Hilhorst, 2017). Consequently, the post-conflict environment created an opportunity to introduce women-focused legal and policy framework

118 *Susan Risal*

frameworks such as Gender Equality Act of 2006, the Interim Constitution of Nepal 2007, and Human Trafficking Act 2007. All these policy frameworks provided an opportunity to address physical, mental, or any other forms of violence against women in the post-conflict period.

Likewise, the establishment of the Nepal Peace Trust Fund, initiated by the GoN and the UN Peacebuilding Fund, presented an institutional structure to assist women ex-combatants, conflict victim women, and other women to ensure their socio-economic rights in the post-conflict period. The Local Peace Committees (LPCs) formed in the district and local government units was another notable structure that guaranteed 33% women representation within its structure and an avenue for conflict-affected women to express their needs and grievances in post-conflict time. Later on, the government also adopted the NAP in February 2011 to carry out the implementation of UNSC resolutions 1325 and 1820 and proposed an 18-member high-level steering committee with the Minister of Foreign Affairs as chair (Thapa and Canyon, 2017).

It has been pointed out that Nepal ranks high in South Asia in terms of its Women, Peace and Security (WPS) index, even in the midst of poor GDP growth. The status of gender rights and the rights of women is also found 42 places higher than its per capita income. Other positive changes observed in the life of women in post-conflict scenarios include a more liberal space for women to work outside home, changed perception towards widowed women, women's political representation, and the changing political space in Nepal. Moreover, an increased awareness of women's rights through proactive efforts made by feminist groups and other rights-based movements is also considered as further progress observed in the post-conflict period. Recent movements include protests against VAT on sanitary items, against the practice of *chhaupadi* (where menstruating women are isolated due to perceptions of impurity), and organising against a proposed law that would require women under the age of 40 to obtain permission from family members and local government bodies before travelling abroad.

Despite these positive impacts on women, the negative impacts that women have experienced in the post-conflict period should also be underlined. Persistent economic insecurity, hierarchies of victimhood, fear of insurgent reprisal, continuation of gender-based and sexual violence, and increased vulnerability due to the killing or out-migration of husbands or fathers, are identified as key problems faced by women in post-conflict society. Such problems are also found differently depending on socio-economic as well as power status of conflict victim women in the society (Berry and Rana, 2019). More importantly, the lack of gender-sensitive outlook from the state mechanism is identified as a core issue of conflict-affected women as it becomes hard to recognise and address the complications faced by women.

Other studies have identified persistent discrimination and stigmatisation of women ex-combatants who returned home after the war (K.C, 2011; Valente, 2011). Such a situation has made them more vulnerable than men ex-combatants in the post-conflict period. In particular, women ex-combatants

Analysing the Peace Process of Nepal through a Gender Lens 119

who participated in inter-caste marriage faced communal backlash. Men also faced a similar experience, but they had the privilege of mobility which allowed them to at least relocate and avoid such discrimination. Female ex-combatants, because of their past engagements, were perceived as an immoral person, thus often discarded as unmarriageable women (K.C and Van Der Haar, 2019). The economic hardships of many of the ex-combatants for a decent living was another factor observed at ground level (K.C, 2019). Receiving compensation from the government bodies was difficult enough, but the paltry compensation was not enough for women to pursue enterprises to support themselves.

Addressing the needs and concerns of conflict widows remained another important issue in the post-conflict period but received less attention in policy discourses. Government data suggests the total number of conflict widows is 9000, of which only 4279 received monetary compensation from the government by 2012/2013 (Thapa and Canyon, 2017). Widows in Nepal have also concealed their status in order to avoid discrimination that is typically associated with widowhood which may lead to forfeiting compensation and an underreporting of the total number of widows (Surkan et al., 2015). Widows facing financial insecurity were forced to sell their assets such as gold and livestock mostly in the immediate aftermath of their husband's death (Ramnarain, 2016). A lack of self-awareness, of facilitating agencies, and of government proactiveness to trace and record the exact number of conflict widows have been observed as a core reason behind the state's ignorance of the agenda of conflict widows in the post-conflict period.

Moreover, the issue of women exposed to conflict-era sexual violence is more critical and often ignored by the government. Out of 64,000 cases filed at the Truth and Reconciliation Commission, only around 300 are related to conflict-era sexual violence (Poudel, 2023). This figure is not indicative of the sexual violence committed by both factions during the war as there is a tendency to underreport such cases. Women face severe difficulties when reporting cases. There is a statute of limitations of a year, increased from 6 months, which meant that civil-era incidents could not even be dealt with by the courts. The existing culture of impunity in Nepal meant that it was extremely unlikely for any action to be taken, especially if it pertained to high-level political figures. Filing a case also meant that women risked publicising their status as a victim of sexual abuse which carries a social stigma in Nepal around the concept of purity. Therefore, the risks were too high, and the chances of prosecution and justice were non-existent which dissuaded victims from filing their cases. The state mechanism's ignorance of addressing the problems of victims has led to devastating long-term impacts such as suicide, mental trauma, and psychological vulnerabilities in the post-conflict period.

Situation of Women During the Post-2015 Phase

This section mainly focuses on three important elements to understand the status of women in the post-constitutional phase. First, it provides an overview

120   *Susan Risal*

of the current status of conflict victim women based on the author's personal observations and experiences working with conflict-affected women at the grassroot level. Second, it presents some facts and figures regarding women's participation and representation in political and administrative bodies in the post-2015 era, in particular after the adoption of the federal governance system in the country in 2017. Finally, it also provides an overview of the current socio-economic status of Nepalese women to demonstrate the changes observed in 16 years after the signing of the peace accord. All these three elements are important to understand the impact of the CPA in improving the status of women in Nepal.

Current Status of Conflict Victim Women

The situation of conflict-affected women has not improved even after the promulgation of the new constitution of Nepal in 2015; rather it has further worsened due to multiple unaddressed issues. Recent interactions with conflict-affected women have revealed that women who lost their husbands during the armed conflict are facing severe difficulties providing for their families due to financial hardships. Widows received a one-time compensation of one million rupees which was used for immediate needs such as their children's education and elderly care, leaving very little money to invest in long-term self-sufficiency. Women who were seriously injured during the armed conflict were not provided medical treatment or home-based care, leading to further marginalisation.

Several conflict-affected women living in rural areas often expressed that nominal compensation and treatment support which they received from the government under the Interim Relief Program (IRP) after the signing of the CPA was just a one-time support, which only covered their costs for a couple of years.

Many conflict-affected women and children who need continuous mental health treatment are deprived of such support due to the absence of relevant programs in several conflict-affected districts. Some local governments from conflict-affected districts such as Rolpa, Dang, Bardiya, and Kailali have introduced free medical insurance and livelihood support programs targeting conflict victims. However, these schemes do not include all women in need due to resource constraints as well as the lack of reliable data of conflict-affected populations in each local government unit. Conflict victim women are also doubtful about the continuation of insurance support programs in the long run, if the existing local governments are replaced by other political parties in the future.

Conflict victim women are also facing psychological stress due to the separation of family members in the post-conflict and post-constitution period. As observed in the field, many young members of conflict victim families migrated to other cities within Nepal or abroad in search of employment, leaving their family members back home. Income sent back home from their children has been a source of current household income for many conflict-affected families

Analysing the Peace Process of Nepal through a Gender Lens 121

in highly conflict-affected districts. However, many of those living abroad have not returned home for many years and this has created a shortage of young people at home to take care of conflict victim women. In some families, conflict victim women are in a key role of taking care of dependent family members, in particular elderly people and children.

Conflict victim women also lack reliable local platforms to express their needs and concerns and put forward their demands to the relevant authorities. Several conflict victim women expressed that Local Peace Committees (LPCs) active in the districts were avenues to put forward their demands in front of political parties, civil society, and media. LPCs were a relatively comfortable space, as many of their concerns such as the record keeping of victims and claiming compensations were addressed through them in the post-conflict period. With the dissolution of LPCs after 2015, they either need to go to the police or District Administration Office (DAO) with their concerns, where they found such authorities not fully sensitive to their needs. On some occasions, they had difficulties in accessing these government institutions.

Local Peace Committee has made a great contribution to advance socio-political reconciliation in Nepal. People affiliated to LPC were our point of contact to express our needs, concerns, and grievances. It is not easy for us to go to the police or a government official to share the plights of conflict victim community.

(Woman from Rolpa district, December 2021)

Conflict victim women are also disappointed with the dysfunctionality of the TRC in providing justice and compensation. There is no immediate action on the cases they have filed at the TRC. Those who registered their cases are also worried about data protection, as they are unaware of where and in what conditions their data are stored by the TRC. Likewise, some conflict victim women I have encountered in the field did not get a chance to register their cases when TRC was collecting complaints. Thus, several of these conflict victim women yet to be in the record of the TRC.

The situation of women whose husbands disappeared during the time of conflict also warrants observation. Many of them are deprived of receiving social security benefits provided by the government to single women, as they are hesitant to make a death certificate of their husband to receive such allowance. As a study by Ramnarain (2016) details, selling assets was the preferred method of widows to acquire money but this was difficult for those whose husbands had disappeared as properties may have been registered under the name of their husbands. There were legal complications and bureaucratic hurdles as the transfer of property under the spouse's name without confirming the death of the husband had a waiting time of 12 years.

My husband is disappeared during the time of armed conflict and it has already been 14 years. I am deprived of receiving single women allowance from the government, as I am psychologically not prepared to make a death certificate of my husband. Without a death certificate, government people do not consider me as a single woman.

(Woman in Kailali district, December 2021)

Women whose husbands disappeared or were killed during the conflict are also having a hard time inheriting the property of their husbands. Land is an extremely valuable resource in Nepal and inheritance is often very contested. This issue is further amplified in indigenous communities who follow their own customs of inheritance which is vastly different and not well understood by government officials who are mainly from Brahmin-Chhetri groups. For example, from my field-level interactions in Bardiya and Kailali it was apparent to me that property inheritance amongst Tharus was based on family consensus. Properties are distributed orally and therefore it is not reflected in official government records. There is a situation where extended family members claim the share of the property from those whose husbands have disappeared during the war, making the process of inheriting property very difficult for women.

Women from disappeared families are also facing other problems, even in the post-constitution period. One such problem shared during the field-level interaction was that the daughters of disappeared families have faced difficulties in getting married and some of those who got married are also facing stigma and discrimination from society and their own family members. Women shared that their disappeared family members are often referred to during family disputes which has led to trauma. The Citizenship Act of 2063 (2006) meant that Nepali women could not pass on their citizenship to their children. This meant that those whose husbands disappeared during the war faced severe difficulties acquiring citizenships for their children. This limited the opportunities for these children as they were essentially stateless. However, some progress has been made with an amendment to the act in late 2022. Now, a Nepali woman may pass on the citizenship to their children if the mother declares that the father cannot be identified. However, the law still remains largely unequal. A child of a single Nepali man can obtain citizenship by descent without having to declare the status of the mother. Similarly, the child of a Nepali man and a foreign woman can also gain citizenship by descent whilst the child of a Nepali woman and a foreign man can only get a naturalised citizenship which means that they are barred from some of the highest elected political positions in the country.

As stated earlier, conflict victims who are accounted for in government records have received some compensations in the past. However, victims of sexual violence and torture as well as those who are yet to be in the government records for various reasons have received nothing even after the promulgation of the new constitution in the country. Updating the records of conflict victims has been further complicated due to the lack of local peace institutions that could be accessed by the conflict victim women.

Analysing the Peace Process of Nepal through a Gender Lens   123

Women who suffered sexual violence are living a highly vulnerable life, which has been overlooked by the former conflicting parties, powerholders, service providers, as well as conflict victim communities. A sign of progress that we have observed over the years is that some victims of sexual violence who are now empowered by NGOs and conflict victim community groups are slowly airing their grievances. Some of these women have also registered their cases at the TRC and even reported to national and international human rights organisations. The submission of such cases in front of responsible author-ities has generated solid evidence to act against the perpetrators of conflict-era sexual violence in the future. It has also facilitated the psychosocial counsel-ling and other medical treatments of women suffering from conflict-era sexual violence. However, encouraging women to be vocal about conflict-era sexual violence is an extremely difficult task for several reasons. Firstly, these women are not confident about obtaining justice for what they went through during the time of armed conflict. Second, conflict victim women found that many perpetrators are still powerholders or close to power, thus they have fears for their own safety and security if such cases are brought into the public domain. Third, most of these women are either in a conjugal relationship or bounded with other forms of social and family relationships and exposing their past may jeopardise their existing relationships. Fourthly, some of the conflict victim women who we interacted with in the field also expressed that they have lost faith in the existing state institutions and actors, thus discouraging them to be vocal about their plight. In sum, the women who suffered from conflict-era sexual violence are hesitant to bring their problems to the surface, as there are no incentives behind disclosing their pain. NGOs, conflict victim communi-ties, as well as the state agencies, are yet to communicate with victim women adequately and give enough assurance to provide them necessary support to come out of trauma and live a dignified life. This was also the case during the immediate post-conflict era which shows that there is a distinct lack of progress regarding justice for sexual and gender-based violence (SGBV).

It was also noted that many conflict victim women lack original documents issued by the government that officially authorise them as a conflict victim. This is because many of them have submitted the original copies of the docu-ment while registering their cases at TRC and Commission of Investigation on Enforced Disappeared Persons, as well as in the course of obtaining relief materials and other support from NGOs and donors in the past. Additionally, many conflict victim women have not even kept the photocopy of those documents, simply because of the lack of knowledge on the importance of keeping those documents safely. Lack of authorised documents on hand may prevent them from obtaining necessary assistance from the government and non-government actors in the future.

Conflict victim women who got very little during the immediate post-conflict era were very hopeful with the new political environment formed after the election of the local, provincial, and the federal government in early 2017. However, all three tiers of the government have not met the expectations of

124   *Susan Risal*

conflict victim women, as they found the elected governments in all three tiers are not so open to address the issue of conflict victims. They found that federal government often points out local and provincial governments as an ultimate authority to address the need of conflict victims in the newly introduced federal governance system, whereas the local and provincial governments always have an excuse for not having enough funds to allocate a budget to conflict victims. Particularly, local government officials remain silent on the agenda of conflict-related sexual violence. Many elected representatives feel that women who were the victim of sexual violence have reverted to a life of normalcy, as they are engaged in daily routines and have started a family life with children. However, while talking to the victim women separately, they are living in a horrendous situation due to what they had gone through in the past. Most of the women who suffered from sexual violence are in an urgent and continuous psychosocial support, but the local government as well as the local health institutions from conflict-affected communities are unable to provide such support, partly due to the lack of trained human resources, and partly due to the lack of awareness among the local authorities regarding the needs of such services.

Women's Participation and Representation in Political and Administrative Bodies Post-2015

Despite the unchanged situation of conflict victim women, Nepal has made significant progress in terms of women participation and representation in political and administration bodies in the post-constitution period. The structural reform towards women's representation began after the success of the second People's Movement in 2006 through a number of constitutional and policy reforms. This has been further institutionalised through creating a constitutional ground for enhancing women's representation in all three tiers of government as well as in the bureaucratic and judicial structure of the state. Representation of nearly one third women in the federal and provincial parliaments and mandatory election of women in several local government positions are some examples of Nepal's progress towards women's political representation. For example, the new Constitution of Nepal in 2015 has made a provision of at least 33% representation of women in the provincial and federal parliaments through the mixed representation system. If the first-past-the-post system does not fulfil this percentage, then the remaining representatives must be fulfilled through the proportional representation system envisioned by the new constitution. The constitution has also guaranteed women leadership in various constitutional positions as equal to men. For example, when the speaker of the federal parliament is a man, then the deputy speaker should be a woman. Similar provisions are made in the case of local government Mayor/President and Deputy Mayor/Vice-President, where one of these positions should be a woman from the same political party. The constitution has also guaranteed the representation of one woman and one Dalit woman at the ward level, the lowest local governance structure.

With all these constitutional reforms, Nepal has set a remarkable history in terms of women's political representation and contestation in the elections. For instance, a total of 14,352 women were elected in the 2017 election of the local government, of which 18 women were elected as Mayor or President of the local government units; 700 women were elected as Deputy Mayor/Vice Chairperson; 62 as Ward President; and the rest were elected as ward members (Manandhar, 2021). For the first time in Nepalese electoral history, such a large number of women got elected at the local government level, though the number of women holding major positions is still nominal. Compared to 2017 data, a total of 55,599 women stood as candidates of the local government election in 2022, of which 14,402 got elected (National Women Commission, 2022). Among them 21 got elected as Mayor/President; 564 as Deputy Mayor/Vice-President; 69 as Ward Chairperson; and the remaining as ward members. There was a slight increase in women being elected as Mayor/President at the local government level, and a significant decrease in the number elected Deputy Mayor/Vice-President due to a coalition-based model of local election practised in recent times by the political parties.

Likewise, in 2017 a total of 189 (out of 550) women got elected in the seven different provincial assembly bodies. In 2022, the elected number of women in provincial assemblies reached 200. In 2017, 90 (out of 275) women got elected in the federal parliament in 2017. This number reached 91 in the 2022 election. There is a slight increment in the number of elected women in both federal and provincial parliaments. However, questions are often raised regarding the quality representation of women and their power and position in the parliamentary decision-making bodies.

It is also not only increased women participation in political decision-making bodies, the number of women in the civil service is also increasing. For instance, the female participation in civil service has increased from 12% in mid July 2008 to 27.2% in mid March 2022 (Ministry of Finance, Nepal, 2022). The participation of women in constitutional authorities is 7.8%. Whilst the overall increase in women's political representation is a welcome sight, it is important to note that they are still vastly underrepresented in leadership positions such as mayors, ward chiefs, and key ministries as these are still dominated by men.

Current Socio-economic Status of Nepalese Women

A common issue that is strongly raised by women's movements is that the root causes of conflict are yet to be addressed. They have strong discontentment with the post-constitution political environment as it has not contributed significantly towards positive socio-economic indicators. In fact, there has been little progress on the gender-related socio-economic indicators. In 2011, the overall literacy rate for the country was 65.9% with disparity between the genders being 18%. The 2021 census revealed that the overall literacy rate had increased

126 *Susan Risal*

to 76.3% with a 14% difference between men and women (National Statistics Office, 2023). Nepal also has a constitutional clause regarding marriage, with both men and women having to be at least 20 when they get married. However, around 37% of Nepali girls still get married before they turn 18. There are also regional disparities within these statistics as these rates are higher in Madesh (52.5%) and Sudurpaschim (45.4%) (National Statistics Office, 2023).

Violence against women remains a serious issue in Nepal. In the year 2021, INSEC reported that a total of 6,285 people were the victims of different violent incidences in Nepal. Among them 5,215 were female, accounting for 83% of total victims (INSEC, 2021). According to the United Nations Population Fund, 48% of Nepali women experienced some form of violence at some point in their lives. This is particularly relevant for Madhes and Sudurpaschim Provinces where gender disparity is at large. Likewise, Nepal Police record shows that 9,240 cases of crime against women were recorded with the police across the country between the period of August–December 2021. Among the various nature of crimes, 7,329 complaints registered with the police were related to domestic violence. Other data from Nepal Police shows that out of the total registered cases relating to violence against women and children in the fiscal year 2020/21, approximately 75% of cases were of domestic violence; 13.41% rape cases; 3.89% attempted rape; 1.48% child sexual abuse; 0.32% witchcraft allegation; and 0.20% related to untouchability (Nepal Police, 2021). The other forms of violence experienced by women in Nepal are related to dowry, polygamy, female infanticide, Chhaupadi, and trafficking of women and girls for sexual exploitation. In addition to these, with the change in lifestyle, technology-based violence such as cyber bullying is also increasing. Other reports also suggest that cases such as polygamy, extramarital affairs, and trafficking of labour are increasing trends commensurate with the increase in foreign labour migration.

Being a patriarchal society, women in Nepal are facing multiple forms of discrimination within family, community, and in the labour market. These discriminations are deep rooted in the socio-cultural, religious values, and norms practised at home and outside. The power given to males by the patriarchy system makes them dominant and superior to women which in turn gives leverage for them to behave violently against women. In many cases women experience violence due to their gender, age, caste, ethnicity, class, as well as disability.

The Constitution of Nepal 2015 has guaranteed women's rights as a fundamental right and states that no woman shall be subjected to physical, mental, sexual, psychological, or other forms of violence or exploitation on grounds of religion, social, cultural tradition, practice, or on any other grounds. The rights guaranteed by the constitution have also paved the way to secure their rights through legal means and seek legal remedy. However, there are several limitations reported in accessing the legal remedy. For instance, victims often keep quiet due to stigma, shame, and trauma associated with the violence or because of a fear of the perpetrators. Even if they build courage and try to

Analysing the Peace Process of Nepal through a Gender Lens   127

lodge a complaint, the victim must go through a series of interviews by police, doctors, lawyers, and judges. The repeated telling of their experience makes them re-victimised. Further, most of these officials are males, which make it difficult for women victims to narrate their stories. Even during the process of getting legal remedy, their privacy and safety is ignored. Likewise, their psychological, medical, physical, and financial needs are also overlooked and often treated as an 'item of evidence' and 'non-person'.

Nepal has made some important achievements during the peace process. With the promulgation of the new constitution in 2015, a three-tier federal governance system was introduced at the national, provincial, and local levels, with the aim to change the political landscape of the country. However, due to the internal power battle amongst the major political parties, now Nepal's democracy itself is on the verge of a crossroads of crisis where once again the agenda of gender justice, particularly one that concerns conflict-affected women, has been side-lined. On top of this, other anticipated and unanticipated events such as elections, the 2015 Nepal Earthquake and the Covid-19 pandemic also led to the exclusion of gender justice for conflict-affected women from the political agenda. In this context, this chapter is an attempt to explore how conflict-affected women continue to be subjugated and excluded from the formal peacebuilding process in Nepal.

Discussion

A peacebuilding process has to go through different stages and processes. Lederach divides it into four phases: (i) immediate action/crisis intervention (2–6 months); (ii) short-range planning/preparation and training (1–2 years); (iii) decade thinking/design of social change (5–10 years); and (iv) generational vision/desired change (20+ years) (Lederach, 1997). Conflict transformation should be seen as a long-term progression in which we can distinguish timeframes appropriate for planning and action. Specific intermediate interventions must consider long-term goals. Such framing addresses the structural and relationship challenges that generate systematic conflict, and helps a country move in the direction of desired change (Lederach, 1997). Without building the necessary capacities at the individual level, and within communities that have experienced direct impact of an armed conflict, desired social change and sustainable peace cannot be achieved. However, Nepal's peace process has only concentrated on political and civil rights on a surface level but failed to consider the deeper impact of the conflict and address structural violence. The peace process also failed to consider the social conditions of women who experienced violence during the conflict, or to uncover the assumptions that would allow for a full and true understanding of how the world works for these women.

Another flaw of the peace process is that the state has not tried to adequately address the social problems that still exist in society. It therefore couldn't offer practical solutions to these problems and make holistic changes when it comes

128 *Susan Risal*

to gender justice. As argued by Horkheimer (2002), there is also a gap in seeing the social totality of the women and how each individual relationship in relation to their other web of relationships is impacting their daily lives. Another major gap in the peace process of Nepal was the failure to empower women who were brutally impacted by the armed conflict, particularly those women who faced sexual violence, or to address the constraints placed on those women by race, class, caste, region, and gender.

The peace accord of Nepal was supposed to be an open avenue for political, social, and economic transformation that ensured a dismantling of all forms of discrimination and inequality. However, the condition and position of women who faced the brutal impact of the conflict remains unchanged. Neither political leaders, nor the state have made an effort to invest in addressing such grievances that continue to subjugate women. Victims of armed conflict continue to live with physical and psychological pain. The nuances and the real narrative of women survivors of the conflict has been decentred. Furthermore, not a single case of human rights violation was brought to attention. The analysis of the current context also observes the state's inability to manage the transition phase delicately. Nepal is side-lining issues of women who have faced severe human rights violation and this is taking the country to the crossroads of another crisis. Now people have lost trust in the mainstream political parties, and many are choosing to vote for alternative parties who range from populists to conservatives who want a reinstatement of the abolished Hindu monarchy. This mistrust is the outcome of Nepal's fragile peace process which is moving towards a political and social fault line. The country failed to listen to the citizens' voices and demands for justice. Until and unless the state and the ruling parties try to address the structural issues of the armed conflict and listen to the people while setting aside their vested interests, sustainable peace will not prevail in Nepal.

Conclusion and Way Forward

It has been argued that in times of violent conflict, men and women face new roles and changing gender expectation, which offers opportunities for reshaping both public and private relationships and making positive steps towards gender equality (Schirch and Sewak, 2005). In the context of Nepal, though the 10 years of violent conflict opened the avenue towards gender equality, the status of women and particularly conflict-affected women has not changed the way it had been projected in the CPA as well as in the new constitution. Instead, their status and condition are seen to be worsening. The initiative to challenge the framework of normative violence was not in the priority of government's plan and actions. Due to this gap, Nepal's peace process has not been able to create positive steps towards gender equality, despite promises ensured in CPA and in the 2015 Constitution of Nepal. Anderlini (2007) argues that gender-neutral peace agreements and the belief that mere references to broad human rights would encompass women have legitimised women's exclusion from the

Analysing the Peace Process of Nepal through a Gender Lens 129

formal peace process. This example can be seen in the case of former Maoist combatants. Many women combatants returned to their previous household core activities where their identity was limited to somebody's wife or daughter, despite having served alongside their male counterparts during the insurgency. Having to go back to unpaid care work in their households has had a psychological impact on these women. Likewise, it can be observed that conflict-affected women who are from the remote areas, economically poor families, have received little to no support from the government and non-governmental sector to repair their broken life in the post-war period.

Considering these facts, the following area of intervention must be considered to address the issue of gender justice which could contribute for the effective peacebuilding process as well as for sustainable peace in Nepal.

Making Women Visible as Agents of Change

Women's experiences of conflict and peace are not homogeneous and merely participating in the process of peacebuilding is not sufficient. Without taking gender into account, real conflict transformation will not occur. One of the major flaws of the peace accords and the peacebuilding process of Nepal is that it failed to acknowledge the contribution of conflict-affected women for systemic change or acknowledge that they have a capability to be an agent of change. This can be validated from the interim compensation policy formulated in 2009 which excluded women who faced sexual violence from the category of conflict-affected women, despite these women's contributions to change. There is also a tendency to see women as solely war victims and their contribution and potential for peacebuilding as change agents within their societies tends to get forgotten or neglected. In Nepal, many women are still compelled to live under a notion of victimhood (Risal, 2020). To maintain peace and security at every level, women must be included in every plan, policy, and peacebuilding process of the country, which can largely contribute to the peace at large. This is needed to ensure that peacebuilding efforts are gender sensitive. Real gender perspective is critical to local dialogues, better policies, and more equitable peace deals, which can dismantle the systemic structure of society that subjugates women. It is important to move from exclusive to democratic decision-making, from gender inequality to gender justice and from conflict and violence to sustainable and feminist peace.

Nepal has made some effort to include women, peace, and security agenda in its peacebuilding process, to address the gender impacts and consequence of violence and war. This agenda has transformative potential to address cycles of conflict, to create inclusive and more democratic peace-making and to turn from gender inequality to gender justice. However, the prevailing patriarchal mindset in the society, discriminatory power structure, lack of political will, and many unanticipated events in Nepal have side-lined the agenda that could have potential to acknowledge women as agents of change. It has prevented the formation of inclusive peace in Nepal that could have seen a restoration

130 *Susan Risal*

of women's dignity. Women's experiences and knowledge of conflict and peace must be taken into consideration in every peace process. Furthermore, many human rights advocates argue that rights must be protected at all stages of armed conflict and human or natural disaster. They cannot be left until later, after a political deal has been made. Human security paradigm recognises and encourages the potential that individuals can use creative change (Anderlini, 2007). However, women's human security did not get any priority in the peacebuilding process of Nepal. The Global Study on the Implementation of the Women, Peace, and Security Agenda of 2021 also advocates for peace processes to be holistic and not reduced to actors around a negotiating table. Any given peace process must be a comprehensive, inclusive, and diverse process in the interest of the whole society, and it must support women's participation in the political architecture of transitional justice processes (UN Women, 2018). However, a very nominal meaningful representation can be seen in Nepal's political structure and conflict-affected women were rarely engaged in the transitional justice process.

Maintaining Rule of Law and Ending Impunity

The other major drawback of Nepal's peace process is its inability to address the issues of impunity and corruption. Perpetrators who committed gross human rights violations towards women at the time of the conflict remain unpunished. Looking at the current trend of the peace process, it can be observed that there is a lack of will among political parties and the state to deal with and address the cases of severe human rights violation. This also exemplifies how impunity is politically sanctioned in Nepal. During these 15 years of the peace process not a single perpetrator of a major human rights violation has been legally tried. There are several reasons why this investigation and prosecution matters. Many women who faced sexual violence are explicitly saying the name of the perpetrator who inflicted sexual violence on them, but in the name of so-called transitional justice these cases are being transferred to the Truth and Reconciliation Commission which is one of the weakest mechanisms of the peace process where every decision is guided by political parties. This move has side-lined the regular justice system. It also exemplifies how Nepal's rule of law has weakened drastically in this peace process, with institutionalised impunity everywhere in the government, public, and the private sphere. Peace is an essential condition for a flourishing society where people can live their lives in dignity. Civil war, however, has devastating effects on individuals, communities, and entire societies. It causes not only civilian deaths but massive ongoing suffering as a result of the long-term impacts of human rights violations and atrocities, displacement, epidemics, sexual and gender-based violence (SGBV), the breaking down of family and community structures, environmental degradation, the collapse of service provision (including medical and education systems) and food production structures, and the destruction of the social fabric that binds a peaceful society together (Westendorf, 2015). Women in

Analysing the Peace Process of Nepal through a Gender Lens 131

Nepal from marginalised communities suffered a lot due to many forms of human right violations. To heal the wound of women who faced the brutal impact of the conflict it is necessary to avoid the notion of denial from the state and the political parties. It is important to avoid the conception that compensation alone can provide justice. Instead, it is important to call for an effective implementation of the promises made in CPA related to truth and justice, to restoring the dignity of women and assuring people that rule of law exists in Nepal. It is also equally important to dismantle structural violence which continues to ostracise women in Nepal today, especially those from marginalised groups.

With the introduction of federalism in Nepal, there were new opportunities to address wartime crimes concerning gender. At the central level, the transitional justice mechanisms were hindered due to politicisation as well as a lack of financial and human resources and therefore the TRC was not able to expedite the process. However, local and provincial governments can aid in the process of transitional justice and can also contribute to repair the harm inflicted to women at some extent by supporting women for their social, cultural, psychological, and economic justice.

There were also promises made in regard to human rights, fundamental rights, and adherence to humanitarian law and principles. Article 7 of the CPA reiterates the commitment to respect and protect human rights, and to international humanitarian law and accept that nobody should be discriminated against on the basis of colour, gender, language, religion, age, race, national and social origin, wealth, disability, birth and other status, thought, or belief. The signatories also committed to impartial investigation and action as per the law and would punish those who were responsible in creating obstructions to the exercising of the rights envisaged in the letter of agreement and guarantee not to encourage impunity. Apart from this, it has also guaranteed the right to relief of the families of the conflict and torture victims and the disappeared. However, at the writing of this chapter, the current transitional justice process has not met the principle of international human rights and has not been able to recommend any of the cases of perpetrators who committed heinous crimes against women for legal processes. Nor has it set any example where it has recommended any of the women for their right to access the immediate and long-term reparative measures. The Universal Periodic Review by the UN included several recommendations in respect to ending impunity by ensuring investigation and prosecution of human rights violations respecting the decision of the Supreme Court of Nepal and guaranteeing access to justice and effective reparations to the victims of human rights violations. However, no effort has been made by the government to date in taking into account these recommendations. This move of the government has contributed to further marginalisation of these women and compelled them to live with stigmatisation. Although the Supreme Court of Nepal, many national and international organisations including UN agencies, call on government to end impunity with a number of recommendations, the government has chosen not to act on

132   *Susan Risal*

them. A strong recommendation has also been made for the amendment of the TRC Act to fulfil the international standards and to ensure women who faced sexual violence in the time of armed conflict have access to effective remedies. However, the lack of political will to address the serious human rights violations has been observed which impacts negatively on efforts to improve the rule of law and accountability and increase public trust in public institutions. No effort has been made to analyse the real dimensions of human rights violations, including their causes and consequences and their relationship with historical discrimination against women. Without taking these issues into account in the peacebuilding process of Nepal the real reconciliation will not occur in the society which can contribute for sustainable peace. It is necessary to urgently address the pervasive impunity for those who are involved in such violations. Nepal is once again elected to the United Nations Human Rights Council for a three-year term and now we are yet to see whether it will issue the standing invitation to the UN Special Rapporteur on the promotion of truth, justice, reparation, and guarantees of non-recurrence procedures to visit Nepal which it has ignored in the past.

Furthermore, Nepal is a signatory to many other international human rights treaties which prohibit sexual violence, including rape and torture, and call upon providing remedy and justice to the victims of rape and torture. These international human rights treaties include the Geneva Convention, International Covenants on Civil and Political Rights, Elimination of all Forms of Discrimination Against Women, and Convention on Torture, and other cruel inhuman or degrading treatment and punishment. However, at the time of writing this chapter, Nepal has never met these international standards. It is necessary for the government and political parties to make efforts to maintain the rule of law and punish perpetrators and end impunity, whereby women can have justice in their lives.

Discourse on Ending Systemic Structure of Violence

Nepal's peace process was conducted as a technocratic one which moved on to the basis of set guidelines. The result of this technocratic approach was that the peace processes were effectively depoliticised, in that they did not respond to the political and social contexts that defined how individuals and communities engaged with peace consolidation or worked against it (Westendorf, 2015). In other words, they overlooked the relationship between the society and the state and did not engage with the politics of conflict and peace in the post-war society, particularly in terms of how power and authority are organised and contested, and how competing interests intersect with either peacebuilding or the continuation of conflict. Consequently, the peace processes were often manipulated and captured by elite interests, and inadvertently contributed to perpetuating the very conditions of insecurity and conflict that they were attempting to alleviate. As argued by Westendorf (2015), Nepal's peacebuilding process was also mostly captured by the elite classes of

Nepal, mostly upper-caste men from the hill region. They failed to listen to the elective knowledge of the people on the ground and especially of women who were never given a space to share their lived experiences of war and peacetime and their needs. Women were never consulted about their ideas of justice. Also, effort has never been made to understand how the systemic and patriarchal structure of the society supresses women in the country. The aspirations of women for a strong governance system and their notions of security (phys-ical, economic, psychological, economic, and social) and transitional justice is never considered. It was necessary to bring these women into the dialogue pro-cess, which could have played a vital role in dismantling the structures that dis-criminate women based on their caste, sex, and race. There were no safe spaces for dialogue between conflict-affected women and their communities, local and national political leaders, and other stakeholders, to make everyone under-stand that the violence the women suffered was not their choice or their fault. These dialogues are equally necessary to cut down the multi-layer trauma of women, which they have been carrying long term. The dialogues can also help people understand how the engraved societal norms and patriarchal mindset of society discriminates these women and excludes them from exercising their choice and voice. Identity, acceptance, recognition, security, and justice are at the core of basic human needs. In Nepal many women who faced the brutal impact of the conflict are living with the sense of losing their identity and security, due to the discriminatory structures that prevail in our society. These structures need to be dismantled by bringing the unspoken stories of women to the surface. Having dialogues at the community, local, and national levels are important to repair the harm that the women suffered, and to ensure col-lective support from families and communities. These ongoing dialogues could have also provided a space for the community to say or hear something that was never said or heard before, and from which they could emerge irrevocably changed. The approach emphasises listening, learning, and the development of shared understanding in a non-hierarchal manner. Such dialogue could help break the cycle of violence, help the conflict survivors restore their identity, and acknowledge their contributions towards societal change.

Necessity of Empirical Studies that Incorporates a Gender Lens

There are very few empirical studies done through gender lens found in Nepal. Data collection on how women were impacted by the armed conflict and incorporation of their lived experiences into a peacebuilding discourse have been largely conducted by NGOs and typically ignored by the state. This is exemplified by how the state-sponsored relief package excluded women who faced sexual violence in the interim compensation policy of Nepal. It can also be validated from the nominal cases of sexual violence reported in Truth and Reconciliation Commission in Nepal. This act of government is, in a way, promoting impunity by failing to provide a safe space to women where they can confidentially talk about the human rights violation that occurred, which

134 *Susan Risal*

could have also helped collect information on the harm suffered by those women. Many factors such as social and cultural norms, and patriarchy, also stopped women from reporting cases of sexual violence. Due to fear of family relationships breaking down, and without a gender-sensitive peace process, women were unable to take legal action. Similar cases have also been observed in countries like Peru, Greece, and Guatemala, where social stigma kept women from reporting cases of sexual violence, and consequently excluded them from the justice process (Stefatos, 2016). Physical and sexual violence, particularly towards women and children, occur with greater regularity during and after an armed conflict. Impacts of armed conflict such as forced displacement and gender-based violence are not understood as human rights violations, but rather as cultural or private issues that are best left alone (Jack, 2003).The atrocity of rape gets considered a private matter, and women remain silent. It has been extremely painful for women to include trauma in their narratives, and when they have decided to share their traumatic stories, there has been an obvious reluctance to talk about the sexual nature of their victimisation. Women were more comfortable discussing physical abuse and psychological violence they suffered, although their narration was brief, succinct, and lacking in detail. As with the case of Greece, this transitional justice process of Nepal, the lack of a conducive environment keeps women from venting their trauma and talking about real incidents. Women throughout the world report that fear of stigma keeps them from seeking services after the rape, even though timely intervention can be lifesaving. Likewise, echoing the findings of the report LOGiCA (2011), women in Nepal who faced sexual assault have also been impacted psychologically, physically, economically, culturally, and socially. The communities that these women belong to question their morals and blame themselves for what happened to them. Shifting the blame from the victims to the perpetrator is important, and it is only possible if those women can break their silence and overcome the notion of self-blaming.

References

Anderlini, S.N. (2007) *Women Building Peace: What They Do, Why It Matters*. Lynne Rienner.

Arostegui, J. (2013) 'Gender, Conflict, and Peace-building: How Conflict can Catalyse Positive Change for Women', *Gender & Development*, 21(3), pp. 533–549. Available at: https://doi.org/10.1080/13552074.2013.846624

Basini, H. and Ryan, C. (2016) 'National Action Plans as an Obstacle to Meaningful Local Ownership of UNSCR 1325 in Liberia and Sierra Leone', *International Political Science Review*, 37(3), pp. 390–403. Available at: https://doi.org/10.1177/0192512116636121

Berry, M.E. (2018) *War, Women, and Power: From Violence to Mobilization in Rwanda and Bosnia-Herzegovina*. Cambridge University Press. Available at: https://doi.org/10.1017/9781108236003

Berry, M.E. and Rana, T.R. (2019) 'What Prevents Peace? Women and Peacebuilding in Bosnia and Nepal', *Peace & Change*, 44(3), pp. 321–349. Available at: https://doi.org/10.1111/pech.12351

Cohn, C. (2004) 'Mainstreaming Gender in UN Security Policy: A Path to Political Transformation?', *Boston Consortium on Gender, Security and Human Rights*, Working Paper No.204.

Horkheimer, M. (2002) *Critical Theory: Selected Essays*. Continuum Publishing Company.

INSEC. (2021) *INSEC Annual Report 2021*. INSEC Annual Report. Informal Sector Service Centre.

Jack, A.E. (2003) 'Gender and Armed Conflict', *Institute of Development Studies, Bridge-Development and Gender* [Preprint], MSc Thesis, Wageningen University.

K.C., L. (2011) *Securing Livelihood: Reintegration of Mother Ex-Combatants in Post Conflict Nepal*. MSc. Wageningen University.

K.C., L. (2019) 'Everyday Realities of Reintegration: Experiences of Maoist "Verified" Women Ex-combatants in the Aftermath of War in Nepal', *Conflict, Security and Development*, 19(5), pp. 453–474. Available at: https://doi.org/10.1080/14678 802.2019.1658969

K.C., L. and Van Der Haar, G. (2019) 'Living Maoist Gender Ideology: Experiences of Women Ex-combatants in Nepal', *International Feminist Journal of Politics*, 21(3), pp. 434–453. Available at: https://doi.org/10.1080/14616742.2018.1521296

K.C., L., Van Der Haar, G. and Hilhorst, D. (2017) 'Changing Gender Role: Women's Livelihoods, Conflict and Post-conflict Security in Nepal', *Journal of Asian Security and International Affairs*, 4(2), pp. 175–195. Available at: https://doi.org/10.1177/2347797017710743

Lawoti, M. and Pahari, A. (2010) *The Maoist Insurgency in Nepal: Revolution in the Twenty-First Century*. Routledge.

Lederach, J.P. (1997) *Building Peace: Sustainable Reconciliation in Divided Societies*. United States Institute of Peace.

LOGiCA. (2011) *Learning for Equality, Access and Peace (LEAP), Semi-Annual Progress Report January-June 2011, Learning on Gender in Conflict Affected Countries in Africa, LOGiCA)*

Manandhar, S. (2021) 'Women Representation in Nepalese Local Election 2017: Issues and Challenges', *Journal of Political Science*, 21, pp. 34–48. Available at: https://doi.org/10.3126/jps.v21i1.39283

Ministry of Finance, Nepal (2022) *Economic Survey 2021/22*. Economic Survey. Government of Nepal.

National Statistics Office (2023) *National Population and Housing Census 2021: National Report*. National Population and Housing Census. National Statistics Office, Government of Nepal.

National Women Commission (2022) Gender Equality and Social inclusion in Local Level Election 2079.National Women Commission. Available at: www.undp.org/nepal/publications/gender-equality-and-social-inclusion-local-level-election-2079

Nepal Police (2021) *Police Mirror 2021*. Nepal Police.

Poudel, B. (2023) *Women Survivors Silenced, Kathmandu Post*. Available at: http://kathmandupost.com/columns/2023/03/15/women-survivors-silenced (Accessed: 15 August 2023).

136 Susan Risal

Ramnarain, S. (2016) 'Unpacking Widow Headship and Agency in Post-Conflict Nepal', *Feminist Economics*, 22(1), pp. 80–105. Available at: https://doi.org/10.1080/13545701.2015.1075657

Rayamajhi, A. and Shrestha, D. (2022) *The Lasting Scars of War: Sexual Violence During the Conflict – The Record*. Available at: www.recordnepal.com/the-lasting-scars-of-war-sexual-violence-during-the-conflict (Accessed: 15 May 2023).

Riley, H., Ketola, H. and Yadav, P. (2022) 'Gender, Populism and Collective Identity: A Feminist Analysis of the Maoist Movement in Nepal', *Journal of Human Security*, 18(2), pp. 35–46. Available at: https://doi.org/10.12924/johs2022.18020035

Risal, S. (2020) 'Defining Justice and Dignity Through Gendered Peace Building: A Case Study of Gender-Based Violence During Armed Conflict in Nepal', *Social Inquiry: Journal of Social Science Research*, 2(1), pp. 56–81. Available at: https://doi.org/10.3126/sijssr.v2i1.28908

Schirch, L. and Sewak, M. (2005) 'Women: Using the Gender Lens', in P. van Tongeren et al. (eds.) *People Building Peace II: Successful Stories of Civil Society*. Lynne Rienner.

Shekhawat, S. (ed.) (2015) Female Combatants in Conflict and Peace. Palgrave Macmillan UK. Available at: https://doi.org/10.1057/9781137516565

Stefatos, K. (2016) 'The Female and Political Body in Pain: 1 Sexual Torture and Gendered Trauma during the Greek Military Dictatorship (1967–1974)', in A.G. Altinay and A. Pető (eds.) *Gendered Wars, Gendered Memories: Feminist Conversations on War, Genocide and Political Violence*. Routledge.

Sthapit, L. and Doneys, P. (2017) 'Female Maoist Combatants during and after the People's War', in Å. Kolås (ed.) *Women, Peace and Security in Nepal*. 1st edn. Routledge.

Surkan, P.J. *et al.* (2015) 'Non-disclosure of Widowhood in Nepal: Implications for Women and Their Children', *Global Public Health*, 10(3), pp. 379–390. Available at: https://doi.org/10.1080/17441692.2014.939686

Tamang, S. (2009). The Politics of Conflict and Difference or the Difference of Conflict in Politics: The Women's Movement in Nepal. *Feminist Review*, 91(1), pp. 61–80. https://doi.org/10.1057/fr.2008.50

Thapa, L. and Canyon, D.V. (2017) *The Advancement of Women in Post-Conflict Nepal*. Daniel K. Inouye Asia-Pacific Center for Security Studies.

Tripp, A.M. (2015) Women and Power in Post Conflict Africa. Cambridge University Press (Cambridge Studies in Gender and Politics). Available at: https://doi.org/10.1017/CBO9781316336014

UN Women (2018) *Women's Meaningful Participation in Negotiating Peace and the Implementation of Peace Agreements: Report of Expert Group Meeting, New York, UN Women*.

Valente, C. (2011) What Did the Maoists Ever Do for Us? Education and Marriage of Women Exposed to Civil Conflict in Nepal. Available at: https://elibrary.worldbank.org/doi/abs/10.1596/1813-9450-5741 (Accessed: 15 August 2023)

Westendorf, J.-K. (2015) *Why Peace Processes Fail: Negotiating Insecurity After Civil War*. Lynne Rienner.

Yadav, P. (2020) 'When the Personal is International: Implementation of the National Action Plan on Resolutions 1325 and 1820 in Nepal', *Gender, Technology and Development*, 24(2), pp. 194–214. Available at: https://doi.org/10.1080/09718524.2020.1766187

9 Governance Challenges and Opportunities in Young Federal Nepal
Growing Pains

Shuvam Rizal

Introduction

In May 2022, Nepal held its second nation-wide local-level elections amidst much fanfare and optimism. This event marked a milestone of significant measure in the country's young history as a democratic republic structured around a three-tier federal governance framework as it signified the successful completion of one full election cycle in the federal system.

Federalism was officially introduced in the country with the promulgation of a new constitution in 2015 following over six decades marked by political instability, bureaucratic struggles, and an armed conflict. The newly introduced foundational governance structure includes a three-tier model, consisting of one central, seven provincial, and 753 local government units. For practical purposes, it could be understood that the central tier carried forward the ongoing works of the previous unitary system while leading the process of power devolution to its provincial and local counterparts. Administrations in the provincial and local levels are afforded a variety of constitutionally defined powers. The central tier also retains involvement in some cases through provisions delineating concurrent powers shared between two or three tiers.

This new, currently governing constitution was historic for several reasons. Firstly, it restructured the country's entire political skeleton away from the traditional unitary system, which featured a constitutional monarchy at its centre with evolving levels of influence over the years. Secondly, it is the first constitution in the country's history which is written not by those in power, but by a Constituent Assembly representing its citizens freshly elected for the purpose of drafting a constitution that fits the people's needs. It is also unique for being the only Nepali constitution written with the primary agenda of ensuring inclusiveness, secularism, and active participation of all groups and subgroups within the country's diverse population. Finally, the 2015 constitution is distinctive because it is written to be decidedly flexible in nature. It allows the passing of key future amendments as deemed necessary by the people, and in doing so, signifies the importance of malleable leadership with changing times to ensure that further changes need not occur at the backs of mass movements and revolutions.

DOI: 10.4324/9781003289876-10

138 *Shuvam Rizal*

In the seven years that have followed, the topic of federalism has remained a sensitive one among politically groups and average citizens alike. Even now, its establishment and implementation as the nation's foremost governing guideline remains contested and unsettled (Bhattarai, 2019). While constitutional guarantees officially outline the governing framework, local elections have played the role of gateways into the practical implementation of the new structure, its operational and administrative challenges, and insights into the post-2015 governance context in Nepal. The remainder of this chapter is an attempt to analyse and critically evaluate what has worked, what hasn't, and what improvements can be made to further iron out the shortcomings of Nepal's young federal governance framework.

The Constitution-Making Process

To properly understand the current governance context in the country, it is useful to recount the scenario in which the constitution was made. Conceptually, the idea of electing a Constituent Assembly in Nepal can be traced all the way back to the 1950s, when the country first adopted a democratic framework of governance following over a century of autocratic Rana rule. The idea remained unfulfilled then as King Mahendra promulgated a post-Rana rule constitution in 1959 triggering parliamentary elections, but again promulgated an updated version in 1962 introducing the *Panchayat* system recentralising power to the palace. Since then, one other notable constitution was brought into effect: the Constitution of the Kingdom of Nepal, 1990, which diluted the monarchy's power by introducing a multiparty parliamentary system.

Following a 2005 decree from King Gyanendra, which took power away from the Parliament back to the palace, a joint movement was launched in 2006 by a unified faction consisting of the prevalent Seven Party Alliance and the Communist Party of Nepal, Maoist. The backbone of this people's movement was a 12-point agreement spelling out the demands and terms of unification. Resultingly, the king backtracked on his decision, the parliament was reinstated, and the landmark Comprehensive Peace Agreement (CPA) was signed. An Interim Constitution of Nepal was promulgated in 2007, which announced the official abolishment of the monarchy and set the wheels in motion to begin the process of drafting a new, permanent constitution.

History was made on 20 September 2015 with the promulgation of the currently governing federal, secular, democratic republican constitution. However, the process which led to this milestone had already been underway since April 2008, shortly after the aforementioned Interim Constitution was introduced, when the country elected its first constituent assembly, hereafter referred to as CA1. Although the CA1 was ultimately unable to successfully draft a full-fledged constitution within its given timeframe of expiration in 2012, leading to the election of the second Constituent Assembly, CA2, much of its work was eventually endorsed by the latter and used in the drafting of the currently governing constitution (IDEA International, 2015).

Governance Challenges and Opportunities in Young Federal Nepal   139

The journey from the election of the CA2 to the promulgation of the constitution was not a smooth one. The assembly faced several challenges in the process of drafting the constitution, including political and nonpolitical roadblocks. Notably, the ongoing momentum of work was halted by the 2015 earthquakes. Throughout April and May of 2015, global headlines were dominated by the news of a series of devastating earthquakes occurring in Nepal. The disasters ultimately took the lives of over 8,500 citizens. Thousands more are believed to be injured. The earthquakes also caused large-scale permanent damage to infrastructure, especially in urban centres around the capital city of Kathmandu. Historically and culturally significant buildings, including world heritage sites, were also damaged. Perhaps unsurprisingly then, the ongoing works related to the constitution-building process took a back seat as citizens, government bodies, and concerned organisations around the world became immersed in disaster response and relief efforts. Public speculations at the time predicted that either the constitution promulgation would be delayed or further accelerated given the post-disaster scenario of the country.

Other challenges in the constitution-making process were more political in nature. Longstanding negotiations on territorial demarcations with Madhesh-based and Tharu political parties characterised the entire constitution-drafting period. Inclusivity and representation concerns were similarly raised by various ethnic minority communities, women's rights organisations, and indigenous groups throughout this period. Concurrently, a number of small factions also arose in an effort to reinstate the monarchy, which never fully materialised on the national or region scales but did cause an added feeling of uncertainty and doubt among citizens whether the CA2 would be able to plan the promulgation of a new constitution as originally intended. Nonetheless, the people's aspirations of officially entering Nepal into a new era of democratic governance sustained over time.

It is worth noting that even after the provisions of the new constitution became public knowledge, activist groups continued to express discontentment due to the feeling of only selected concerns being raised in the drafting processes and having been inadequately reflected in the final draft. The sharpest and most notable voices expressing this dissatisfaction belonged to the Madhesh-based parties. Several elected members belonging to these factions did not participate in either the CA2 meetings endorsing the constitution, or the official signing of the statute stating that the draft was unacceptable due to its discriminatory provisions (Mint, 2016). Concurrently, violent protests erupted along the Terai belt, and continued even after the constitution was officially promulgated.

Divisive Perceptions Towards the Constitution

Following the 2015 promulgation amidst deadly protests by Madhes-based and Tharu groups across the southern plains, Nepal emphatically adopted its new federal framework with the local elections of 2017 serving as a gateway into its implementation. The successful completion of the local elections would

140　*Shuvam Rizal*

signify a positive outlook towards the new government skeleton framework envisioned by the constitution. Over a full decade after the signing of the CPA and the end of the civil war, the country saw the formation of its first federal government in 2017.

As the ideological and spiritual successor to the CPA, the constitutional provisions that introduced federalism aimed to alleviate many of the prevalent social concerns that led to the armed conflict of the 1990s in the first place. Primary among them was the improved political representation and participation of historically marginalised groups such as Madhesis, Janajatis, Dalits, and women. In fact, the philosophical backbone behind the localisation and provincialisation of geographical territories rests on the theorised improved visibility and increment of avenues for political participation among marginalised groups in their respective areas.

However, despite the constitution guaranteeing the protection and representation of marginalised groups on paper, analyses of the current situation suggest that measures of political inclusiveness and participation has seen little improvement since before the war (Bhattarai, 2019). The protests, which had deep support in the ethnic Madhesi Terai belt, were founded on a sense of profound alienation from the constitution-drafting process at the capital.

Such sentiments have been palpable in the national scenario before, during, and after the promulgation of the constitution in 2015. A coalition of Madhes-based civic and political groups led a 135-day supplies blockade, which ultimately ended with no endline solutions arising nationally or regionally (Jha, 2016). Multiparty disputes over the placement of provincial boundaries and the naming of province headquarters have also continued since.

Moreover, tensions between different facets of the federal system, which was designed to foster an environment of strong local politics, has instead consistently undermined the scope of the local tier. Political jurisdictions have been superseded by the Kathmandu-based central government. This scenario has caused an environment of national and regional tensions between different entities within the three-tier federal structure. In such a scenario, however, it should be noted that it is a positive sign that Nepal has not shown strong signals of reverting to a state of violence despite a lack of significant governance improvement.

Local Elections as Gateways into Federalism

In 2017, citizens across Nepal took to the polls for the first time to elect their local leaders within the newly adopted federal framework. The elections thus held a special significance as they formed a key part of the country's transition from its historic unitary governance model to a federal state. On February 2017, then-Prime Minister Pushpa Kamal Dahal announced that the elections would take place on 14 May, giving the Electoral Commission of Nepal, the body responsible for organising and conducting elections, a short window of around 80 days to ensure all required preparations were in order (Bakken,

2017). Although the local elections were originally foreseen to be conducted on a single day, logistical specifics, preparation issues, and security concerns triggered by the ongoing protests along the country's southern belt saw them being held in phases.

Given that the country was in a delicate transitional period, the political and historic significance of the successful completion of the 2017 election cannot be overstated. For all practical intents and purposes, the election is viewed as one of the major landmark steps taken by the country towards its path of implementing the federal state envisioned by its newly promulgated constitution. The completion of the local elections in a peaceful, organised, and conflict-free fashion was also important as provincial and central level polls were planned for November later that year. Thus, the local election was in a position that it would set the very first precedent for the nature of election management and operations in federal Nepal. Finally, its historic importance was also marked by the fact that it would create the first set of government units in Nepal that followed the federal vision of the constitution. This also meant that the results would determine answers to key questions and concerns surrounding the practical implementation of the provisions on paper. Elected leaders in the local and provincial tiers would also set the precedent of laws, policies, mandates, and division of responsibilities within their newly created infrastructure. The 2017 local elections were thus extremely important as the first, true gateway into federalism for Nepal.

A major facet of the 2017 local elections was the environment of ethnicity-based protests they were conducted amidst. Scholar communities and influential outlets within the international media had even speculated that the first, true test of Nepal's young federal constitution was the peaceful completion of the elections amidst political dissent and turmoil throughout the Terai region (Groves, 2017). Vocal dissatisfaction among Madhes-based ethno-political groups were poised as the biggest obstacle faced by Nepal's young, yet untested federal governance system.

As mentioned in the previous section, Madhes-based groups represented a unified conglomerate of a large chunk of the national population that were historically marginalised by Nepal's hills-based political elite circles in the capital city of Kathmandu for centuries. Quickly upon the announcement of the 2017 local elections, several Madhesh-based political parties threatened to boycott the elections completely in protest of dissatisfactory and discriminatory constitutional provisions following the promulgation of the fast-tracked draft following the 2015 earthquakes. A successful boycott of the first local elections—let alone the first Nepali elections of any kind held in decades—would prove to be a major blow to Nepal's future as a federal republic as that would go against the very ethos of inclusivity and participation that was at the core of the new constitution. Eventually, such concerns were assuaged when an agreement was met wherein the protesting groups agreed to cancel their planned boycott and vote in the elections under the conditions that a specific set of constitutional amendments would be tabled in the parliament, which

142   *Shuvam Rizal*

ultimately failed to secure the required majority votes. The elections proceeded successfully through their last phase over the months and concluded in a timely manner with minimal disruption.

At the time of writing in May 2022, the second round of local elections has also been completed with minimal operational disruption or peace disturbance reported so far in the polls. This round of local elections was also subject to rumours of delays due to logistical backlogs in preparation following multiple dissolutions of the parliament in the prior year (Gaunle, 2022). Nonetheless, the widespread public disagreement with the rumours of delay and their successful completion does indicate that, while federalism in Nepal is still unsettled, there is a significant level of importance and reverence given to the democratic value of timely elections.

Pacifying Elements of Local Elections

Given the tense environment of protests and threats of boycotts in which the 2017 local elections were conducted, several public concern-pacifying aspects have come to light since their successful completion, indicating the key role elections can play in promoting societal peace and positive governance transformation. Not only did the relatively hassle-free realisation of the 2017 local elections plans reaffirmed the country's faith and determination to continue on the path of federalism, but they also served to alleviate the concerns arising from the observed socio-ethnic fragmentation of the time.

In accordance with the Local Level Elections Act 2017, which outlines the governing and monitoring guidelines for local elections, voting municipalities are geographical divisions that are further subdivided into wards, where one ward chair and four ward members are elected to represent the residents of their respective territorial delineations. The Act mandates that at least two representatives from each ward must be women, among which one of the two must be from the Dalit community. Further, voters in each municipality also vote for a mayor and a deputy mayor, for which all participating political parties are mandated to field one male and one female candidate. Such quota provisions are designed to ensure that elections results are representative of the constituency the winning leaders are elected to serve, and that the concerns of historically marginalised groups are brought to the attention of local leadership through improved political participation. The European Union Election Observation Mission had reported during the election of the CA2 that such strong quotas make Nepal the frontrunner among all South Asian nations in terms of guaranteeing its female citizens an accessible pathway to political decision-making positions (European Union, 2013).

Post-impact studies analysing the long-term effects of the completion of the 2017 local elections on societal peace have found that the elections helped significantly to improve political participation and responsiveness of local governments, driven by a diverse set of mechanisms, thereby contributing to promote an environment of fostering societal peace through democratic

Governance Challenges and Opportunities in Young Federal Nepal 143

processes (CSC, 2022c). The elections were characterised by an unprecedented level of enthusiasm and optimism around the country, reflected by high voter turnout rates across all provinces.

Notable factors that led to high participation included the long absence of local elections in the country, increased hope in political processes inspired by the new federal governance model, increased political awareness following the armed conflict, expectations of improved public service delivery, and the introduction of new and (for some groups) more relatable candidates through the aforementioned quotas. While the quotas are found to be the most popular factor driving election participation in 2017, it should be noted that many voters reported feeling disappointed by the role played by personal financial resources in the distribution of local posts and campaigning potential, thus limiting equitable access to participation as candidates. Still, studies have found that the role played by the 2017 elections on societal peace have been overwhelmingly positive (ibid.).

Studies have also found that the 2017 local elections increased political trust through increased accessibility to locally elected leaders. The vertical relations between state and society were thus observed to have been thereby improved substantially, as increased civic trust in leadership is also associated with improvements in conflict resolution, sustained long-term political participation, and tangible improvements in service delivery outcomes (Fiedler et al., 2022). The 2017 elections were thus notable for pacifying many pertinent doubts and misunderstandings of the social effects of the newly adopted federal system.

Although it is too early to make any conclusions about the 2022 local elections at the time of writing, the observed strong voter turnout and the increased visibility of independent candidates in the polling proceedings also indicates a healthy evolution of local elections as a federal tradition contributing to improved state-society relations.

Pertinent Challenges of Implementing Federalism

Aside from the elements outlined in the previous section which have been met with positive transformation over the last seven years, there are still several challenges associated with the effective implementation of federalism in Nepal. This section recounts some of the most pertinent ones observed in the current scenario and is not written to be an exhaustive list of all relevant challenges.

The major issues currently under debate with regards to the early-stage implementation of federalism in Nepal can be classified into two broad-stroke categories. Firstly, the constitutionally outlined power-sharing model between the three tiers of the government is still relatively raw in both vision and implementation, and thus needs to be reconciled with concrete policies and laws establishing precedent. A primary ongoing debate that has remained unsettled since the constitutional drafting process remains the allocation of provincial headquarters and naming of the provinces, which stands as an example of a lack of institutionally mechanised power-sharing structures within key decision makers in the federal system.

Secondly, there is a wide array of operational issues with regards to the practical and stable implementation of federalism over time and into the future. Only a robust, easily referenced, transparent system can ensure long-term stability as federalism evolves out of its early stages. Key issues within this category include the vision and overall direction of the federal structure with regards to its continued devolution of power to local and provincial actors, the mechanisation of tools to ensure accountability of public service delivery, communication and coordination systems between actors belonging to different government tiers with regards to common issues, and the operational costs associated with the smooth working and sustainability of the federal system over time. Anecdotal evidence suggests that political conversations around federalism are dominated by administrative, political, and fiscal dimensions, leaving very limited interactions around the social, behavioural, and civic participation aspects of federalism (Bhattarai, 2019).

Perhaps the most publicly debated and currently visible challenge is the administrative process of managing the bureaucracy and power hierarchies between the central, provincial, and local governments. There have been instances of the central government retaining abilities to make certain decisions that fall constitutionally under the jurisdiction of the local level with the justification of inadequate capacities. The management of this bureaucracy within the federal structure and the recruitment or training of adequately competent staff at local and provincial governments is thus a pertinent challenge in the operational and mechanised implementation of federalism in the current scenario. Similarly, the formulation and enforcement of operational provisions, laws, and policies that guide movement within bureaucracy of the three-tier structure without curtailing the rights of citizens and undermining the scope of any governmental entity is equally important to ensure the long-term sustainability of the federal system as a pro-people governance system.

A recent, prominent example highlighting such an instance of bureaucratic confusion came in the form of the announcement of the Covid-19 pandemic that disrupted the education sector across the country. The administrative and operational jurisdiction of primary- and secondary-level education falls under the local government units as per the provisions outlining the delineation of power. Meanwhile, the management of national-scale crises such as a pandemic fall on the de facto jurisdiction of the central tier. Despite no cases of Covid-19 being identified in several areas, nationwide school closures were announced by the central government which some education sector activists believe undermined and weakened the young local government administrations (Farid et al., 2021). Through such examples, the Covid-19 pandemic is believed to have revealed the extent to which Nepal's federal transformation is still yet incomplete.

Economically, the transition into the federal structure is a costly process as it institutes the creation of complex new physical, legal, and administrative

Governance Challenges and Opportunities in Young Federal Nepal 145

infrastructures. The formation and maintenance of key entities to design, enforce, and monitor the federal transformation alone is cost intensive. Furthermore, a stable and reliable resource-sharing mechanism is yet to be built, which adds to the economic burden, as most operations carried out in provincial and local governments are still reliant on central-tier funding. Over the long term, it can be argued that federalism has the potential to prove economically favourable with the exploration of locally viable economic development opportunities throughout the country, locally tailored anti-corruption policies, and contextual capital investment models. However, in its early stages, its implementation costs are evident.

In addition to the above-mentioned economic challenges of federalism implementation, the smooth transition of existing economic structures, infrastructures, and their difficulties into the new governance system is equally important.

Nepal's economy is primarily based on the agriculture sector and is also characterised by high remittance in-flows. For most of its history, Nepal was listed by the United Nations as a Least Developed Country (LDC), although it has recently been scheduled for a 2026 graduation under the condition that it makes a smooth post-pandemic recovery while continuing to implement polices and strategies needed to establish a strong economic base. Given that it is in such a critical period of its economic development, it is highly important that stability in existing trajectories of economic growth is ensured as a cornerstone of the ongoing federal transformation process. Additionally, as power-sharing mechanisms are further strengthened with legal and policy provisions across geographical jurisdiction, the careful management and utilisation of natural resources dispersed across the country's territory is a challenge of utmost economic importance. Three major natural resources of economic value in Nepal are water, minerals, and forests. Studies have found dispersed availability of each of these resources throughout the country, further highlighting the economic importance of a well-planned devolution of administrative power (ADB, 2020).

On a related note, issues hindering effective, peaceful, and optimal power-sharing concerns across levels, sectors, and operational delegations can itself be considered a prominent threat to the successful implementation of federalism in Nepal. Tensions between central, provincial, and local governments have been observed most notably in the control of local public services, security agencies, and their respective bureaucracies (Acharya & Zafarullah, 2020). Similarly, isolated instances of tensions between local mayors and deputy mayors, sometimes representing different political parties, have also been observed (Kamati, 2022). In such cases, it is constituents of the local areas that bear the brunt of disputes as development projects become stalled and people are deprived of their entitled public services. Despite all contesting candidates pledging to work together to develop their constituencies during the 2017 local elections, such disputes have arisen to create doubt among people about the effective implementation of federalism.

There are also pertinent governance challenges related to public service delivery, both development and administrative in nature, which have carried forward in the last seven years from the old unitary system to the current federal framework. Concerns regarding the quality, accessibility, inclusiveness, and participation levels of education enrolment in local government-run schools, availability of scholarship opportunities, financial support for students, and equitable education across social dimensions such as ethnicity and gender are still longstanding public service challenges that are relevant in the federal context today (CSC, 2022a). Similarly, the availability of essential medication in health centres, basic treatments, first-aid care, access to nearby medical centres, essential vaccination equity, etc., are all pertinent challenges in the health sector that experts believe have carried forward from the old system (CSC, 2022b).

Aside from public service-related challenges, there are also concerns that unproductive, wasteful, and inefficient development processes carried out by the pre-2015 leadership might find thoughtless continuation as old governance traditions. To combat this, new governance bodies, especially at the local and provincial tiers, should be given the required training, autonomy, and support to bring structural changes in public policy agendas instead of just continuing work readjusted to the new bureaucracies. Similarly, the launching, renewal, or realignment of existing projects should not be carried out without adequate planning under the new bureaucratic structures, as they could inadvertently undermine the jurisdiction of newly formed administrations. Given the increased level of localised autonomy, contextualised sensitivity training on existing social dynamics, socio-economic viability and relevant ecological aspects of development projects should be prioritised by the central government as well as other parties such as civil society organisations and the active international community for newly formed entities to ensure the successful transition of long-term projects.

Finally, there is growing concern regarding the gradual decline in availability and accessibility of civic space for citizens to express their grievances towards their respective government units within the federal framework. It is believed widely among the research community and the political intelligentsia that local and provincial governments still have a long way to go to ensure a true, pro-people, effective bottom-up governance mechanism as envisioned by the constitution (Bhattarai & Adhikari, 2020). In cases where conflicts have arisen, they stand to become further exacerbated by the lack of active conflict-resolution mechanisms, grievance-handling operations, mediation councils, and interactive multistakeholder platforms.

Even when disagreements are handled internally, having the availability of discussion platforms and interactive forums stand to improve local trust towards the government and increase the citizens' self-driven capacities to tackle local problems systematically. Having such open and accessible grievance-sharing connections with government bodies can also help local citizens groups to realise the complexities of governance processes and to

Governance Challenges and Opportunities in Young Federal Nepal 147

understand the reasonings behind policy and legal decisions, which can then lead to improved trust and cooperation between different parties.

Intergovernmental Concerns

Given the fact that the political and ideological notion of federalism is still relatively new in Nepal, both in theory and in practice, the challenges recounted in the previous section regarding its effective implementation are natural. However, the current situation, operational concerns, and perceptions at the local and provincial levels are worth noting separately from the issues described above from the lens of intergovernmental relations.

Some province-level representatives have expressed that there is no need for local governments, as a two-tier system would be easier to navigate, more efficient to communicate between, and more cost effective to run. On the flipside, local-level representatives have also reportedly expressed similar concerns regarding the lack of need of provincial governments. Hon. Subhash Chandra Nembang (2020), who served as the chairman of the CA2 when the constitution was passed, expressed in his article "From Constitution Writing to Implementing Federalism" that such disputes are unproductive for the success of the federal model, and that representatives from all three tiers should realise that federalism is the outcome of extensive analysis of the country's governance historic challenges and future goals. He argues that the core structure of the federal framework should no longer be a topic of debate. Instead, the country's energies are better suited to further enhance the three-tier model so that provision, delineations, and communication between its various entities becomes easier over time.

As mentioned in the first section of this chapter, one of the key defining features of the currently governing constitution is its deliberate flexibility. Given that the CA1 and CA2 had already been working on drafting it for many years, and supplemented by the fact that the constitution's promulgation was fast-tracked due to disruptions caused by the 2015 earthquakes, it was necessary for political parties and their leaders to reach consensus while working among a diverse set of ideologies and visions. Many old, existing laws and policies were thus allowed to continue into the federal era with timelines establishing them to be revisited. The deadline for such laws has now passed, and change has been put into effect in some areas whereas others are still lagging. Jurisdictional conflict is also natural to be expected in such a situation as technically all three tiers of the government have the right to make laws, but practically doing so in the provincial and local levels still require that the central level outlines the relevant areas of autonomous, concurrent, or overlapping competencies (Adhikari, 2020).

One example of confusion caused by overlapping jurisdictions comes from the provision that announces that matters concerning the country's security falls under the central government. Through multiple rounds of reviews during the constitution-writing process, the decision was made to delineate security

148 *Shuvam Rizal*

to the central tier for multiple reasons: to maintain uniformity of training and recruitment processes, to keep channels open for the sharing of confidential information across provincial and local governments, to help develop and facilitate a national forensic laboratory, and to make it legally easier to arrest people who may be residing in one jurisdiction after having committed a crime in another. Yet, still to this day, there is palpable tension between representatives in the provincial and central levels about the details of how intergovernmental power should be shared in the security sector. This example highlights how topics that were left unsettled among the stakeholders during the drafting of the constitution have since evolved into areas of active intergovernmental conflict.

Another common area of intergovernmental jurisdictional confusion has been the legalities associated with policies in the education sector. In "The State of Constitution Implementation and Federalism in Nepal", Hon. Radheshyam Adhikari (2020) writes about the observed trend of province and local-level governments making laws to exercise their exclusive powers, ignoring the fact that they could potentially be counterproductive to existing provisions in the central tier. In the essay, he recounts an example where the mayor of Triyuga Municipality, Gaighat, shared that existing recruitment and administrative decisions had led to a strong imbalance between numbers of teachers and students in different schools and subjects. He thus expressed a desire for the municipality to make laws to transfer teachers to ensure a better balance in the teacher-student ratios across schools, despite the fact that doing so would contravene the Education Act and go against the central government's existing law.

Untimely and insensitive handling of such situations can give rise to intergovernmental disputes, while also clogging up the legal systems with increasing numbers of complaint cases in courts, thus creating further tensions between different entities of the federal government. In such cases, Adhikari (2020) argues, it is better to draw the attention of the central tier government regarding the issue rather than creating local laws that contravene federal laws, giving way to dangerous precedents that could result in legal anarchy between intergovernmental actors.

On a positive note, experts have claimed that one of the strongest aspects of Nepal's federalism is that it explicitly outlines the basic principle and spirit of intergovernmental harmony, coordination, communication, and cooperation in the constitution itself (Devkota, 2020).

Political Scientist R.L. Watts (2003) theorised that intergovernmental relations can have one of two distinct dimensions. First among these are vertical relations between entities belonging to different tiers of the government, such as central-local or provincial-local relations. Increasingly around the world, political order is defined by multiple levels of such vertical relations, including international entities such as the European Union. Second are horizontal relations that exist between entities of the same federal tier, such as relations between two local municipalities or two provincial government administrations.

Governance Challenges and Opportunities in Young Federal Nepal 149

Both types of intergovernmental relations are equally important for smooth operation within a federal model, and thus, effective communication, conflict resolution, and project coordination should be mechanised in both types of relations.

Part 20 of the constitution outlines provisions, guidelines, and operational delineations of intergovernmental relations. In it, Article 232 states that "the relations between the Federation, Provinces, and Local levels shall be based on the principles of cooperation, co-existence, and coordination".

Despite the existence of intergovernmental tensions and instances of conflict as in the cases outlined above, it should be noted that there are several institutional arrangements set up in Nepal's federal framework that allow for improved intergovernmental relations. Six notable ones include:

1. **Constitutional Bench**
   Article 137 of the Constitution allows for the creation of a Constitutional Bench in the Supreme Court to resolve matters of conflict or disputes between intergovernmental entities. The Bench is headed by the Chief Justice of the Supreme Court.
2. **Interprovincial Council**
   Article 234 of the Constitution includes a provision outlining an Interprovincial Council, a dispute resolution body meant for entities belonging to either the central and provincial tiers, or different bodies from the provincial tier.
3. **Provincial Coordination Council**
   The Provincial Coordination Council plays a special role in maintaining and improving intergovernmental relations as it is the body that facilitates and mediates on issues surrounding policymaking, planning, and budgeting between provincial and local governments.
4. **National Natural Resources and Fiscal Commission**
   Similar to the Provincial Coordination Council, the National Natural Resources and Fiscal Commission's role in the management of intergovernmental relations is specific to delivering on tasks related to fiscal disputes. It also holds the authority to mediate on disputes between intergovernmental actors on matters involving the use, protection, and management of natural resources.
5. **Intergovernmental Fiscal Council**
   The Intergovernmental Fiscal Council is a standalone discussion platform created by the Intergovernmental Fiscal Arrangement Act of 2017. It was introduced to create an unbiased common ground that can be used to resolve financial matters between entities from different tiers of the federal government. Since 2017, it has grown into a frequent forum used to discuss fiscal disputes between members from all three tiers of the government.
6. **National Coordination Committee**
   The National Coordination Committee was introduced by a provision in the Intergovernmental Coordination Law of 2019. Its primary task involves

150 *Shuvam Rizal*

the formulation of laws and policies that involve entities from different tiers of the government to ensure national standards are met, uniformity is maintained in service delivery, and issues of national interest are aligned correctly among multiple stakeholders. In doing so, it also holds significant potential in maintaining strong intergovernmental relations.

Despite the existence of the six institutional entities mentioned above, it is arguably still expected to see cases of intergovernmental disputes arise given the early stages of federalism implementation in Nepal. The administrative and political infrastructures upon which the three tiers exist also have an impact in how intergovernmental disputes are perceived.

The central tier continues to utilise many of the infrastructures present in the unitary model. Meanwhile, the newly formed local governments were created in many places as restructured versions of existing local units. On the other hand, provincial governments are entirely new. Thus, as key administrations adjust to the new federal model, it can be expected that tensions boiling over from the previous governance framework will dissipate over time. Similarly, the fact that the development of new laws, policies, and acts are still in the national political discourse is a positive sign that Nepal can expect stronger, more detailed, and more sophisticated provisions in the future regarding intergovernmental relations.

Conclusion: The Way Forward

Nepal has come a long way since the days of the unitary government. While the journey towards reestablishing its national identity as a federal republic has not been free of obstacles, the national discourse is now well set on the path to continuing the improved implementation of the new framework.

Most influential voices in the political discourse today agree that the way forward is not to entirely scrap the constitution, but instead, to amend its provisions to further enhance the federal framework. Still, there is an active and vocal minority group that entirely opposes the idea of federalism and advocates for the 2015 constitution to be completely scrapped and for the country to revert to the unitary system. In such a scenario, the importance of improving Nepal's federal functioning thus cannot be overstated.

After over a decade since the signing of the CPA and seven years since the promulgation of the constitution that introduced a new governance framework to the country, the merits and demerits of federalism is still a hotly debated topic among academics, researchers, government officials, civil society organisations, and individual citizens alike. The federal structure has already produced many positive outcomes in this short time, including a sustained period of peace following the state of war and the enabling of greater political representation among marginalised groups such as Madhesis, Janajatis, Dalits, and women. Nonetheless, the current system is far from perfect.

Governance Challenges and Opportunities in Young Federal Nepal 151

Despite the constitution pledging the protection and representation of marginalised groups on paper, the de facto situation on the ground, especially in rural areas, appears to have seen little improvement. Ongoing conflicts between key actors of the government, including instances of intergovernmental disputes, also suggests that there is tremendous potential for improvement in Nepal's governance structures and systems. Some of the most pertinent opportunities, based on this chapter's review and analysis of the currently observed challenges, are outlined below.

1. Above all, the constitution and policies that have followed its promulgation need to be thoroughly reflected and revisited through a critical review in relation to the CPA, and the context in which it was originally signed. Prominent stakeholders from all three tiers of the government should be involved in such review processes on a regular basis, perhaps after every election cycle, so that the original spirit of the CPA is retained.
2. A culture of creating regular, specific, measurable national targets and goals should be normalised. For example, the above-mentioned review exercises could produce distinct one-, five-, or ten-year plans relevant to the jurisdiction of the different tiers of government. Not only would this culture promote higher accountability and transparency among government representatives, it would also make it easier for those working on ground-level projects to plan and adjust their work expectations accordingly.
3. The development of adequate knowledge and capacity development opportunities to enhance the scope and quality of local and provincial governments should remain a high priority. Not only should administrative works such as human capital development, resource sharing mechanisations, financial management, etc. be carried through, but a thorough monitoring mechanism should also be introduced to ensure that provincial and local government growth occurs in a uniform and standardised way to ensure better service delivery in all areas of the country.
4. True to the spirit of the CPA and the constitution, the federal structure should continually thrive to identify and address the needs of marginalised communities. Aside from ensuring social equality through equitable public services, this task should also take the dimension of maintaining strict political representation quotas and creating mechanisms to monitor them to ensure that they are not being exploited by the powerful.
5. As Nepal slowly adjusts to the federal structure, governments should continue to identify and advocate for necessary structural changes to further enhance the scope, efficiency, and inclusiveness of the three-tier structure. Representatives becoming accustomed over time with their day-to-day tasks related to fiscal governance, financial management, service delivery, etc. should not be at the cost of losing momentum on enhancing governance structures. Intergovernmental relations should remain a priority in this effort.

152 *Shuvam Rizal*

6. Finally, governments from all three tiers should take active efforts to create provisions, platforms, and forums where citizens, opposition parties, and civil society actors can express their views and share grievances. Such platforms should also be equipped with capable personnel trained in dispute resolution and conflict management.

Discussions around the six recommendations outlined above are already present, in evolving degrees, in the current national discourse surrounding federalism. Still, their importance in the determination of the successful next phase in Nepal's journey towards peace and democracy cannot be understated. Despite being accepted as a positive next step for governance in Nepal, many of its citizens are not happy with how federalism is functioning. It is thus of utmost importance that political representatives, opposition parties, civil society groups, knowledge production communities, and concerned citizens across the country continue to strive towards improving the federal system into a customised model that fits the historic challenges, current needs, and future goals of the country.

References

Acharya, K. K., & Zafarullah, H. (2020). Institutionalising Federalism in Nepal: Operationalising Obstacles, Procrastinated Progress. *Public Administration and Policy*, *23*(2), 125–139. https://doi.org/10.1108/PAP-03-2020-0013

ADB. (2020). *Country Integrated Diagnostic on Environment and Natural Resources for Nepal*. Asian Development Bank.

Adhikari, R. (2020). The State of Constitution Implementation and Federalism in Nepal. In *Nepal's Constitution and Federalism: Vision and Implementation (Ed)*. National Forum of Parliamentarians on Population and Development, Nepal (NFPPD)

Bakken, M. (2017). *Local Elections at the Epicenter of Nepal's Federal Democratic Future*. International Institute for Democracy and Electoral Assistance. Retrieved 12 March 2022, from www.idea.int/news-media/news/local-elections-epicenter-nepal%E2%80%99s-federal-democratic-future

Bhattarai, P. (2019). *The New Federal Structure in Nepal: Challenges and Opportunities for Quality Governance*. External Democracy Promotion. Retrieved 10 March 2022, from www.external-democracy-promotion.eu/the-new-federal-structure-in-nepal-challenges-and-opportunities-for-quality-governance/

Bhattarai, P., & Adhikari, P. (2020). *How Are the Local Governments Doing?* MyRepublica.

CSC. (2022a). *Education Governance in Nepal: Based on One Year of Real-Time Governance Monitoring*. Retrieved 12 March 2022, from https://myrepublica.nagariknetwork.com/news/how-are-the-local-governments-doing/

CSC. (2022b). *Health Governance in Nepal: Based on One Year of Real-Time Governance Monitoring*. From https://socialchange.org.np/wp-content/uploads/2022/01/GMC-Health-Policy.pdf

CSC. (2022c). *Local Elections and Societal Peace in Nepal*. From https://socialchange.org.np/wp-content/uploads/2022/01/Local-Elections.pdf

Devkota, K. L. (2020). Intergovernmental Fiscal Relations in a Federal Nepal. *International Center for Public Policy Working Paper 20-13.*

European Union. (2013). Final Report: Constituent Assembly Elections. *European Union Election Observation Mission.*

Farid, N., Hayes, B., & Sirkhell, R. (2021). *Nepal's Challenges in Delivering Education Amidst the COVID-19 Pandemic.* Asia Pacific Foundation of Canada.

Fiedler, C., Mross, K., Berg, A., Bhattarai, P., Drees, D., Kornprobst, T., Leibbrandt, A., Liegmann, P., & Riebsamen, M. (2022). *What Role do Local Elections Play for Societal Peace in Nepal?: Evidence from Post-Conflict Nepal.* German Development Institute.

Gaunle, S. (2022). *Why Government Plan to Delay Local Elections Puts Nepal Democracy in Peril.* OnlineKhabar. Retrieved 1 March 2022, from https://english.onlinekhabar. com/local-elections-delay-impact.html

Groves, S. (2017). *Local Elections: The Coming Test for Nepal's Constitution. The Diplomat.* Retrieved 10 March 2022, from https://thediplomat.com/2017/03/local-elections-the-coming-test-for-nepals-constitution/

IDEA International. (2015). *Nepal's Constitution Building Process: 2006–2015: Progress, Challenges, and Contributions of International Community.* International Institute for Democracy and Electoral Assistance.

Jha, P. (2016). *End of the Madhesi Blockade: What it Means for Nepal.* Hindustan Times. Retrieved 13 March 2022, from www.hindustantimes.com/opinion/end-of-the-madh esi-blockade-what-it-means-for-nepal/story-JixO1gsdWLprj8Lc6G0hQL.html

Kamati, S. K. (2022). *People Bear the Brunt of Dispute between Mayor and Deputy Mayor.* Centre for Investigative Journalism, Nepal. Retrieved 11 March 2022, https://cijnepal.org.np/people-bear-the-brunt-of-dispute-between-mayor-and-dep uty-mayor//

Mint. (2016). *Nepal's Madhesi Front Refuses to Back Constitution Amendment Bill.* Mint. Retrieved 23 March 2022, from www.livemint.com/Politics/lDWeTDTXk3a F6TFtwFdwDM/Nepals-Madhesi-Front-refuses-to-back-Constitution-amendm ent.html

Nembang, S. C. (2020). From Constitution Writing to Implementing Federalism. (Ed.), *Nepal's Constitution and Federalism: Vision and Implementation.* In *Nepal's Constitution and Federalism: Vision and Implementation (Ed).* National Forum of Parliamentarians on Population and Development, Nepal (NFPPD).

Watts, R. L. (2003). Intergovernmental Councils in Federations, Constructive and Co-operative Federalism? A Series of Commentaries on the Council of the Federation. *Institute for Research on Public Policy.*

Conclusion

Raunak Mainali

A thorough analysis of Nepal's peace process from 2006 until now clearly confirms that even though the nation has largely avoided a return to large-scale armed violence, the peace process itself is incomplete. This section will aim to summarise the findings within this book as well as provide the necessary steps in order to close the gaps regarding peace process implementation. Due to the authorship of this volume consisting largely of practitioners, there will be several policies discussed relating to the themes that were covered in earlier chapters. This section will also outline several avenues for further research pertaining to post-conflict Nepal.

Lack of Political Will

A theme that was consistent between the different chapters is the impact political will had on the apparent successes and failures of the peace process. As the first chapter by Prakash Bhattarai suggests, even the conflict itself came to an end partly due to the political will of the respective parties; the Maoists moved away from their tactic of a protracted conflict due to the stalemate situation and their unpopularity with the urban middle and upper class of Kathmandu as well as the international community. Both sides were also encouraged by the Jana Andolan movement which occurred as a reaction to King Gyanendra's regime adopting autocracy. The movement clearly demonstrated a willingness of both parties to work towards the progressive future of the country. Therefore, there was sufficient political will to bring about the end of the conflict and the formalisation of a peace process.

A peace agreement can be argued to be a reflection of the political will of the belligerent parties at a specific time. As a post-conflict process is dynamic in nature, the political will of parties pertaining to some aspects of the agreement may differ to that compared to when it was signed. The Comprehensive Peace Agreement (CPA) clearly displays this with a strong commitment to some aspects of the peace process when compared to the others. As outlined by the second chapter, ceasefire clauses, the disarmament, demobilisation, and reintegration (DDR) process, and political restructuring were all detailed within

DOI: 10.4324/9781003289876-11

Conclusion 155

the peace agreement when compared to clauses relating to transitional justice and socio-economic reform. This is clearly reflective of the political will of the respective parties. A restructuring of the state and promulgation of the constitution would be ideal achievements for the parties to gain domestic and international legitimacy as it would display their commitments to a democratic model of governance which was sought by domestic and international actors alike. The success of a DDR process is also heavily reliant upon political will as it can take place in a situation of a security dilemma where demobilisation may place a party in a vulnerable position (Berdal, 1996; Rolston, 2007). For this reason, the Maoists were initially reluctant to enter the DDR process as they believed that rehabilitation would turn the ex-combatants into civilians and, therefore, they would not be politically engaged and in turn be less likely to support the Maoists as a mainstream political party (Subedi, 2014). The voluntary retirement option which gave ex-combatants cash handouts increased the willingness of the Maoist leadership as they believed it would mean that ex-combatants would be more likely to return to the party and be active in grassroot politics. The Maoist leadership often imposed a cash levy on their combatants and the voluntary retirement option meant that more cadres could contribute to the party fund which would be necessary for their entry into mainstream politics.

The importance of political will for any transitional justice process should not be understated and studies have even focused on devising frameworks to measure political commitment (Pham et al., 2019). There was a clear lack of political will in the transitional justice process in Nepal as both the government and the Maoists sought to secure impunity for themselves for their wartime atrocities. This has resulted in the delayed formation of the Truth and Reconciliation Commission (TRC) and Commission of Investigation on Enforced Disappeared Persons which materialised almost eight years after the signing of the CPA. Even with the constitution of these institutions, they were underfunded and constantly faced barriers placed by the political elites of the country. The government consistently ignored the Supreme Court, the TRC, international actors and the victims themselves by attempting to include amnesty provisions for those who committed human rights violations. The only party that seems to be willing to discuss transitional justice is the CPN-UML but their commitments are not substantive and transitional justice for them has been a tool to pressure their political rivals.

A Superficial Peace Process

At a surface level, Nepal's peace process seems like a success. The country has not reverted back to large-scale violence which is so often the case following peace agreements; the Maoist rebels have turned into a mainstream political party; and the country has undergone radical progressive changes which is symbolised in the 2015 constitution which codified the rights of marginalised groups in the country and introduced a federal model of governance.

156 *Raunak Mainali*

The peaceful resolution to the Madhes crisis that materialised during the constitution-making phase is a testament to the institutionalisation of democratic methods of dispute settlement in the country.

However, a closer analysis of the process reveals that there is still a mountain to climb in order to actualise a peaceful, prosperous, and equitable society in Nepal as envisioned by the CPA as well as the Constitution and demanded by the people. As mentioned by Shuvam Rizal, the federal framework is experiencing 'growing pains' especially regarding the coordination between the three tiers of governments. The central government in Kathmandu still retains significant power in relation to budget, developmental planning, and the transfer of bureaucrats. This has led to issues arising between the different tiers of government due to the confusion over the jurisdiction of each body. This is to be expected with the adoption of a brand new framework and issues relating to coordination are likely to be ironed out in the future as a result of institutional practices arising out of informal practices as well as laws introduced by the Nepali government. At the time of writing, Gandaki province is rumoured to be tabling a provincial law pertaining to the transfer of civil servants. What is more worrying concerning the federal framework is the elements within the society that undermine federalism in general. Senior politicians, including a former Prime Minister, have made comments that undermine federalism suggesting that the provincial and local governments are subordinates of the central government in Kathmandu (Kathmandu Post, 2019; Pradhan, 2021). Hindu conservative alternatives are also gaining popularity by espousing an anti-federal and anti-secular stance citing they want a return of the Hindu monarchy. Their popularity is likely to increase due to the absence of a progressive alternative in the country as well as the repeated failures of the mainstream parties who are often mired in corruption cases.

Nepal's path towards inclusiveness on the surface looks to be commendable. The nation had inequalities along the lines of gender, caste, ethnicity, region, and religion. The post-conflict phase has witnessed the erosion of social taboos regarding caste, albeit there is still ample room for progress. The rights of marginalised groups have been included in the constitution and their political representation has been ensured through the provision of quotas. This has led to a rise in the political representation of women, Dalits, Madhesis, and indigenous groups within political bodies as well as across the public sector which all adopt some form of reservation policy. However, with the exception of a few cases, the political representatives from marginalised groups strongly toe their party line and rarely progress the cause of their respective groups. The high cost of elections has led to only the economic elites of marginalised groups contesting elections or those who are well connected to party leadership and therefore have access to the party network and funds. Close relatives of leading politicians are also more likely to be given party tickets to contest elections, further undermining the purpose of reservation which is to empower marginalised elements of society through political representation. The zero-sum game of Nepali politics also means that those from marginalised groups are often given proportional representation seats as parties do not see them capable of being directly elected or the cost involved in contesting the election. Also, pertinent to address here is that there still exists discriminatory practices from the senior party leaders who are often Hill-Brahmin/Chettri men against historically marginalised groups (Bishwakarma, 2017).

Intensification of Marginalisation and Inequalities

Inequality has been a major talking point in Nepal and was one of the primary reasons for the start of the armed conflict against the state. As mentioned above, marginalisation and inequality in Nepal manifests itself along the lines of gender, class, caste, ethnicity, region, and religion. The Maoists, armed with revolutionary left-wing ideals, were critical of the state of inequality in Nepal and their ranks swelled with women, indigenous groups, Dalits, and the rural inhabitants of Nepal. Inequality amongst these identities has been acknowledged within Nepali politics and society and finds itself in the CPA as well as the Constitution of Nepal 2015. Despite this, the post-war period has observed an intensification of some of these inequalities as well the introduction of new inequalities. In his chapter, Ram Prasad Mainali points out that political opportunities, even those reserved by marginalised groups, have been captured by the economic and political elites. As a result, despite the overall increase of marginalised groups within politics, there remains a massive class gap between the individual elites and the common citizens of marginalised groups. This is illustrated by studies which show that those from marginalised groups are more likely to seek employment opportunities abroad when compared to those from traditional elite backgrounds such as Brahmins, Chettris, and high-caste Newars (Adhikari et al., 2021). Women, who have been historically marginalised within Nepali society, have also progressed very little in the post-conflict period. As Susan Risal's chapter states, women who were victims of the conflict have been largely ignored by the state. Those who were victims of sexual violence were not even eligible for state relief. The participation of women in politics has been largely limited to those that are related or close to the senior members of their party and substantiative presence in decision-making roles is lacking.

The conflict also opened further discussions concerning the disparities between urban (particularly Kathmandu valley) and rural Nepal. The Maoists were able to recruit from and gain a stronghold in Mid Western Nepal largely owing to the isolation of that area from the central government. The result of the isolated rural setting was a population that was aggrieved and weakly defended police posts which facilitated the guerrilla tactics of the Maoists. The disproportionate development between the urban and rural was even emphasised within the CPA and was a primary talking point of the Maoists as a mainstream political issue as well as being touched upon by other parties. However, the post-conflict era of Nepal has not closed the significant gap between urban and rural Nepal. As an earlier chapter by Raunak Mainali

158 *Raunak Mainali*

covered, the conflict primarily took place in rural Nepal. The damage that was done in the rural areas during the conflict is incalculable. Rural inhabitants lost their lives, family members, homes, businesses, and years of schooling which has pushed an impoverished demographic further into poverty. Also communicated by the inhabitants was the loss of communal trust in the villages that has fractured rural society even further. The peace process in Nepal also failed to provide sufficient relief to victims of the conflict, leaving many in worse situations than before the conflict as they lost breadwinners and lost the ability to work themselves. Many of those rural inhabitants that were consulted seemed to accept that their generation were lost causes and wanted the government to create opportunities for employment and education so that their children had a better chance at life. This was a common perception as many victims seemed to prioritise the creation of future opportunities as opposed to redressing the past as suggested by other studies (Selim, 2018). Once again, the outflow of migrant workers provides a good metric for understanding the lack of opportunities in rural Nepal. The Mid Western districts of Rolpa (3,466), Salyan (2,347), and Pyuthan (2,314) see far more people seeking to work abroad than Kathmandu (1,966) despite the latter's population being significantly higher (GoN, 2020).

Interestingly, the chapters of Ram Kumar Bhandari and Chirajibi Bhandari also suggest the introduction of a new marginalised identity. The former's chapter outwardly claims that conflict victims have become a marginalised group in the country with the political elites and other actors often using them for their own agendas. For example, the Maoists have often used the victims of the conflict as a testament to the sacrifices they endured to bring a progressive revolution in the country whilst opposition parties convey the victims as a reflection of the Maoists' cruelty. Additionally, the post-conflict era of Nepal has also witnessed a proliferation of NGOs which include those that are concerned with conflict-era victims. These NGOs are often led by the caste and economic elites of the country whilst victims tend to belong to the traditionally marginalised groups of Nepal. By leading the advocacy for victims' rights, these NGOs undermine victims themselves as agents of change and further reinforce long-lasting inequalities of Nepal. Although Chiranjibi Bhandari does not explicitly label ex-combatants as a marginalised group in Nepal, there is a strong case to do so. Firstly, the ex-combatants themselves can be labelled as victims as many were forced into joining the Maoists as combatants, depriving themselves of the years of schooling, employment, time with family, or agricultural work which would be vital for their long-term prosperity. Furthermore, the Maoists were also active in recruiting children amongst their ranks and child soldiers are regarded by most as victims of conflict. The loss of formative years and injuries have left many combatants without the physical capacity, skill, or education to seek meaningful employment which has effectively marginalised them from society. There are cases where ex-combatants have found a place within Nepali politics largely owing to the opportunities opened by federalism. However, a larger proportion of ex-combatants now

Conclusion   159

find themselves working as migrant labourers in the Gulf, Malaysia, Japan, and parts of Eastern Europe.

Further Avenues of Research

One of the areas concerning peacebuilding and post-conflict Nepal that lack extensive research is that relating to Local Peace Committees (LPCs). Whilst there has been some work by and Babcock (2013), Suurmond & Sharma (2012), and Tandukar et al. (2016) there needs to be further effort to create a more nationally representative study. This is essential as one within the focused discussions that took place as part of research for this volume, several individuals mentioned that those that were Maoists during the conflict faced much prejudice by their community as they were perceived to have joined the armed conflict for selfish reasons. This shows a failure on the part of the LPCs as they were supposed to conduct dialogues in localities and it should have been revealed that many who joined the Maoists did it on the assumption that they were to bring progressive change to their country, because they were forced by the Maoists, or to gain security in order to escape the violence propagated by the state security forces. Had this been revealed in a community setting, it may be argued that there would be more harmonious relationships between ex-Maoists and those that they share their localities with. Furthermore, the research could also reveal new ideas and reinforce existing concepts regarding the factors that made LPCs successes or failures. This is important in order to avoid conflicts in the future and ensure a long-lasting peace in the country.

A recent work by Mac Ginty (2021) delves into how ordinary citizens engage in their own personal conflict transformations in conflict and post-conflict societies. Mac Ginty posits that peace agreements are often signed at a national level with political and military elites and revolve around institutions which may not always engage with citizens. This forces these citizens to be creative and proactive in avoiding conflict on a personal and community level with those around them. Even within this volume, there are several instances where this is apparent. Manchala Jha recounts, during a field visit, an individual telling the representatives of the TRC that they were not needed and that the local people had reconciled amongst themselves. Chiranjibi Bhandari also explains how many ex-combatants chose not to return to their origin village after their cantonment as they had already built communities with other ex-combatants. This could be regarded as an action of everyday peace as there was clearly a stigma associated with ex-combatants and many chose not to return to their village to avoid conflict with their family and community. An earlier chapter also revealed that women from a particular village associated with Maoists were often abused when they revealed their home village to those outside their locality. Choosing not to reveal this information would also be an act of everyday peace as envisioned by Mac Ginty. Further research into this can uncover other methods used by citizens in Nepal to avoid conflict situations in their everyday life. There have been some studies conducted relating

160 *Raunak Mainali*

to everyday peace in Nepal such as Lundqvist (2019) and Nepali & Bhandari (2019).

Finally, whilst there has been research conducted regarding the DDR process in Nepal, a long-term study of Maoists who chose to join the Nepal Army would be extremely beneficial to a comprehensive understanding of the DDR process.

Policy Implications

As the authorship of this volume consisted entirely of practitioners or scholar/practitioners, it would make sense to suggest some policy suggestions drawn from research. Firstly, there has already been talk within domestic circles on the need to change the structure of civil service recruitment. Critics of the current reservation policies have pointed out that those who take opportunities of marginalised quotas are often the 'creamy layer' or economic elites of their respective groups. As of right now, you can apply for a 'reserved' seat if you are a woman, from an indigenous group, disabled, or from a 'backwards' region. This system of recruitment completely disregards class inequalities or pre-existing connections to the civil service. Therefore, this has resulted in a situation where reserved seats are occupied by elites of those marginalised groups. For example, the spaces allocated for women have been largely occupied by those from upper-caste backgrounds or relatives of civil servants. Similarly, upper-caste Newars are overrepresented in the bureaucracy and are allowed to apply for the reserved spaces despite being designated as an advantaged group. As Nepal's inequality is intersectional across many identities, civil service recruitment itself needs to reflect this. This can be done by having a points-based system where an applicant scores higher points if they are marginalised across multiple identities and therefore should be a higher priority for recruitment. There needs to be further studies conducted to determine the weighting of each marginalisation. A similar issue is also prevalent in regard to the reserved seats for political representatives. This issue may be fixed by a proper implantation of the pre-existing laws which limit election spending. However, there must be significant political and judicial will for this to take place.

Another issue that is highlighted mainly by Shuvam Rizal is the need to create laws relating to the coordination between different tiers of government. This is vital in creating a federal system that does not have much friction between the different political entities which may be a future source of conflict. As Rizal points out, there are already institutions created by the constitution to mediate any conflict between the local, provincial, and federal government and their proper use is required. The flexible nature of Nepal's constitution enables pragmatism and amendments can be made as necessary in order to foster good governance. Already parliament is in talks of changing the deeply unpopular citizenship laws which curtail the citizenship rights of women compared to the men in Nepal. Additionally, Rizal also talks of creating more

Conclusion 161

civic space in Nepal in order for citizens to exercise their democratic rights and air their grievances in order to hold the government accountable and inform them of local issues. This is particularly important as exclusion from the state, especially in rural communities, was a major motivator of conflict. Currently, advocacy of this nature is carried out by NGOs which as pointed out earlier removes citizens from being agents of change and reinforces existing dynamics of inequality. The conflict and the succeeding years have shown that the people of Nepal, especially those from marginalised groups, are more than able to be agents of progressive change in the country. NGOs in Nepal are also often associated with a political party meaning that their advocacy is likely to be limited by political agendas. As with every aspect of Nepal, including the peace process, political will and politicisation has hindered positive developments in the country.

Last but not least, the CPA signed between the Maoists and the government is already 18 years old at the time of writing. Yet no effort has been made by the signatories to critically review and reflect on the outcomes of the CPA and draw a conclusion whether or not this agreement has addressed the aspirations of the people as envisioned by the document. CPA evaluation should be conducted by using political, social, and economic lens and should compare against the progress the country has made over the past 18 years on all these three different fronts. A critical evaluation of the pact from signatories by themselves provide opportunities for them to incorporate the unaddressed agenda of the CPA in the new constitution as well as in other policies and programmes of the government. A signatories-led CPA evaluation process can also be an important accountability instrument of a peace process that informs citizens as well as the international community regarding the current status of the peace process from signatories' viewpoint.

We re-emphasise that a successful implementation of the peace process should not be viewed only from the country's success to prevent the resurgence of large-scale political violence in the post-agreement period; it is equally important to look at whether signatories have adopted a balanced approach where an agreement has been able to address the root causes as well as by-products of the conflict in a systemic and timely manner. Another way to look at the balanced way of implementing a peace agreement is its equal attention to the political, social, and economic aspects provisioned in the pact. A victim-centric peace agreement implementation process is also found equally important to increase ownership of the marginal segments of the society.

References

Adhikari, K., Gellner, D., & Bahadur Karki, M. (2021). Dalits in Search of Inclusion: Comparing Nepal with India Cite this Paper. In A. S. Rathore (Ed.), *B R Ambedkar: The Quest for Justice* (Vol. 2). Oxford University Press.

Babcock, J. F. (2013). Samar Basi—'We go there together' the Local Peace Committees and their effect on building peace in Nepal. *Capstone Collection*, 2614.

162 *Raunak Mainali*

Berdal, M. (1996). *Disarmament and Demobilisation After Civil Wars: Arms, Soldiers and the Termination of Armed Conflicts*. Oxford University Press for the International Institute for Strategic Studies.

Bishwakarma, M. (2017). Democratic politics in Nepal: Dalit political inequality and representation. *Asian Journal of Comparative Politics*, *2*(3), 261–272. https://doi.org/10.1177/2057891116660633

GoN. (2020). *Nepal Labour Migration Report 2020*. Ministry of Labour, Employment and Social Security, Government of Nepal.

Kathmandu Post. (2019). Oli makes yet another remark that contradicts the spirit of federalism. *The Kathmandu Post*. Kathmandu Post. Retrieved August 25, 2022, from https://kathmandupost.com/national/2019/05/21/oli-makes-yet-another-remark-that-contradicts-the-spirit-of-federalism

Lundqvist, M. (2019). Post-war memorialisation as everyday peace? Exploring everyday (dis-) engagements with the Maoist martyrs' gate of Beni Bazaar in Nepal. *Conflict, Security & Development*, *19*(5), 475–496. https://doi.org/10.1080/14678802.2019.1658970

Mac Ginty, R. (2021). *Everyday Peace: How So-Called Ordinary People Can Disrupt Violent Conflict* (R. Mac Ginty, Ed.; 1st ed.). Oxford University Press.

Nepali, S. C., & Bhandari, C. (2019). Assessing Everyday Peace Indicators (EPI) in Tandi and Padampur Areas in Chitwan, Nepa. *Journal of APF Command and Staff College*, *2*(1), 118–123.

Pham, P. N., Gibbons, N., & Vinck, P. (2019). A framework for assessing political will in transitional justice contexts. *International Journal of Human Rights*, *23*(6), 993–1009. https://doi.org/10.1080/13642987.2019.1579712

Pradhan, T. R. (2021). Oli's aversion to federalism and secularism becoming more apparent. *Kathmandu Post*. Retrieved August 25, 2022, from https://kathmandupost.com/politics/2021/07/05/oli-s-aversion-to-federalism-and-secularism-becoming-more-apparent

Rolston, B. (2007). Demobilization and reintegration of ex-combatants: The Irish case in international perspective. *Social and Legal Studies*, *16*(2), 259–280.

Selim, Y. (2018). *Transitional Justice in Nepal* (Y. Selim, Ed.). Routledge.

Subedi, D. B. (2014). Dealing with ex-combatants in a negotiated peace process: Impacts of transitional politics on the disarmament, demobilization and reintegration programme in Nepal. *Journal of Asian and African Studies*, *49*(6), 672–689. https://doi.org/10.1177/0021909613507537

Suurmond, J., & Sharma, P. M. (2012). Like yeast that leavens the dough? Community mediation as local infrastructure for peace in Nepal. *Journal of Peacebuilding and Development*, *7*(3), 81–86.

Tandukar, A., Upreti, B. R., Paudel, S. B., Acharya, G., & Harris, D. (2016). *The Effectiveness of Local Peace Committees in Nepal: A study from Bardiya district Researching livelihoods and services affected by conflict Working Paper 40*. Secure Livelihoods Research Consortium.

Index

Adhikari, Radheshyam 148
Adivasi 106, 107
agriculture 2, 43, 49, 52, 54, 102, 105, 145, 158
Amnesty International 66
April Uprising (2006) 1, 5, 10, 13, 14–15, 16, 17–19, 24, 25, 77, 154

Baidya, Mohan 90, 93, 94
Bankariya 109
Bhattarai, Baburam 11, 14, 93, 94, 110
Biplav 53
births 107–8
Bishwakarma, M. 110
bonded labourers 51, 104
Brahmins 44, 105; civil service 104, 108, 109, 122; land ownership 51, 102; migrant workers 111, 157; political leaders 103, 157; socio-economic advantages 100, 101, 102, 103, 104

caste 1, 2, 11, 33; role in civil war 100; role in marginalisation 101–3, 104, 110, 113
census 6, 101, 125–6
centralised governance 38–9, 43, 44, 45, 47, 54, 62
Chand, Netra Bikram 93, 94
Chepang 102
Chettris 44, 45, 105, 157; civil service 104, 108, 109; land ownership 51, 102; socio-economic advantages 100, 101–2, 103, 104
child soldiers 2, 48, 52, 68, 76, 81, 95, 111, 158
China 16, 19, 20, 36
Chunwang plenum meeting 15
citizenship laws 122, 160
civic space 146–7, 160–1

civil service: reservation policies 106, 108–9, 160
civil wars: role of marginalisation 100
coalition party 2
Cold War 35–6
Commission for the Investigation of Enforced Disappeared Persons (CIEDP) 58, 59, 60, 66, 67, 68, 74; delay in formation 63–4, 78, 155; politicisation 66–8, 78; victims' organisations 79, 83
Communist Party of Nepal-Maoist (CPN-Maoist) 24, 67, 69, 85, 87, 94, 138; appeal to marginalised groups 11–12, 30, 80, 100, 103, 115, 157; attacks on the the Kamaiya movement 51; civil war 1, 2–3, 10, 11–14, 58, 60; cultivation of conflict victims 72, 75; strategic shift 14, 15–16
Communist Party of Nepal-United Marxist Leninist (CPN-UML) 2, 18, 24, 67, 69, 94; cultivation of conflict victims 72, 75
Comprehensive Peace Agreement (CPA) 28–31, 40–1, 161; background to 9–10, 14–19, 24–5; commitment to addressing marginalisation 38, 100–1; critical evaluation 151, 161; economic reforms 37, 38, 39; key provisions 31–5; lack of gender equality 115, 120, 128–9, 131; political reforms 37–9; renegotiation of former agreements 21–4; signing 1, 2; third party involvement 19–21, 24–5; wartime crimes 58
conflict victims 72–3; politics of victimhood 74–7; production of 73–4; social movement 2, 79–82, 83; state response 77–9, 82–3

164 *Index*

conservatives 4, 128, 156
Constituent Assembly 29–30, 38, 137, 139, 147; abolition of the monarchy 1; drafting of the constitution 137, 138–9, 140, 141, 143–4, 147–8; elections 15, 31, 89, 112, 138–9, 142
constitution (1959) 138
constitution (1962) 138
constitution (1990) 1, 22, 40, 103, 138
constitution (2015) 3, 150, 151; drafting of 137, 138–9, 140, 141, 143–4, 147–8; federal framework 1, 39, 137–8, 140, 149–50; flexible nature 160; implementation of 139–40; marginalised groups 139, 140; protests against 139, 140, 141–2
corruption 2, 4, 39, 55, 103, 111, 112, 130; civil service 104; local governments 47; mainstream political parties 11, 12, 18, 50, 94, 156; policies against 145
Covid-19 pandemic 6–7, 68, 93, 100, 101, 127, 144

Dahal, Pushpa Kamal (Prachanda) 3, 4, 67, 90, 110, 140
Dalits 3, 45, 100; bonded labourers 104; caste structure 102; civil service 104, 106, 109; government initiatives 107; lack of documentation 111; migrant workers 111; political representation 106, 107, 110, 142; socio-economic inequality 103, 104, 113
Deuba, Sher Bahadur 4, 67, 110
disappeared persons 2, 58, 60, 68, 73, 74, 75; Bardiya 79–80; impact on families 75–6, 121–2, 131; women 116; *see also* Commission for the Investigation of Enforced Disappeared Persons
disarmament, demobilisation, and reintegration (DDR) 2, 3–4, 24, 30, 32, 40, 85–7, 88–90; employment 52, 53, 92–3, 94–5, 158–9; integration 86, 90–1; Nepal Army 3–4, 24, 30, 38, 39, 61, 160; political engagement 88, 90, 93–5, 96; social reintegration 32–3, 86, 87–8, 91–7; voluntary retirement 86, 89, 90, 91, 92, 93, 96–7, 155; *see also* ex-combatants
Doramba massacre (2003) 14

earthquakes (2015) 68, 127, 139, 141, 147
education 43, 45, 64, 69, 120; conflict victims 76; effect of civil war 52, 54, 130; effect of Covid-19 pandemic 144; ex-combatants 52, 92, 93, 94, 158; inequalities 103, 105, 109, 146; laws 148; scholarships 54, 64, 69, 107, 146
elections 30, 36, 37–8, 39, 45–6, 47, 95, 127, 138; 2008 112; 2017 2, 4, 45, 46, 107, 110, 139–42, 145; 2022 46, 69, 107, 110, 137, 142; monitoring 21, 65; pacifying aspects 142–3; representation mechanisms 109–10, 112, 125, 156–7
Electoral Commission of Nepal 140–1
Engels, Friedrich 100
European nations 19, 21
European Union Election Observation Mission 142
European Union (EU) 19, 142, 148
ex-combatants 63, 85–7, 88–90; child soldiers 2, 48, 52, 68, 76, 81, 95, 111, 158; education 93, 94, 158; employment 52, 53, 92–3, 94–5, 158–9; integration into Nepal Army 86, 90–1; as marginalised group 158–9; political engagement 88, 90, 93–5, 96; social reintegration 32–3, 86, 87–8, 91–7; stigma 49, 159; voluntary retirement 86, 89, 90, 91, 92, 93, 96–7, 155; women 116, 118–19, 129

federalism 1–2; challenges 143–9, 150–2; conservative opposition to 4; framework 1, 39, 137–8, 140, 149–50
feudalism 10, 24, 38, 39, 40, 44, 51, 100, 101
Foreign Direct Investment (FDI) 37

general election (2017) 2
genocide 35–6, 37
Gurung 102, 108–9, 111
Gurung, Chandra 1, 2

House of Representatives 22, 23, 39, 40
human capital 103–4, 105, 106, 112
Human Development Index (HDI) 43, 105

India 16, 19, 20, 21, 49, 102; migrant workers 111; reservation policies 106; role in peace talks 3, 14, 17, 19, 21
indigenous peoples: caste system 102, 104; civil service 104, 106, 108–9, 160; constitution 139, 156; government initiatives 107; inheritance 122; and Maoists 3, 103, 112, 157;

Index 165

marginalisation 3, 100–1, 102, 103, 112, 113, 157; migrant workers 111; political representation 107
inequality: role in civil wars 100
instability 2, 4, 103, 137
interim constitution (2007) 3, 23, 24, 58, 60, 63, 85, 101, 118, 138
Interim Relief Program (IRP) 64
International Monetary Fund (IMF) 37

Jana Andolan movement: first 1, 29, 80; second 1, 5, 10, 13, 14–15, 16, 17–19, 24, 25, 77, 154
Janajati 30, 80, 100, 106, 107, 140, 150

Kamaiya movement 51
King Gyanendra 13, 18, 24, 25, 29, 138, 154; removal from power 14–15, 16–17; unpopularity 10, 14, 16, 19
King Mahendra 102, 138
Kiranti, Gopal 94
Kisan 109
kleptocracy 4, 50

Limbu 102
Local Level Elections Act (2017) 142
Local Peace Committees (LPCs) 48, 49, 55, 59, 62, 66, 75, 118, 121, 159

Mac Ginty, Roger 159
Madesh region: protests 2, 53, 140, 141
Madhesis 100, 103; civil service 106; employment 104; inter-caste marriage 45; lack of documentation 111; and Maoists 3, 30; political representation 107, 109, 110, 140, 150, 156; protests 2, 53, 140, 141
Magar 46, 102
Mahara, Krishna Bahadur 14
Mainali, Raunak 104, 105
Maoist army *see* People's Liberation Army
Maoists *see* Communist Party of Nepal-Maoist
marginalisation: intensification of 157–9; and Maoist mobilisation 11–12, 30, 80, 100, 103, 115, 157; role in civil war 1, 2–3, 100, 115; role of caste 1, 2–3, 101–3, 104, 110, 113; of women 1, 2, 3, 4, 30, 100–1
Marx, Karl 100
migrant workers 52–3, 55, 94, 111–12, 157, 158–9

Monarchy 10, 12, 15, 16, 22–3, 24, 29–30, 38, 112; constitutional 1, 4, 103, 137; efforts to reinstate 128, 139, 156; removal of 1, 63, 138
Muluki Ain 102
Muslims 103, 107, 109, 113
Mutually Hurting Stalemate (MHS) 9, 20

National Assembly 39, 40, 106, 107
National Human Rights Commission (NHRC) 31, 34, 35, 40, 66
National Living Standard Survey (NLSS) 6, 101, 104, 105
Nembang, Subhash Chandra 147
Nepal Army 12, 14, 22, 23, 51, 52, 73, 78, 79; army integration process 3–4, 85–6, 89, 91, 96, 160; DDR process 3–4, 24, 30, 38, 39, 61, 160; investigations 68; recruitment of women 116
Nepal Association of Indigenous Nationalities (NEFIN) 103
Nepal Communist Party (NCP) 46, 94
Nepal Foundation for Indigenous Nationalities (NFDIN) 103
Nepali Civil War 2, 10–12, 58; death toll 2, 58; phases 12–13; root causes 35–9, 100; rural areas 43–4, 46–7, 48–50, 51–2, 54, 55; *see also* conflict victims; disappeared persons; ex-combatants; peace process; transitional justice; women
Nepali Congress (NC) 18, 46, 61, 64, 67, 69, 72, 75
Nepali language 102–3
Nepali nationalism 102–3
Newars 102, 103, 104, 108, 113, 157, 160
non governmental organisations (NGOs): conflict victims 78, 79, 80, 81, 123, 133, 158; data 6, 101; ex-combatants 48; peace process 19, 21; reinforcement of inequality 83, 158, 161; rural areas 44, 51, 62; transitional justice 4

Office of the High Commissioner for Human Rights (OHCHR) 21, 30, 31, 34, 35, 40, 66
Oli, K.P. 4, 46, 67

panchayat system 102–3, 138
peace process 2, 3; 12-point agreement 10, 14, 15–16, 17, 18, 21, 24, 138; acts of everyday peace 159–60; elite capture 132–3; gender 115, 116–24, 125–34;

166 *Index*

intensification of inequality 157–9; Maoists' strategic shift 14, 15–16; need for critical evaluation 161; peace talks 13–14, 15; political reforms 38–9; political will 154–5; reduction of caste discrimination 44–5; superficiality of 155–7; technocratic approach 132; third party involvement 19–21, 24–5; *see also* Comprehensive Peace Agreement; transitional justice

pensions 104, 107

People's Liberation Army (PLA) 2, 3–4, 24, 30, 32, 40, 85–7, 88–90; child soldiers 2, 48, 52, 68, 76, 81, 95, 111, 158; employment 52, 53, 92–3, 94–5, 158–9; integration 86, 90–1; political engagement 88, 90, 93–5, 96; social reintegration 32–3, 86, 87–8, 91–7; voluntary retirement 86, 89, 90, 91, 92, 93, 96–7, 155

People's Movement *see Jana Andolan* movement

Piketty, Thomas 100

police 12, 48–9, 51, 65, 78, 121, 126, 127

political connections 7, 48, 66, 102, 104, 108, 109, 111

poverty 2, 3, 43, 76, 80, 93, 115; decline in 108, 111; rural areas 52, 53, 81, 158

Prachanda 3, 4, 67, 90, 110

progressive policies 1–2, 3, 37, 55, 154, 155, 161

protests 2, 53, 81, 95, 140, 141; against the constitution 139, 140, 141–2

Rai 102, 108

Raji 109

Ramnarain, S. 121

Rana, Jung Bahadur 102

Rana Prime Ministers 38, 101–2, 138

reservation policies: civil service 106, 108–9, 160; criticisms of 106, 108–9, 110, 112,.156–7, 160; political representatives 106–7, 109–10, 160; women 48, 106, 108, 109

Royal Nepal Army (RNA) 12, 14, 19, 20, 21, 73

rural areas 1, 3, 43–4; caste discrimination 44–5; decline in community trust 49–51; local governance 45–9, 53; socio-economic issues 51–5, 157–8

Rwanda 35–6, 37

Sajha Party 46

scholarships 54, 64, 69, 107, 146

security sector reform (SSR) 2

Seven Party Alliance (SPA) 10, 14, 16–17, 18, 21, 24, 25

sexual violence 58, 115, 116, 118, 119, 122–3, 124, 126, 128, 129, 130, 132, 133–4; confidentiality 61, 133–4; social stigma 74, 119, 123, 133, 134; TRC Act 60, 65, 132

Shah dynasty 1, 101–2

Sherpas 102

Soviet Union 36

Stiglitz, Joseph 100

Sunuwar, Maina 79

Sunuwars 108

Tamang 102, 108–9

Terai region 51, 83, 100, 103, 104, 109; protests 139, 140, 141

Thapa, Ram Bahadur 14

Tharu 30, 44–5, 47, 107, 108–9; bonded labour 51; caste system 102; disappearances 79–80; land theft 102; political parties 139; property inheritance 122; protests 139

torture 58, 74, 79, 122, 131, 132; Kamaiyas 51; police 48–9; TRC Act 65

tourism 2

transitional justice (TJ) 2, 4, 54, 58–64, 68–9; challenges 64–8; politicisation 4, 66–8, 72–3, 78; *see also* Commission for the Investigation of Enforced Disappeared Persons; Truth and Reconciliation Commission

Truth and Reconciliation Commission (TRC) 2, 24, 30, 34, 58, 60–2, 69, 74, 155; amnesties 78; challenges 64, 65, 66, 67–8; delay in formation 60, 63–4, 77–8, 155; politicisation 66–8, 78; sexual violence 119, 130, 133; victims' organisations 79, 83

United Nations Mission in Nepal (UNMIN) 3, 21, 66, 116; social reintegration 85, 86, 87, 88, 90, 97

United Nations (UN) 29, 31, 66, 81, 85, 87–8, 132, 145

United People's Front (UPF) 11

Watts, R.L. 148

widows 115, 118, 119, 120, 121–2

women: army recruitment 30, 49–50, 116; citizenship laws 122, 160; civil service 106, 108, 109, 160; ex-combatants 116, 118–19, 129; government initiatives 107–8; marginalisation 1, 2, 3, 4, 30, 100–1; peace process 115, 116–24, 125–34; political representation 46–7, 106, 107, 124–5, 142; violence against 48–9, 116, 126–7, 128, 129, 130–2, 133–4

World Bank 37

Young Communist League (YCL) 87

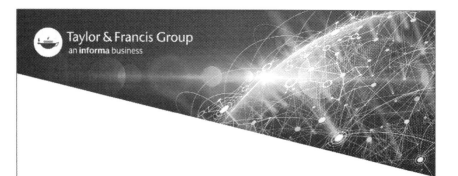